Filming History
The memoirs of John Turner, newsreel cameraman

by John Turner

British Universities Film & Video Council

British Universities Film & Video Council
77 Wells Street, London W1T 3QJ
Tel: 020 7393 1500 Fax: 020 7393 1555
e-mail: ask@bufvc.ac.uk   www.bufvc.ac.uk

ISBN 0 901 299 72 3

Cover picture
Main picture: Frame still of John Turner from the 1943 documentary film CAMERAMEN
AT WAR (IWM). Inset pictures: Frame stills from Turner's newsreel footage of the sinking
of HMS *Barham*, 1941 (IWM).

Produced by Gem Graphics, Trenance, Nr. Newquay, Cornwall TR8 4BY.

Dedication

To SB

John Turner, 1944

Contents

CONTENTS

Foreword

As we move into the twenty-first century, and look back on what was recorded of the twentieth, a significant part of that historical record is provided by the newsreels. Between 1910 and 1979 in Britain, and between roughly similar dates in many other countries, the newsreels were shown weekly or twice-weekly in cinemas and gave millions their picture of national and world events. Their libraries now supply television documentaries with basic archive footage that illustrates the personalities, passions, pastimes, tragedies and events both significant and trivial that filled the cinema screens, and now provide such a substantial moving picture record of the past.

The people who made the newsreels were the editors and cameramen, and their personal stories help to illuminate this record of the past, as well as being documents of a lively, compelling time when moving picture news was primarily an entertainment medium. There have been too few such memoirs, however, which makes this publication of John Turner's 'life with the newsreels' so valuable. John Turner has enjoyed a truly remarkable career. He joined *Gaumont-British News*, one of the five major British newsreels of the sound era, as an assistant cameraman in 1936. He soon graduated to cameraman, going on to film many key events in the late 1930s, including the coronation of King George VI, the launch of the liner *Queen Elizabeth*, and Neville Chamberlain returning from Munich, promising 'Peace for our time'.

The Second World War first saw Turner serving as a naval war correspondent, mostly notably filming in the Mediterranean with the vital Malta convoys. It was at this time that he secured one of the most celebrated of all newsreel shots, that of the battleship HMS *Barham* exploding and sinking after being hit by torpedoes. He went on to film the invasion of Sicily and D-Day, before ending up in Singapore, where he got exclusive film of the surrender of the Japanese forces.

Continuing his career as a newsreel cameraman in the 1940s, Turner was sent to India in 1947 to film events surrounding the independence celebrations, and was the only British cameraman in the country when Gandhi was assassinated. The 1950s saw him appointed as the royal rota cameraman, assigned to cover stories concerning the British royal family, footage which would then be shared among each of the newsreels. He spent much of the decade in the company of the young Queen Elizabeth and Prince Philip, including the Commonwealth tour of 1953-54.

As the 1950s came to a close, the cinema newsreels started to fade in the face of the growing competition from television news. *Gaumont-British News* folded in 1959, but Turner remained as royal rota cameraman while *British Movietone News* and *Pathe News* became the only surviving newsreels into the 1960s. Turner's final royal tour was to cover Prince Philip's

1963 visit to South America. He then joined *Pathe News*, no longer as a cameraman, but eventually as news editor, where he was responsible for organising the filming of such notable events as the funeral of Winston Churchill and the 1966 World Cup.

Pathe News folded in 1970 (Movietone would follow suit in 1979), and Turner ran his own film business until retiring in 1981. At the invitation of the British Universities Film & Video Council, he has now written the account of his life with the newsreels, which serves both as a record of a remarkable career and as a history of the sound newsreels in Britain. It documents in absorbing detail his filming of such key historical events as the Malta convoys, Indian independence, Gandhi's funeral, and the royal tours of the 1950s, but it also illustrates the working life of the newsreel cameraman, and his particular view of the world and its news.

The popular image of the newsreel cameraman has been well-described by Philip Norman, who calls them 'fun-filled, large-overcoated and bibulous men with loud voices and connections as close to Gatty's Music Hall as to any technical union' (*Sunday Times*, 10 January 1971). It certainly could be a fun-filled life, with a robust cameraderie among its practitioners. However, Turner's memoirs in their modest way are more revealing of the process of producing news on film than some of the more jocular account that exist. Turner reveals the methodical, practical approach to filming the news, be it routine trivia or national calamity, that characterises the professional cameraman. He maintains his distance from disaster, taking such pictures as may be necessary, checking that exposure, lens and focus are all properly set, aware at all times of what the news editor needs, or what sort of scenes will be of value to the production office and which may be ignored. It is a cost-conscious sensibility (35mm film was a far more expensive and precious medium than the video of today), sensitive also to the caution necessary with news as an entertainment medium.

Maintaining a professional distance does not preclude a sympathy with one's subject, and if there is one aspect of John Turner's memoirs that stands out in particular it is his ability to empathise with people of every kind, high and low, all treated as equally interesting, equally newsworthy. As he writes, 'a cameraman has to be alert, imaginative, unemotional, able to cope with the unexpected. He must be able to approach the greatest and the lowest in society equally. He is not concerned as to "who" a person is, only his or her newsworthiness'. Turner displays justifiable pride in his service as the royal rota cameraman, but he shows equal interest and understanding of the fans at football matches, the crew members of the ships in which he sailed during the war, the crowds at Gandhi's funeral, whoever came before his camera. He is no less aware of those who were to see his films, and what they needed and wanted to see. 'I have tried to travel with a seeing eye, for what I saw the audience saw.'

Moving image news has changed greatly since the heyday of the newsreels, and against the sophistication, ubiquity and generally hard news values of television news today, the cinema newsreels can seem quaint. There were no newsreaders or analysis of the news in any real sense; commentators boomed out above jaunty music scores in a style that can be all too easy to dismiss, or parody. This would be a grave mistake. The history of recent times which we have bequeathed through the newsreels is a valuable one, if only we understand the process by which it was made, the circumstances which controlled its contents and exhibition. The testimony of those who made the newsreels is essential to our understanding of this heritage. We are now the audience for the newsreels, and John Turner's 'seeing eye' allows us to view that inheritance all the more clearly.

Luke McKernan
Head of Information
British Universities Film & Video Council

Acknowledgements

In writing this story I have used notes I made at the time of the various assignments. I have also tested my memory, which may have failed me occasionally. But in particular I acknowledge the help I have received from the following:

James Ballantyne, whose friendship, encouragement and observations have helped me so much.

Luke McKernan, who refreshed my memory from the newsreel database at the BUFVC and whose skill in editing made my efforts readable.

Dr Nick Hiley, who gave me many useful observations.

Angus Robertson, who supplied information from researches from his own work and the photograph of Castleton-Knight from his collection.

Dr C. M. Woolgar, Archivist at Southampton University and the Mountbatten Archives, who gave me valuable information and obtained for me permission from the Trustees of the Broadland Archives to reproduce verbatim a letter from Lord Mountbatten, and I thank the Trustees for that permission.

The libraries which helped me check facts and dates.

The captains and commanders of the various ships in which I sailed during the war, who gave me technical and other explanations of attacks and battles necessary for me to supply with the films I took and which have helped me in recounting those operations in this book.

My journalist colleagues on royal tours, who kept me informed with details and specific facts relating to what I had filmed.

Connie Boyd, who made available photographs from her albums of war events in the Mediterranean collected by her late husband, an officer on HMS *Valiant*.

The Imperial War Museum, for pictures of ships in which I sailed during the war.

ITN Archive/Reuters for frame stills from copies of *Gaumont British News*.

British Pathe for frame stills from copies of *Pathe News*.

Marilyn Sarmiento for her copy-editing.

Hetty Malcolm-Smith, Publications Officer, BUFVC for seeing this book through to publication.

Murray Weston, Director of the BUFVC, for making possible the publication of this book.

Chapter One
Early Days

Author's collection

The author before he was dropped on his head.

All life begins in the same way until, at the age of none, when we sever our connection with Mama, we start on the pathway to our particular destiny.

When I was just twelve months old my nanny accidentally dropped me on my head, presenting me with an inverted view of the world, and so, perhaps, determined my future as a cameraman.

What follows is the story of the newsreels as I knew them, right way up. It covers a wide spectrum of events. The world has been my canvas, my camera, my brush, light and shade, my paints. I have crossed many seas, many borders – to Australia, New Zealand, the Cocos Islands; to Canada, North and South America, India, Ceylon; to Kenya, Malta, Egypt and Tanzania; to fifty-seven countries and every county in the United Kingdom. My story tells of World War II – of my war on the seas, of fun and tragedy. In the East, the North, the West, the South I sweated, I shivered, I was brave, I was afraid. There were many personalities – Gandhi, Earl Mountbatten, Churchill, George Bernard Shaw and the less well-known men and women who made the news. From a privileged position I filmed the Queen and the royal family, and the scoops which often made small events big occasions in our world: sport, politics, flying, industry. News has no boundaries.

Long before I had any notion of entering the film industry my interest in films was aroused when, quite young, my brother and I were taken to a film studio in London by an uncle to take part in crowd scenes in a film in which comedian George Robey was the star. This unreal world stayed with me throughout my formative years. I was also able to see the industry trade papers and was an avid reader of the *Daily Film Renter*, the *Cinema* and the *Kinematograph Weekly* with their glossy full-page, colourful advertisements. Those three papers were the embodiment of the creative side of an industry which had grown up from the showground. The heady showbiz atmosphere of greasepaint, attractive people, arc-lights, costumes, tinsel, cameras, film sets – the whole paraphernalia of film-making – was contained in their pages, confirming what I had experienced first-hand in those early days in the film studio. It excited me, fascinated me and still does. Although my path was to be on the road and not the studio I have never lost my love for films and film-making – and never will.

I began work in a publicity department, straight from boarding school. Music often moves me greatly – a sentimental streak – and in the school on a Sunday evening we would attend chapel and after the service listen to an organ recital or the angelic voice of a young chorister. Later our housemaster would play *Lohengrin* or Tchaikovsky on his gramophone and we would go to bed satiated with music. In my school holidays I was fed daily doses of Wagner, Chopin or Mozart by my music-loving grandmother and so, with that kind of background, my entry into Wardour Street was, to say the least, traumatic.

Jobs were not easy to get in the 1930s and I was over the moon and the envy of my school chums when I learned I could start work with Ideal Films at £1 10s a week, a reasonable salary then. It went a long way. For lunch one could walk to Mooney's Pub in Oxford Street and for sixpence have a bottle of Guinness, a ploughman's lunch – a large piece of fresh crusty bread, masses of butter and a huge piece of cheese – or in the little cafe by the side of Film House there was steak and kidney pudding and treacle tart for less than a shilling. But at school my headmaster was not overjoyed. The film industry! He was appalled. His pupils were being prepared for the academic life, for university, for an Establishment career. The entertainment industry – oh my goodness! I had gained an Oxford and Cambridge School Certificate with several credits; I was wasting my education. It was indeed a shattering interview. Nevertheless to London's Soho, to No. 76 Wardour Street I went in my new suit and my new bowler hat which almost covered my eyes. Not exactly the right gear even in the 1930s.

What a strange life I entered. The closeted environs of my school had not equipped me for the hurly-burly of commerce. Knowing nothing about business, I was so naïve. In fact I knew very little about the everyday world, for my father had died when I was eight and soon after I was sent away to boarding school. I was right in at the deep end. My first experiences in the publicity department of Ideal Films were quite startling for a young beginner. My immediate colleagues appeared to spend most of their time in competition with visiting sales representatives to see who could make the loudest noise when passing wind. A senior executive spent many a lunch hour screwing his massive middle-aged secretary across his massive desk. Strange people appeared: poster artists – scruffy, nicotine-stained, carpet-slippered individuals nearly always skint although they were some of the highest paid in the business. Brilliant in their work, they produced wonderful huge posters advertising films with a few deft strokes, usually caricatures of the actors, telling the story of the film. Another frequent visitor, my first meeting with 'royalty', was 'Ras Prince Monolulu', the extrovert racing tipster who had appeared in one of our films – an Edgar Wallace thriller, THE SPORT OF KINGS. The 'Prince' was a tall articulate black man of great charisma, probably Ethiopian, always wearing an ostrich-feather headband and blue and red robes and looking for free stills of himself to display on the racecourses. As payment he regaled the office with some of the filthiest jokes imaginable. Even my hardened windy fellow-workers went quiet at some of them. I was to meet him again some years later at big race meetings and wherever there was betting, shouting his catch-line, 'I gotta 'orse'. He would give me free tips which I am afraid I never backed. I believe he handed out the names of all the horses so someone had to win. He died in 1965.

In this world of posters, stacks of stills, promotional publicity and the untidy paraphernalia of a department which operated with very little supervision, I gradually acquired some knowledge of what cinema managers needed when they rang to order front-of-house displays. When my colleagues were on holiday, usually together, I was promoted to the main desk and took the incoming calls. These were occasionally so garbled, hurried and ambiguous that I sometimes sent the wrong orders or failed to note what had been sent, causing chaos at the designated cinema. I was a nervous wreck when the holidays were over. I did not like the job and concluded that I was not a desk person.

Was this the glamorous industry I had expected? I began to understand my headmaster's attitude. It was indeed an eye-opener on a different species of mankind and perhaps, while the goings-on in our publicity department were not the norm for the whole industry, films were not regarded as one of the highest of professions. Wardour Street played host to prostitutes and pimps and certainly had its sleazy side. There was glamour, however. There were brilliant trade shows in the plush West End cinemas. In the streets, lit by arc lights, dense crowds waited hours to see the stars arrive, to see the splendid dresses, everyone in evening dress. Most films had a promotional gimmick – imaginative stunts like metal tickets for a futuristic film about a floating platform in the sea called F.P.1 – and there was always a gift for the ladies. As a member of the publicity department I had to attend many of these shows at which we had to make sure those we wished to publicise were brought into contact with film critics and photographers. I, as a junior, had only a supporting role, but what I learned then I found very useful later when I had to arrange and film such occasions. Yes, there was glamour, an atmosphere, a way of life, a drug difficult to shake off once hooked. The film industry was a world of creative people of many skills. It was an industry dedicated to entertain, for that was the criterion around which films were made. Entertainment was the key – a fantasy world maybe, but it pleased the public and filled the cinemas. In those days of Depression, films provided escapism with fun, glossy sets, beautiful music, stunning girls, handsome men – the sort of life we all dreamt about. The programmes always contained two films and usually a stage show or organ recital of popular music, sometimes both. Value for money. And, supporting all this were the cartoons, the travelogues, the magazine-type shorts – and the newsreels.

France began to put together reels with news as early as 1896. These were mainly a series of unrelated short items and this format became the basis of future newsreels. In 1908 *Pathé Journal* showed the first newsreel in a cinema followed in the same year by another French reel, *Gaumont Actualités*. It is particularly interesting to me because these two 'first' reels were the parent names of the companies with which I began and ended my career in newsreels. I first joined *Gaumont-British News*; I was with *Pathe News* when it closed. The first British newsreel was *Pathe's Animated Gazette* in 1910, soon followed by reels all over Europe and America. Like the feature films, they were silent and relied on titles and captions to supplement the pictures. By the 1930s the newsreels had sound, and there were five of them in Britain: *Gaumont-British News, British Movietone News, British Paramount News, Pathe News* and *Universal Talking News*.

In the very early days cameramen hand-cranked their cameras mounted on light tripods, which were themselves turned by handles to tilt and pan. The whole contraption was moved from position to position as necessary – no easy thing to do as well as turn three handles, keep a constant turning speed on the camera and keep the picture in the viewfinder. These men were real pioneers, some processing, editing and even projecting their films. It was remarkable what was achieved when one considers the lightweight 16mm cameras with their zoom lenses and fast films used subsequently, and the even more sophisticated electronic cameras of television.

Wardour Street took its name from Sir Edward Wardour, who had owned the land. At that time, the 1600s, antique dealers lined the street. It was an American, Charles Urban, who brought films to Soho in the early 1900s. He opened a small film studio and laboratories in a building in Wardour Street which he called Urbanora House. It still stands today close to No. 76 where I first started work. In the years just before the Second World War it was a changing time, particularly in the film trade. Mergers took place: Ideal Films joined Wolfe and Fox and they were taken over by Gaumont-British Distributors, itself later to become part of the Rank Organisation. Somehow I managed to survive all these changes and ended up on the top floor of Film House, 142 Wardour Street, a building which also still stands today. I was still in publicity. The publicity department had become an odd mix of personalities. My colleagues at No. 76 Wardour Street had departed. Now there were the two daughters of Isidore Ostrer, the millionaire owner of the company – Pamela, who later married the actor James Mason, and Sheila, whom I rather fancied but who showed little interest. Perhaps I was attracted by the wealthy father. Then there was Charlie Pearce, a talented designer of advertisements, and a secretary, Nancy Pritchard, who was a friend of Castleton-Knight. He was then a director of G.B. Distributors, and later became managing director and editor-in-chief of *Gaumont-British News*. I completed the department. Apart from the designer and the secretary we did little real work. There was a lot of fun, horseplay, flirtations, lunches and trade shows, but not much progress towards a business career. Castleton-Knight used to come up frequently to see his girlfriend and would put his head through a cubby-hole to see who was in the office. As soon as he appeared the two Ostrer girls would creep up with a pair of scissors and he would depart with half a tie. Until he got wise to this and tucked his tie into his shirt the girls gained quite a number of expensive trophies.

Publicity was not my cup of tea. I did not have the kind of extrovert personality that went with the job. When I learned there was a vacancy for an assistant cameraman with the newsreel, *Gaumont-British News*, I thought, being in the company, I might have a chance and I applied for the post. At the interview I had to confess that I did not know one end of a camera from the other but nevertheless they agreed to give me a chance. So, from the bright lights of the fifth floor I descended to a dingy room in the basement of Film House where the newsreel administration and technicians were housed.

My entry into the film industry had been traumatic. My entry into newsreels was equally so. From the easy-going, playful set-up of publicity here I was the 'boy' again. At that time assistant cameraman meant very hard physical work humping extremely heavy 35mm equipment in and out of cars, on location, any place where filming in sound was scheduled. With no unions and no training schemes one learned the hard way. Working conditions for television crews are fantastic compared with those the cinema newsreels experienced before the war. We could not join a club to play any team game because they were mainly played at weekends and we could not guarantee that we would be available. The telephone often dragged us out at dawn, continually intruded into our lives, so that even today when it rings we groan. We were on call twenty-four hours a day, seven days a week, with not very good pay, no over-time, and few if any bonuses. We received expenses, which helped, and generally we were treated very generously by the managers. With much unemployment in the country, as a single man I found the long hours and the disruptions acceptable, although it needed a very understanding, tolerant family to cope. We lived the job. This is the common lot of news people, I know, but such terms as we had to accept would not be tolerated now and, of course, led to the

Castleton-Knight, my boss.

Angus Robertson

formation of the technicians' union, the Association of Cine Technicians – the ACT – later the ACTT to include television. Although it was exhausting, and frequently dangerous, it was an exciting life, for we were always at the centre of whatever was happening in the world.

When I arrived on the scene the reels were no longer silent. Sound had come to Britain with Al Jolson in the feature film THE SINGING FOOL and in 1929 British Movietone was the first to use the new medium in its newsreels. The other four were slow to follow their lead and it was not until 1931 that sound became a 'must' for all reels. Then the old stories became new stories in sound. The commentator appeared and cinema-goers were able to hear as well as see the pictures. Commentary and music replaced the captions and the piano. Sound cameras were powered by heavy-duty batteries and could run 1,000 feet of film without reloading. The sound system was incorporated inside the camera, accounting for the extreme weight as everything was in one casing. The 35mm film ran past an oscillograph, a device which converted the sound waves into light waves which were then photographed on to the negative alongside the picture. It was not easy to edit for it had to be cut absolutely precisely; otherwise it became out of sync. The Gaumont cameras were either Vintens or Mitchells.

Because of the cumbersome equipment it was necessary for the sound camera to work from an elevated fixed position or from the top of a camera car – 'trucks' we called them – anything from a van, a Rolls-Royce or a Humber limousine, all with reinforced roofs. Those vehicles were mostly driven by the sound men. When I became a cameraman I sometimes travelled with the sound crew when it was necessary to keep the team together. Gaumont employed a motor mechanic to look after the cars and he occasionally drove the truck when he was acting as an extra assistant. I remember one time, when he was driving, coming back from Newmarket races, seeing one of our rear wheels passing by at speed. I wondered what the mechanic thought of that. He did manage to pull up without further mishap. Rarely did the sound crew work from ground level. This meant that it had to be supplemented by another camera and on most stories this was the hand-camera. The cameramen who used these, being mobile, were able to get different angles and into areas not available to those using the heavier equipment. Like sound-camera work, hand-camera filming was a specialised job. Many stories were covered only with a hand-camera and later I found this was the kind of coverage that suited me. Some cameras were battery-driven; some ran by clockwork. I preferred a heavy, cumbersome, clockwork camera – about thirty pounds it weighed – the Newman Sinclair, aluminium and box-like, very strong and very reliable. It ran for 100 feet without rewinding, had two springs and 200-foot magazines which could be changed quickly in daylight. At first the viewfinder system was tricky as it was situated on top of the camera with the lens half-way down, causing problems of parallax. I used this camera most of my filming life, updating it as improvements were made. It served me well during the war when battery-driven cameras were a constant worry due to the difficulty of recharging batteries in many war zones. All one needed with the Newman was a spare spring. There were other lighter cameras, for example the Eyemo and the LeBlay, both of which were spring-driven but only running 100 feet before reloading. The Aeriflex was a very good battery-driven camera which I did use on occasions but I was generally happier with my sturdy Newman.

Gainsborough Pictures, with whom Gaumont-British was associated, opened studios in Lime Grove, Shepherd's Bush in west London in 1932 for the production of feature films – classics such as Alfred Hitchcock productions and films with the stars of the day: Jack Hulbert, Ralph Richardson, Jessie Matthews, Walter Huston. These studios and their laboratories were later acquired by the BBC but were at the very heart of my first cinema newsreel.

Although cameramen and administrative staff were based in Wardour Street all our negatives were processed, edited and printed at Shepherd's Bush. The film was often developed by hand, the black-and-white 35mm film wound on to large wooden wheels not unlike those huge cable drums which telephone and electricity engineers use to carry heavy-duty cables. They were revolved slowly through the developer watched minute-by-minute, almost lovingly, by the studio laboratory technicians. Because they were so closely monitored under a dark-room safe-light and not timed through machines some very fine results were obtained, particularly when a cameraman had been up against very poor light and had come back with a much under-exposed negative.

The cinema newsreels were issued twice weekly, on Mondays and Thursdays, and the logistics were formidable. A print had to be made for every first-run cinema – those showing the reel when issued. For companies like Gaumont and Pathe with large cinema circuits this meant printing over 200 copies of each issue. Before the war the reels ran for fifteen minutes, 1,350 feet of 35mm film each reel, a minimum of 270,000 feet to be printed overnight twice a week. The war reduced lengths to ten minutes to conserve film and the reels remained at this level after the war. But it still meant printing 180,000 feet twice a week.

Editing was done on a machine called a Moviola which enabled the film to be run backwards and forwards. Since the editor was always working to a deadline the original negative was usually handled, as there was no time to make duplicates. The risks were terrifying, the constant to-ing and fro-ing on the editing machine making the negative liable to bad scratching. For a cameraman who might be in the cutting room watching his masterpiece being carved up it was little short of nightmarish.

With all stories edited and joined a print was made and the film was 'dubbed', that is, sound tracks were added. This involved original sound, sound effects, music and commentary being recorded on to one track. If the commentator fluffed the film had to be laboriously wound back to the beginning of the reel, as this was the only

Gaumont-British News camera crews on parade.

BUFVC/Ted Candy collection

way to keep the picture and sound synchronised, and the whole procedure started again. So, when time was everything a fluff was catastrophic and more than one sent a harassed editor-in-chief crazy. Later the projectors were able to roll back in sync to the point of error and time lost was minimal.

Since I had come to the newsreel from another department in the company I was regarded with some suspicion and it took me some while to be fully accepted by the cameramen and sound men. The turning-point came when I was sent to the zoo as an assistant to film a new arrival, the okapi, a zebra-like creature from Africa with horizontal white stripes on its legs and a reddish-brown coat. My cameraman, Jimmy, liked a noggin and when the story was completed we adjourned to a pub near Regent's Park. Unlike Jimmy, whose eyes were heavy in a face that bore all the marks of the expert, I was not a very experienced drinker. But I managed to drink on level terms, which impressed the cameraman and I learned later I was being tried out. From then on I was 'one of them'. The Gaumont technicians in fact were not hard drinkers; some were even committed tea-drinkers. Mostly they were conscientious, courageous, loyal and skilled men. All were characters to be sure but it was rare for a story to be missed through misbehaviour. The editors-in-chief were showmen, most having come up through the ranks, so they were sympathetic. The popular conception of the newsreel cameraman or Fleet Street photographer was as a very tough, uncouth, unemotional, constantly-smoking, hit-the-bottle, a piece on the side type of gent – a mixture of the ingredients which make up individuals in most walks of life from kings downwards. Our own media, films and television, have not helped to dispel this conception. Of course, there is a little bit of truth in everything and much of the myth surrounding a throne is built up by the people who surround it. It was incidents illuminated by such characteristics which built up the stereotype of the newsman. The men behind the cameras were in fact normal human beings and very good judges of character who rarely stepped out of line, however much provoked.

Soon after I joined the newsreel another assistant was employed – Chris Challis. Castleton-Knight gave us both Leica cameras and fully equipped a superb darkroom for our use. The idea was to take still pictures while on a news story, and go through the processes of developing, printing and enlarging in the darkroom in order to learn the basics of photography. If the pictures were good they could be used for publicity. The Leica was a very nice camera, but the idea did not work out as hoped as we were always too occupied as assistants when the story was worth photographing. Challis was an enthusiastic amateur before he joined the newsreel. He had a wealthy father and had many cameras of his own and a darkroom in his home. This was fortunate for me for he taught me a great deal about darkroom techniques and the basics of photography. He did not stay long with the newsreel but went into a film studio and became a number-one cameraman on feature films.

This then was the background to the newsreels in the 1930s. Life was slower. There were no Concordes, no spaceships, no television screens to bring world events to our armchairs. It was the cinemas which showed us other lands, other ways of life, gave us romance, humour and adventure and, through the newsreels, it has been my mission to bring a slice of this outside world to the large screen. I have tried to travel with a seeing eye, for what I saw the audience saw. The cameraman chooses whether to film in close-up or wide-angle, where to put the emphasis, how to represent tragedy and joy. He must not distort the facts, nor must he be just a button-pusher, for unless he is very lucky and gets a scoop, his newsreel story will not be interesting. There have been cameramen who have been technically brilliant, but it does not matter how beautifully they have filmed the occasion, if having concentrated on getting a perfect picture they have missed the point of the story. The result is that their efforts are consigned to the bin. They do not last long as news cameramen. A cameraman has to be alert, imaginative, unemotional, able to cope with the unexpected. He must be able to approach the greatest and the lowest in society equally. He is not concerned as to 'who' a person is, only his or her newsworthiness. So I will try to show what it was like behind the camera.

Life with the newsreels began for me in 1936.

The 1930s had already proved eventful years when I joined *Gaumont-British News* in 1936, giving the newsreels a wonderful opportunity to feature major stories in the early days of sound. The *R101* airship had crashed in France on its maiden flight. The new Sydney Harbour Bridge was opened. Hitler became Führer of Germany in 1934. A year later Mussolini invaded Abyssinia. We received overseas stories from associates in countries which had their own reels, reciprocating with important events from the UK. In areas where no newsreel existed coverage was commissioned through freelance cameramen or we sent a staff man if a story was sufficiently newsworthy. At home, with much depression caused by protracted unemployment, the Tories led by Stanley Baldwin replaced the coalition government of Ramsay MacDonald.

1936 was as notable a year as any. From Jarrow unemployed workers banded together and made a historic march to London, carrying a casket containing thousands of petitions seeking government help, which they delivered to Downing Street. The story featured prominently in the newsreels. Civil war broke out in Spain. In Berlin the Olympic Games were staged with the political overtones of the Brown Shirts and the German Youth Movement. The liner *Queen Mary* sailed on her maiden voyage. In England the year began with the death of King George V and the accession of King Edward VIII. It closed 325 days later on 10 December with his abdication.

As a learner I was only on the fringe of such major events. I lived near Kew Gardens and on 30 November I was standing in our garden on a cold winter night observing a very red sky to the east. The sky got progressively redder as I watched. This was something different from the normal night sky over London which always had a red and orange tinge. It was only later that I heard on the wireless the Crystal Palace at Sydenham was burning. All the cameramen were phoned and sent to the fire. No call for my services. That taught me what a small cog I was in the newsreel world. Next day, when I went with one of the cameraman who had to film the aftermath, I could not wait to get my 'wings' – to handle a camera myself. Fires like the Crystal Palace tragedy were an exception but ordinary fires were almost an everyday assignment. Many an abortive one I chased. I came to adopt my own ideas on fire coverage. I had followed so many at speed, leaving home in the middle of a meal or half-dressed and half asleep, rushing madly away to get to the scene.

I learnt how daft this was. If a fire was worth filming it would burn for a long time and while it was necessary to be on the spot as quickly as possible to get the highlights, the mad fire-engine-type of dash was mostly unnecessary.

Through most of 1936 there was the serious situation arising from the King's involvement with Mrs Simpson. Long days and nights were spent camped outside Belvedere Castle near Windsor trying to get pictures of them. Cold, unpleasant waits as winter approached. There was another icy area – Downing Street – in which to film the comings and goings of the political figures involved in the crisis. There is no draughtier place than Downing Street at any time of the year and we would stand, Fleet Street and the newsreels, huddled together opposite Number Ten in the archway leading into the Foreign Office quadrangle – the warmest place we could find. When anyone arrived at or left Number Ten there was a dash across the street. We usually had a small pair of steps which enabled us to get above the pushing, struggling mass of photographers and so get reasonably steady pictures. Accredited cameramen and photographers were issued with special police passes which enabled us to work in places in London where restrictions might be imposed. Pre-war the public were allowed into Downing Street so our valuable documents were of little importance as everyone in the street tried to see what was going on. I was to spend many hours outside Number Ten and the Foreign Office when I graduated to cameraman, particularly at election times or during important political events. It was not an easy job for one needed to know the faces of all the current Government ministers, all the key Opposition figures, most of the important foreign ambassadors and all the heads of state of foreign countries and the Commonwealth. It was also necessary to keep very up-to-date with current situations so that one knew who to expect. No one liked this assignment for, often on one's own, we could not relax for a moment, could not get a cup of tea, a drink or answer nature's call. To take a chance risked the absolute certainty that whoever we were after would arrive or leave at that very moment.

In addition to the donkey-work humping equipment I often had to hold the microphone when we were seeking an interview with a VIP. He or she would be brought to the camera because the microphones, heavy box-like contraptions, twelve inches square, were very directional and had only a short run of cable. If there was no interviewer I had to collar the victim, get him to the camera, pick up the microphone and ask for 'a few words for *Gaumont-British News*'. Most obliged, flattered at being on the news. There was one gentleman who would rarely cooperate – George Bernard Shaw. We would try to get him to say anything because everything he said was witty or caustic and made good 'sound'. One time – I think it was at Malvern Festival – he stopped, which was a good start, quizzed me from head to foot, saw the camera and proceeded to lecture me at length on why he would not give an interview. We filmed it all. When he had finished he said, 'Young man, I hope you've got all that.' Quite unpredictable.

The day came I had been waiting for – my first solo story. The choice of stories, apart from the hardy annuals, royal occasions and obvious hard news stories, was often very casual or seemed to be. The news staff would go through the daily papers see some way-out event and we would be given the newspaper cutting and sent off. More often than not the story was some journalist's dream – fantasy built up from a tiny fragment of fact.

I was alone in the camera room when such a story materialised and so, being the only one available, I was given my chance. The newspaper cutting told of a discovery and mining of bauxite in the hills of the Lake District. How excited I was! I had learned to drive in an old Daimler car, taught by a lorry driver around Hyde Park Corner, notorious for traffic even then. The car belonged to my grandmother but was too chancy to risk on a long journey so I was off by train, arriving in the early evening at Appleby near Penrith. I then realised how lonely and scared I was and that I had little idea what bauxite was. I had to make a success of this story but I had no idea where to look for it other than that it was somewhere in that area. I could only hope there would be a lot of activity with miners and the stuff coming up in quantities. A taxi-driver found me somewhere to stay – a pub – and there luck was with me. The landlord had heard of the find and knew the farmer who owned the land. With this help I was able to arrange to go to the spot the following day. It was high in the hills and after a short taxi ride it could only be reached by a very tiring uphill trek with camera and tripod. What a disappointment when I arrived. All the things I had envisaged were non-existent. Mining had not begun. A few signs had been erected to mark the area but of activity there was nothing. A depressing start but to return without a story was unthinkable. This was my first story. It was a fine clear day so I set about building up a pretty-pretty scenic of the landscape – sheep, nice clouds, rock formations and later some local people looking at the ground and so on. I had found out that bauxite is a clay-like substance, the chief source of aluminium, so in the town I filmed some aluminium utensils to show the end-product. Such stories, not strictly news, do not date, and it went down very well as a 'filler' when news was short, the commentator telling the story over the pictures. I had survived my first solo test! This bauxite find was very different from the rich bauxite mines in British Guiana which I was to visit twenty-five years later.

Every kind of subject was covered in the years leading up to the end of the 1930s and war. Sport occupied many hours of screen-time and horse-racing was always a great favourite. Those two popular classics, the Lincoln and the Grand National, started the year for us at the end of March; the Derby, Royal Ascot and Goodwood followed in the summer and the Autumn Double – the Cesarewitch and Cambridgeshire at Newmarket closed our racing season. The Lincoln was run pre-war at Lincoln on a Wednesday; the Grand National was staged on Friday in the same week. Today, of course, the Lincoln is run at Doncaster and the Grand National in the following week at Aintree.

Cameraman Eric Owen and his sound man Alan Prentice.

The Lincoln course was a one-mile straight run alongside a public road. It was here, for the first time, a camera car followed alongside the horses – a very dicey operation on a crowded public highway at over 30 m.p.h. We certainly would not get away with it today. We pioneered a similar run on a closed section of road alongside the Grand National course when the motor-racing circuit was built and which television was quick to follow. The camera car at Lincoln was a one-off effort. Usually, as there was no natural elevation, we built a thirty-foot tower rostrum half-way down the course on the opposite side of the public road and another lower one opposite the finish. With a man on the ground at the start we were able to cover the whole race with three men.

On a memorable occasion on 25 March 1936, just after I had joined the newsreel and was in an early stage of learning, it was decided to film the race from the high rostrum with a very long telephoto lens – forty inches long – to follow the horses in extreme close-up from start to finish. I believe we were the first newsreel to use such a long lens; we were certainly in the forefront of such specialised filming, pioneers in movie photography in the same way as the Fleet Street photographers have been for still cameras. We worked closely with trade manufacturers of equipment and companies like Kodak and Ilford in the development of film stock. There have been many special lenses since, including the zoom lens, making it simple to take wide-angle and close-up pictures without having to stop the camera to change lenses. The forty-inch lens was mounted on the tripod first, the camera screwed on to a plate at the back of the lens which was then fitted into the camera. It required a very experienced cameraman for long-focus work of this type. It was difficult enough to film a fast-moving object with a twelve-inch lens. With such extreme close-ups with the forty-inch lens everything was very critical with regard to focus and keeping the subject in the viewfinder. With the Lincoln focus was particularly difficult as the horses came from almost infinity to less than twenty yards in front of us and away again into the distance. This meant altering focus as the race approached and receded and was a two-man exercise, one to operate the camera, one to follow focus. The lens was focused and marked for various points along the course and it was my job to make sure it was turned to those marks as the race progressed. It was not easy for the camera moved rapidly. The lens was very large in circumference as well as in length and required a small rod to turn it smoothly from mark to mark. Down towards me to the nearest point and back again as the horses moved away. 'They're off!' and the horses came thundering towards us at 35 m.p.h. Suddenly the camera stopped panning as the horses were at their nearest point. One of them had fallen and there was a pile-up of horses and jockeys. My colleague, George Golding, with everything in close-up might so easily have followed the leaders without seeing the accident. However with one eye on the rest of the field he did see what happened and I, fortunately, reacted to the camera and did not move the focus out again. We spent that night, fingers crossed. Had we got a scoop in close-up? Horses rarely fall in a flat race and in a Classic too.

The following day we received many congratulations on a marvellous picture. We drank a large toast to each other. But it was also a sad occasion for one horse died in that fall and it is a sickening experience to see a horse put down in those circumstances. The stewards at Lincoln also asked for a copy of our film for their enquiry on how the accident happened. Sadly too, George Golding died shortly afterwards from appendicitis. He was a cheery, plumpish chap, very generous, teaching me a great deal about filming in the brief time I knew him. I owed a lot to him.

With the Lincoln on a Wednesday and the Grand National meeting starting the next day it meant that everyone connected with racing had to get from Lincoln to Liverpool in double-quick time, that is, by Wednesday evening. This applied to us as well as we would have briefings on our Grand National positions on the Thursday. There were no motorways then, cross-country by road was slow and not everyone owned a car. So, to get everyone across by Wednesday night, an imaginative railway company laid on a special race-train. Bookies, touts, tipsters, jockeys, conmen, tic-tac men, fortune-tellers, dedicated punters, cameramen, photographers, journalists, the whole conglomerate of the racing fraternity, boarded that train immediately after the last race at Lincoln. It was a mad scramble, no seats were reserved, first come, first served, every carriage open-plan with tables, meals and drinks being available. We only had to film the big race but packing up the equipment, writing out dope sheets (details of each shot taken), which had to be done on every story, enclosing any official information such as a race-card or whatever was relevant to the occasion, then despatching the exposed negative to London and getting to the station left us with little time to spare. However, between us we usually managed a table near the diner service and a timely tip ensured we got a meal and drinks. The whole atmosphere was always extremely convivial; with such a mixture of personalities it could not fail to be. Everyone had an hour or two to relax. Winners celebrated and even the bookies looked contented. Card schools were soon in full swing. It was an unreal and very enjoyable experience.

Soon after the train began moving the ticket inspectors would come along in pairs, sometimes in threes – and what fun! Those who had had a bad day would lock themselves in the toilets or come rushing ahead of the inspectors looking for somewhere to hide, underneath one's table if one would let them. Some would offer out-of-date return tickets, underground tickets, even bus tickets. The inspectors always took it in good part and I suspect enjoyed the challenge, as did the dodgers who knew they would have to pay up in the end.

On another noteworthy journey two of us shared a table with two Irish men of the cloth. They were marvellous fellows from County Cork. They had done the racing circuit, finally coming from Edinburgh to Lincoln and were finishing at Aintree before crossing to Dublin and home to preach the evils of gambling. All of us had imbibed handsomely and our friends were full of good talk and anecdotes not always what one might expect from reverend gentlemen. Before we arrived at Liverpool they told us they had been given a number of good tips on their travels and passed one on to us – a horse that would run in Scotland. We were to back it every time it ran until the odds shortened to evens, then leave it alone. How they came by such knowledge one can only surmise. Maybe some guilty fellow had passed it on in the confessional. We did nothing the first time it ran; it won! We backed it the next time – it won! And again, and again until, as forecast, it went to evens – and lost! It gave one a thought or two about racing and the straight and narrow, but that was a long time ago. However we blessed the Church. Lovely fellows those two, men of the world, well able to administer good sense to their flock.

At the Aintree meeting each company had its favourite hotel. Pre-war, Gaumont stayed across the Mersey at Wallasey. On the first evening we would make for the Argyle, the old music-hall at Birkenhead close by and a very merry time it always proved to be. Later we stayed at Southport, much nearer to Aintree, pleasant but not so much fun.

In the 1930s Gaumont had acquired the rights to film the Grand National from Mrs Topham, the formidable lady who owned the course. There were thirty-one jumps on the four-and-a-half mile circuit and key ones like Becher's Brook, Valentine's, the water jump and the first and last jumps were double-covered. This meant hiring a number of freelance cameramen in addition to all our staff men. After the war, because of this expense, the cost of the rights and the problems of keeping other companies from 'pinching' pictures, the National became a pooled event coordinated by our production manager. On the day before the race everyone was told to be at the course in the morning before racing began. It was a ritual. Although we all knew the course and jumps backwards we had to walk to our positions, inspect the special stands or rostrums erected, receive identification armbands, be allocated an assistant, often an elderly gent not fit enough to carry the heavy equipment. This meant we had to hump most of it ourselves. The men came from the British Legion and were there each year. Collection points were arranged for the exposed negatives because everything had to be flown to London for processing. Each newsreel was allotted a section of the racecourse and was responsible for processing its negatives, making duplicates (called lavenders) for the other reels and seeing they were delivered on time for, as always, getting the pictures into the cinemas as quickly as possible was a priority and many saw the race on the screen the same night, in the West End of London and as far afield as Scotland.

Gaumont's Sid Bonnett (the first cameraman to fly over Mount Everest) with sound man William Burningham.

BUFVC/Ted Candy collection

Still on racing in 1936, our editor-in-chief, Castleton-Knight, a true showman, chanced to tip the Aga Khan's grey colt, Mahmoud, in the reel to win the Derby. He filmed it in the stables and exercising on the Downs, and its picture was splashed in reels prior to the race. It won – at 100-8. The public were ecstatic for it had been well backed on the strength of our tip – 16-1 – when it first appeared on the screen. I fear all the cinemas would have been wrecked had it lost. There were many congratulations at this scoop including a cable from our managing director who was in New York when the race was run. It read, 'Well done, very many congratulations – but don't do it again!' The Derby appeared in three reels: on 25 May 1936 – GB NEWS TIPS 'MAHMOUD' FOR THE DERBY; 28 May – THE DERBY WON BY 'MAHMOUD' – TIPPED BY GB NEWS; and on 1 June – £1,000,000 WON BY GB NEWS 'MAHMOUD' DERBY TIP – TWO BACKERS SPEAK.

Grand Prix motor racing was in its infancy in the 1930s and Brooklands racing circuit at Weybridge, Surrey, was an early venue for this sport. Built in 1906 and closed in 1939 the circuit was about two and three-quarters miles round and only 100 feet wide with two steep banks twenty-nine feet high. The cars used to come hurtling round the top of these close to where I sat filming, praying they would stay on the track. Such steep banking would not be permissible in today's Grand Prix racing. Paul Wyand of *British Movietone News* did have a car go over the top near where he was filming and the driver, Clive Dunfee, was killed. Paul got a very tragic scoop.

Football always accounted for a high percentage of newsreel footage and was hell to film. We could not film the whole match as television does today. It would have been too costly and too time-consuming to edit. To shoot a whole game would have needed about 8,000 feet on the main camera alone for a possible use in the reel of 200 feet. So we had to try to keep our coverage to the highlights. It was amazing how many goals were obtained in roughly 800 feet, about nine minutes of actual filming which was about average for the main camera. For the chap on the touchline, usually my stint, 400 feet would probably be the maximum. Football crowds could be very dangerous, even pre-war. Some grounds, particularly in the North, had the front row of standing spectators at worm's-eye level with the result that anyone sitting on the touchline, perhaps only a yard from the crowd, blotted out the view of those behind. Football crowds do not talk, they act, and a heavy beer bottle can hurt. We tried to gain their goodwill by filming those we intended to sit in front of. This worked while the match was dull but come an exciting moment and the missiles flew. At first class grounds like Arsenal's at Highbury in London we had properly constructed stands with plenty of room on the ground so that one was far enough away from the crowd not to interfere with their view. Luxury filming. A very different picture presented itself at Chelsea's ground at Stamford Bridge. Here our main position was from a special rostrum, fifteen feet high, situated on a cinder bank in the middle of the standing crowd. They were a rough lot, mostly full of beer which they continuously discharged unceremoniously where they stood, often on the person in front. It was a sordid scene, and not easy to concentrate on filming. In spite of the barbed wire which surrounded the base of the stand there was always someone trying to climb on it for a better view. The result was we were constantly being shaken and sworn at and we worked in an atmosphere of urine and beer. I am glad to say it is a different Chelsea ground today.

One of the oldest and strangest forms of football is the Eton wall game. It is played on one of Eton's playing fields against a high brick wall which runs parallel to the Slough Road. They start playing in September but the only time we and the public can see the game is at the end of November when the Collegers and the Oppidans (the Scholars and the Townsmen) play their most important match of the season and the only time they face each other. It is rather like a local derby in normal football. The pitch is a narrow strip about six yards wide by 120 yards long. There is a goal at each end, one a door in an adjacent wall, the other an old elm tree with the goal, marked in white on the trunk. The complete rules are too complex to give in detail. There are ten men a side with two periods of half an hour and a five-minute interval. The ball is small and round. Passing is only allowed sideways, there is no handling of the ball and no heeling backwards. A player may only touch the ground with his hands and feet but filming down from the top of the wall and seeing the mass of bodies below, it seemed to me the object was to annihilate each other in the thick mud the ground had become after a rainy autumn. As far as I know it is still played today.

Much has been written about cricket and the rivalries between newsreels when one had the rights to film a test match. Searchlights were shone into lenses, often unsighting the players; high rostrums were built outside the ground – all well documented in other publications and books. A similar problem arose, as in football; we could not film the whole game over four or five days. Wickets were what was wanted instead of goals. To keep the footage to a reasonable length we had to have a fair idea of each player's potential. There were obvious times to film. Opening batsmen, a new batsman, a new bowler, a new ball. But wickets were difficult to get, almost as difficult as it was for the bowler. Luck was a factor and was well illustrated at a test match when there was no rights and all companies were filming. The five cameras were all set up on one stand. On a hot summer's day one of the cameramen had indulged his thirst more than was wise. With the soporific warmth of the sun his eyes closed and he drowsed away at the foot of his tripod. The other four cameraman stuck gamely to the job, switch on, switch off – a hot day and wickets would not fall. The footage mounted. A hundred feet, 200 feet, 300 feet and upwards. The other camera was silent, turned off as the cameraman slumbered. Suddenly he woke. 'Hell,' he cried, 'why didn't someone kick me?' The others were thoroughly browned off sitting on their cases giving the match a chance to liven up. The sleeper jumped up, switched on his camera set for a close-up on a wicket and with the first ball he filmed a wicket fell. Luck! The others would have been only too pleased to have followed his invitation to kick him.

Then there was boxing, which always made good pictures. We concentrated on heavyweight fights and I was usually at the ringside. It was a difficult place from which to film because, apart from the sound camera at the back of the hall, no other proper position could be obtained, there being very little spare room. I had to be sure not to obstruct the view of the ringside big-shots, so it meant finding a spot below one of the corners and bobbing up to film when anything dramatic happened. At the end of a round I would film the boxer in my corner being sponged down, revived or whatever, but the greatest hazard for me was when he took a swig at the water bottle and spat into the spittoon on the side. Often the aim would miss and one would be fortunate to dodge the full contents of a bloody mouth.

A boxer I had a lot of time for was Tommy Farr, a Welsh miner before he became professional in 1926. In 1937 I went to the village of Tonypandy in the mining area of the Rhondda Valley to film him at home prior to his fight with Ben Foord. He won, gaining a Lonsdale Belt, and became British heavyweight champion. I saw for the first time the hard life of the Welsh miners of those post-World War I days. I saw the small terraced houses with their primitive facilities. I saw the giant wheels turning at the coal-face taking the men to the gloom below and the weary black-faced shift trudging the streets to their homes when the wheels turned the other way. For me it was full of interest, the place where Tommy Farr was brought up rather than the boxer himself, although he could not have been more cooperative and, of course, he was the story. I was very glad he won the British title but he never managed to get a world title. The nearest he got was against Joe Louis, also in 1937 in America, taking Joe the full fifteen rounds, only one of three boxers to take him the full distance. Tommy died in 1986 aged seventy-two.

A different day and a different sport. One could be at Twickenham filming rugger from a top gantry battling with the sun, which sat behind our position casting a shadow across the pitch. One half was dark and the other brilliant causing a tricky exposure problem. When we see the great interest in sport these days one could say that the newsreels were ahead of their time by allocating so much of their space to sport all those years ago.

However there were many stories other than sport to cover. I could be at Southampton watching the *Queen Mary* berth, 81,000 tons of ship, over 1,000 feet long. It was always a thrilling sight to see this massive vessel brought alongside so smoothly with scarcely a bump. Then up the first gangway with the officials to the purser's office to try to find the particular personality I was there to film. Not an easy task to locate anyone in that vast floating hotel when everyone was about to disembark; somehow we always managed to find them.

Another story concerning ships was the fleet exercises to Gibraltar. A senior cameraman from each company was accommodated in a different battleship and

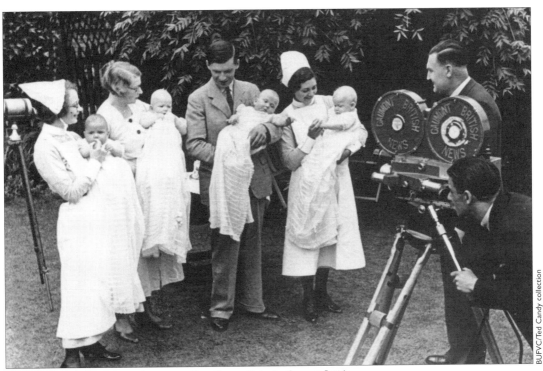

The St Neot's quads. Bert Bishop and cameraman Peter Cannon filming for Gaumont-British.

their films pooled. What magnificent pictures they made, those great ships steaming in line astern, turning together, approaching the Rock. Those were the days when we had a huge navy. Little did I know, as I wished to be picked for this annual assignment, that a few years hence I would be very much involved with warships.

There was Olympia at Christmas time, filming hundreds of children screaming their heads off with laughter at the antics of the clowns at Bertram Mills Circus and becoming suddenly silent as they watched the daring performance of a high-wire act. A very noisy job, but the children's faces were always a joy to photograph.

A different sort of circus with animal connotations was the Chelsea Arts Ball each New Year's Eve. A seething mass of people of all ages would fill the Royal Albert Hall. We would have a camera placed in a box with huge ten-kilowatt arc lights stationed all round the top gallery to light the dancing revellers below. One of us, often me, would be on the floor for close-ups with a hand-camera and an electrician with portable lights. Those hand-lights, as we called them, were invaluable, enabling us to film many events at night or in areas where the light was poor, such as in this story. Couples would be coupling in the corridors, students in fancy dress would stagger outside to be sick and the general mixture of high spirits and bottled spirits would erupt in smashing up set pieces and anything else handy as the clock struck twelve and hundreds of balloons descended from the ceiling. For those of us who were there to work it was not the most enjoyable of occasions. A debauch *par excellence*.

Fertility drugs were not a feature of the 1930s, so when quadruplets were born at St Neot's in Huntingdonshire on 30 November 1935, shortly before I joined *Gaumont-British News* in 1936, it was a big story and all the reels rushed north-wards to film the tiny tots. But Gaumont had secured exclusive filming rights and the other reels were forced to snatch what they could. Gaumont issued several reels during 1936 showing the progress of the babes including their daily routines, their first shopping outing in St Neot's, and their first birthday party. Was this an early case of cheque book journalism? Perhaps.

After the tragedy of Edward VIII's abdication came pageantry with the coronation of King George VI and his queen in May 1937. There was no television so it was the cinema newsreels that showed the great processions of state. Facilities were certainly not like those provided for the coronation of Queen Elizabeth II but there was much to film. This was a time when the King was crowned as King of Great Britain and Ireland and of the British Dominions beyond the Seas; King, Defender of the Faith, Emperor of India. It was, however, the first time at a coronation when the dominions had acquired a status of free and independent nations not answerable to the British Parliament. The crowds along the route from Buckingham Palace to Westminster Abbey had plenty to look at. There was the Lord Mayor's procession and the Speaker of the House of Commons in his coach. There were the King's Bargemaster and Watermen and the Yeoman of the Guard marching with massed bands, detachments from the various services at home and overseas, field marshals, the Honourable Artillery Company – so much pageantry. There were sixty-two countries represented, among them representatives from Afghanistan, the Argentine, Bulgaria, Cuba, Czechoslovakia, Guatemala, Honduras, Nicaragua, Salvador and Yemen – most unlikely to attend such an occasion today. Such a lot for the cameras to film. Now the royal family. The Dukes of Kent and Gloucester; Queen Mary and the Queen of Norway in the glass coach; the young Princesses Elizabeth and Margaret and then the King and Queen in the State Coach drawn by eight fine grey horses. Weeks of planning went into such stories, requiring all our resources, not only to film but to solve the complicated problems of rushing the negatives to the laboratories for developing and editing to get the reels into the cinemas that same evening. We were in our positions at dawn, each cameraman allotted a section of the route. As always in a major story, key areas were double-covered in case of camera trouble. Those were pioneering days which set the pattern for the extensive television productions we see today. My position was at the top of the Duke of York's statue overlooking the Mall. I had not been filming on my own for very long and this was quite a simple job filming general scenes. It was also a lonely one, 124 feet up, almost not part of the spectacle below, and it seemed a very long day before I returned to earth again.

In this same year there were many deaths of well-known personalities, a number of whom had featured in our reels. Jean Harlow, Sir Austin Chamberlain, Viscount Snowden, John D. Rockefeller, Marconi, George Gershwin, John Drinkwater, Ramsey Macdonald and Ravel among them. Pictures of the civil war in Spain came to us, a prelude to the coming world war, as we saw Guernica bombed by the Germans. There was the fantastic film of the German airship *Hindenburg* crashing at Lakehurst, New Jersey, in the United States a few days before the coronation – horrific scenes of survivors running from the burning hulk sent to us by our American associates. And there was the tragedy of the disappearance of pioneer aviator Amelia Earhart over the South Pacific in July 1937. Library film had to be used in stories of this nature.

In July 1938 I had my first flight. Flying was really an experience then. We used single-propeller planes with open cockpits from which to film. We dressed like airmen with helmets, goggles and intercom, sitting next to the pilot to direct him on positioning to film the subject below, probably a shipwreck or major disaster. We got a special danger fee for flying and I think, generally speaking, we deserved it. Later, coping with slipstream, flying off aircraft carriers and in fighter jets we had to do

Loading camera equipment into our private plane from one of Gaumont's early 'trucks'.

BUFVC/Ted Candy collection

almost impossible feats against G-force. A camera can be almost impossibly heavy when you are power-diving at 400 m.p.h. or more.

My first flight was not to film from the air. The company had hired a plane to fly me to Dublin from Croydon Airport (after the war we owned our own plane based at Croydon). This first ascent into the skies was very exciting for in a small plane one got the real feel of flying. We trundled along the grass runway of Croydon at something like 80 m.p.h. to rise slowly above the houses. As we gathered speed I remember very clearly looking down, seeing the red roofs and the green pattern of fields and circling the town as we headed for the coast to cross the waters to the distant Emerald Isle. What a wonderful invention was this man-made bird, I thought. I was on my way to film an American, Douglas Corrigan, – 'One-Way' Corrigan as he came to be styled – who had flown the Atlantic in a nine-year-old monoplane which had cost him under £200. No one in New York knew he was intending to make such a flight. Everyone thought he was bound for Los Angeles when he took off from Floyd Bennett Field. The flight was a remarkable effort for his only instruments were an oil pressure gauge, a bank-and-turn indicator and that was all. No wireless or compass. He landed at Baldonnel Airfield just outside Dublin with very little petrol left, twenty-eight hours after leaving New York. I got some good pictures and after filming I was taken in tow by our Dublin branch representative, a true Irishman with the un-Irish name of Shakespeare. He suggested I had earned a drink. I did not know much about the Irish and the drink and a hectic evening followed. Many Guinnesses later I stumbled stupified to bed to awake next morning with a terrible hangover. My sole wish then was to get away as soon as I could; I did not want another session. Nor did I relish flying, for in a small plane one does not fly very high and every bit of turbulence is registered as one bumps one's way across the skies. Goodness knows how Corrigan managed the Atlantic in that old plane. However, all I could think of was to get away and back to good old England. It was not a good day.

The weather was poor and the pilot, who did not look too bright either, was not keen to make the flight. I told him I had to get the negative back, so off we went. When we got over Croydon there was dense fog. There followed a most unenjoyable half an hour circling round and round unable to see anything, wondering whether we had enough fuel to stay up or find another airport – and not feeling terribly well. I was quite nervous for this was only the second time I had been in an airplane. Unless we could see, we did not have the instruments to make a landing, and what if we *did* run out of fuel? Mercifully there was a break in the fog and we managed to find our way through the hole and touch down safely – half frozen and white about the gills. I rang the office and *then* I realised I had broken the most important rule of the newsman: when a story is completed ring the office, which I should have done the previous evening. It was a commandment in case one was to be sent on elsewhere. 'Where are you?', they asked. 'We've been trying to get you all last

24

night.' 'Croydon.' 'Croydon! We wanted a follow-up on Corrigan, perhaps a flight in his plane!' That nearly ended my career as a newsreel cameraman but perhaps had I stayed and had a flight in that monoplane my career might have ended for good. It taught me a lesson – never to leave a story without phoning, even in London. Gaumont did try out car radio links but fortunately for us they did not work satisfactorily and the idea was dropped. It was not very appealing never to be away from the office. Pity the cameramen of today with mobile phones. My visit to Ireland also taught me to be wary of the Irish and Guinness. Although I did not enjoy my return flight I had broken my duck as a flyer and in later years had many different flying experiences in flying boats, Hurricanes, Dakotas, Swordfish and Walruses from ships as well as a passenger on regular flights to many other countries.

July 1938 seemed a month of records. It started with an LNER steam locomotive reaching a speed of 125 m.p.h. between Grantham and Peterborough on a test run – some speed before the war on a railway line! There followed the opening of the first passenger and mail service by Imperial Airways flying boat *Challenger* to Sydney, Australia. It took just over seven days, stopping to refuel at a number of places including Singapore and giving passengers an opportunity to stay ashore overnight. When a flying boat lands on the water it sounds as if the bottom is being torn out.

To complete the month's records there was another remarkable flying event. A composite aircraft consisting of a flying boat – the lower half named *Maia* – and a float seaplane – the upper half named *Mercury* – left Foynes sea-base in Ireland with *Mercury* due to fly to Montreal and New York. The composite aircraft with *Mercury* on the wing of *Maia* took off as a single eight-engine plane and by so doing enabled *Mercury* to conserve fuel and make its journey without refuelling. When some way out to sea the planes separated and *Mercury* accomplished the journey to Montreal in a record twenty hours. Among its half-a-ton load, it was carrying newspapers, photographs and newsreels of the King's visit to Paris. It returned to Southampton without the aid of its partner but had to stop frequently to refuel.

Politically there was much coming and going in Downing Street. Neville Chamberlain formed a coalition government, succeeding Stanley Baldwin as Prime Minister. There were increasing signs of coming war. Singapore naval base was opened. Germany annexed Austria. The British fleet was mobilised. We began to concentrate on military subjects.

But there was another very splendid event in that year of 1938. On 27 September, with daughters Princesses Elizabeth and Margaret, Queen Elizabeth (the Queen Mother) launched on the Clyde the largest ship in the world at the time – 'the noblest vessel ever built in Britain', said the Queen. Like her sister, the *Queen Mary*, the *Queen Elizabeth* was a wonderful ship and some statistics with regard to her size may be interesting. She was 1,031 feet long. If stood on her stern, her bow to the sky, she would be higher than the Eiffel Tower and three times the height of St

Queen Elizabeth launches the liner *Queen Elizabeth* at John Brown's shipyard on the Clyde in 1938. From the newsreel.

ITN Archive/Reuters

Paul's Cathedral. She was 118 feet wide and weighed 83,675 tons. There were thirteen decks accommodating 2,043 passengers and 1,190 crew. Her rudder weighed 140 tons; four anchors each weighed sixteen tons with 990 feet of chain cable which itself weighed 300 tons. There were twenty-six steel lifeboats, ten million rivets in the construction of her hull; three steam whistles, each a ton; 650 electric motors, 700 electric clocks and two power stations generating 8,800 kilowatts. In the ship there were 30,000 lamps and 4,000 miles of wiring. The skies were dark and sombre in keeping with the grave times but the crowds of 250,000 who lined the river banks did not seem to mind the occasional drizzle. To stand, as I did, a midget beneath this huge mass of steel perched on the stocks and leaning down towards the river soon to receive her, was a chastening, awe-inspiring, slightly terrifying experience. Four propellers eighteen feet in diameter, each of thirty-two tons – silent, still, soon to thrash the waters of the oceans. Above, a tiny man stood in the bows. A clear deck with no superstructure, no funnels. The Queen in pale grey with the princesses in pink was waiting with a bottle of Australian wine to launch the ship. Close-ups of hammers knocking away the supporting wedge-shaped chocks until there was almost nothing to prevent her moving. What if she were to topple over? Such thoughts go through one's mind. A shot along the keel. I would never see below the water-line again. Close-ups of proud men, tense and waiting. 'I name this ship...,' and the last of the chocks were knocked away. Silence. Then, imperceptibly, a slight shudder as liner No. 552 braced herself for her big moment. The huge drag chains secured to her sides to slow her journey down the slipway began to move, throwing up clouds of dust and she slid away faster and faster, the chains pulling hard as she dipped into the cold waters of the Clyde and was afloat, successfully launched. Relief on the faces of the men who built her, whistles and cheers from the many craft on the river. A job well done and a vital one. She served as a troop transport during the war, steaming over 492,000 miles carrying 811,000 troops.

Two days later there was a very different story. The Germans were becoming increasingly aggressive and the prospect of war was an early possibility. Neville Chamberlain for the UK, Mussolini for Italy and Daladier for France had flown to Munich to meet Hitler. Their fears of war were allayed when the Munich Agreement was signed in which Hitler promised to negotiate by peaceful means in any future territorial claim. So back in London from John Brown's Shipyard, on 29 September 1938 I was at Heston Airport to film the return of Neville Chamberlain from Munich. Winged collar, black tie and hatless he stood grey-faced on the steps of his aircraft waving a piece of paper. There was the trace of a smile on the downward curve of his lips. Later, in Downing Street, he uttered the memorable words, 'Peace for our time', to the waiting, cheering crowds. At Heston, at the foot of the aircraft steps I, with other cameramen, press photographers, journalists and officials pushed and jostled in an excited effort to get closer for pictures and interviews. Behind, the five newsreels filmed the historic and extraordinary scenes from the tops of their camera cars. I will never forget that look on Chamberlain's face, the rare smile beneath his moustache, really believing that Hitler was sincere in what he promised. It was a wonderful moment for the Prime Minister but, alas, was to break his heart when a year later he realised that his piece of paper was just that. Everything he felt came across in his voice when he was to announce that we were at war. A sad day ultimately although at the time there was euphoria. Chamberlain was described as 'a knight of peace' – 'the Great Conciliator' – there were thanksgiving services and prayers, congratulations by the King and masses of flowers and tributes were received at Downing Street.

The established newsreels were fighting a war of their own as the decade approached its grisly end. All our coverage was in black and white. To film in colour meant running three negatives, impractical for normal news filming. Only Technicolor had suitable cameras and that was a very costly operation. So no newsreels in colour – we thought. Suddenly a new all-colour newsreel appeared – *National News*. It was a bold attempt to break into the newsreel monopoly but was doomed from the start. The parent companies of the newsreels owned most of the cinemas and controlled what was shown on their screens and *National News* was unable to get sufficient distribution to become viable. In addition to distribution

Peter Cannon, ace Gaumont cameraman, and his sound man William Burningham.

BUFVC/Ted Candy collection

problems it was beset with technical difficulties and very soon the company folded. After the war a single-colour negative was available and we were enabled to film many stories in colour. Film stocks have undergone tremendous changes since those early days. Some are so fast that pictures can be taken almost without light. Such changes have created problems for both movie and stills professionals, for the amateur photographer is very much a competitive force to be reckoned with.

In April 1939 the Spanish civil war ended, an uneasy peace ensued, and most of our stories had a political aspect. To lighten these sombre trends for a while we continued to film the normal social round – society weddings at St Margaret's Church, Westminster, fashion shows and big sporting events like the Boat Race and the Cup Final.

However more serious matters soon took precedence in our presentations. Conscription was introduced in Britain and our filming was exclusively directed at preparations for war. Air raid shelters were constructed, parks dug up, trenches sunk, sandbags filled. Chamberlain restated the British intention to stand by Poland, and the continental countries were mobilising as the chilling reality of impending disaster spread over Europe. I was on holiday in France in August and really became aware just how near war was when travelling back from Nice by road and passing through Dijon I saw a large group of men and women gathered round a notice. It was a call-up for the reserves. I had intended to stay in Paris for a couple of days but I decided if Reserves were being called up I had better get back to England quickly. I am glad I did for the next week the rush started.

The 1930s had indeed been eventful years; in 1939 on 1 September Germany invaded Poland and two days later we were at war.

Chapter Three
War Correspondent

Sunday, 3 September 1939, saw me standing in the centre of London Bridge in the City of London as the first air raid warning sounded shortly after Neville Chamberlain gravely told us we were at war. I was in the City to film whatever might happen in London's Square Mile after the anticipated announcement of hostilities. I do not recall exactly what the office expected or receiving any specific instructions except, maybe, the proclamation of war from the steps of the Royal Exchange. No one had thought there would be an air raid so soon and I was on the bridge wondering what to film. Sunday morning in the City was always very quiet and peaceful and this one, with nobody about, was especially so. It was so still. In the warm September sunshine and with the shimmering water below softly lapping against the banks of the river, war seemed illogical. It was an unreal atmosphere, almost eerie, the lull before the storm. The barrage balloons had gone up across the Thames – a symbol: the balloon had gone up. Suddenly a tin-hatted air raid warden appeared shouting 'Take cover!' as he raced on over the bridge. Those earlier thoughts disappeared and passed into an awareness that we really were at war. No good making for shelter. I was there to film whatever was going to happen. That produced an uneasy feeling, almost fear.

How did one film an air raid? I needed a clear view of the sky and the ground. I needed elevation. I remember contemplating climbing the 311 steps of the 200-foot Monument that, aptly, commemorated the Great Fire of London which started in Pudding Lane. How absurd 'Pudding Lane' sounded just then. No good. The Monument was not open. Nor were any of the office buildings. It had to be where I was, on the bridge in the middle of the Thames. There was an uninterrupted view of the sky; I could look along the river both ways and see buildings on either side. Then the all-clear rang out to solve my problems. I made for the labyrinth of quiet City streets to see if there was anything to film. That first hour or so at the start of a war, alone on the deserted roads of London, made me realise that I, and the rest of the country, were going into the unknown, into an uncertain future. My thoughts were confirmed, somewhat, before the end of the year. Unbelievably the battleship HMS *Royal Oak* had been sunk in the supposedly safe harbour of Scapa Flow with the loss of over 800 men. The German ship *Graf Spee* was scuttled in Montevideo, Uruguay, after the battle of the River Plate.

War came early to the newsreels in an unexpected way. All places of entertainment were ordered to be closed with immediate effect. This meant shutting all the cinemas. The ban fortunately did not last long as the authorities soon realised the importance of theatres and cinemas to public morale. There was no television so the newsreels were a necessary outlet to show what was happening on the war fronts. I am not sure whether we made up reels during the ban; we certainly continued to film.

Decisions had to be made as to which cameramen were to be accredited to the army and the RAF, the Royal Navy believing its own naval photographers would be able to obtain suitable material. A system was established whereby all coverage from all areas was available to each company. This was a sensible arrangement avoiding more than one cameraman filming in the same area, reducing the number of cameramen required overall in theatres of war, and, as important, conserving negative film stock. It was known as the 'rota' system.

It was not long before the first war correspondents were chosen from each of the five companies. I was not very senior and at Gaumont I did not hear my name in the forefront of those eligible. I saw them leave for France with just a little envy, kitted out in the official war correspondent's uniform, that of an army captain, with no pips but 'War Correspondent' sewn on the sleeves and a suitable cap badge. We filmed their departure, giving them quite a prestigious send-off. We wondered how they would get on. Although destined to be in the front lines the men received no advance training from the forces. Also, most found there was little formal explanation of how the war was being directed in their particular section of operations and had to rely on the goodwill of commanders to keep them in the picture. The only exception to this that I personally experienced later was just before D-Day when I was briefed on the forthcoming operation in great detail.

A Ministry of Information had been set up in London with some newsreel editors and technical people on its staff. At the end of January 1940 they decided that the newsreel had to be vetted on what war news was included, and although not termed censorship, some items had to be withdrawn or altered. Later all war coverage was censored before reaching the newsreels.

Although all of us were in a reserved occupation we could, of course, have resigned and joined up, and a few did. Most of us felt the sensible thing was to stay with the reels and use our experience in the hope of a responsible and useful job. With men now overseas, at Gaumont the remaining cameramen were deployed around the country, our brief to obtain anything to do with combat war, particularly dogfights and air raids – or any other form of attack. With nobody having any idea where such happenings might occur, and no service authority being forthcoming about service movements – 'security' and 'fifth column' being the 'in' words – our assignments were thankless tasks.

I was despatched to Chatham and there I stayed for a month. My headquarters was the Bull Hotel in Rochester, next door to the town hall where the air-raid warnings were received. It was the bar of the Bull which eventually enabled me to make friends with town-hall officials and get some idea when air raids were expected. I was not allowed into the dockyard. I was then the owner of an old Riley car for which one received a petrol allowance so when there was a warning I would rush up to a position I had found on a hill in a residential area overlooking the dockyard surround, the best I could do. Frequently the all-clear was received before I reached my position but I had no way of knowing this, not hearing it in the car, and I would wait for long periods on the alert for something to happen, tripod set up, camera ready, binoculars round my neck. After some days of this procedure I was approached by a police officer. Apparently I had been reported by a resident as a possible spy. I had some difficulty convincing the police why I was there.

From Chatham, with nothing in the can, I was switched to Southend where retired naval officers had been recalled to organise convoy assemblies and elderly ladies knitted jumpers for the forces. Not much to film there.

Soon I was on my way north to Scarborough. This meant a nightmare journey in the blackout with masked headlights, on unknown roads, to arrive late at night in a strange town with no hotel booked. Finding one's way around in such circumstances was like driving in thick fog. Eventually I did locate a commercial hotel after enquiries from the few people about and a lot of suspicious looks – people who wandered around at night asking questions were certainly suspect. From the dark streets I went through an outer door, past heavy curtains, and found myself in the midst of a very jolly crowd of people. A buxom lady welcomed me with the friendly warmth of the North, said a room could be found for me and a cold meal provided, and come and join the party. And join the party I had to do, for no one had the slightest notion of leaving it to show me a room just then. The raucous atmosphere was something of an ordeal. I was cold sober, tired. They were very merry, convivially friendly, celebrating the birthday of one of them. The party was made up of some older commercial travellers and the staff of the hotel. Eventually a pie-eyed chambermaid got me into a room and would have stayed had I wished. I never got the cold meal. In spite of this bizarre start I stayed on at the hotel, which was comfortable and had unusually good food for the times. It was still early in the war. I was in Scarborough for six weeks and had more to do there. Whitby was close by and was constantly having survivors brought in from mined ships. The most difficult part of this kind of assignment, as elsewhere, was in establishing sources of information, and one had to be devious. There were a few officially blessed excursions conducted under secret conditions to various areas. On these occasions it was mostly to show army activities of one sort or other. There was no other way of getting pictures of service operations. No amount of goodwill could get one into these areas without official permission. All our tricks and dodges in peacetime were of no avail. So one had to be content with the few opportunities one was given.

In this unsatisfactory way the first months of the war passed and I began to wonder whether I had made the right decision in staying with the newsreels. I had taken nothing of any consequence, very little had been used, and although up to then not a great deal was coming back from overseas, I wished for more involvement in things that mattered. I was soon to get my wish. In early April 1940 as I was preparing to be best man at my brother's wedding in Liverpool I received an urgent call to return to London. The Royal Navy had decided professional cameramen were needed to supplement their own staff to depict the war at sea and had called for three cameramen to proceed immediately to Scapa Flow to be accommodated in ships. I was to be one of them. It meant I would not be able to attend my brother's wedding, which has always been a source of great regret for me. I never saw him again. Just before the war he had been with Gaumont for a while in its sales department. He joined up when war was declared and was getting married before returning to Cranwell to complete his training to be an RAF fighter pilot. He was reported missing in the Mediterranean before there was another opportunity to meet.

Although the navy had realised it needed experienced operators its attitude towards publicity was very stuffy at first and apart from providing the means to get into the war in other ways it certainly did not offer a great deal. The army and RAF had an official war correspondent's uniform. The navy specified we could wear an officer's uniform but without brass buttons or cap badge, no stripes or anything on the sleeves although we were to hold the notional rank of lieutenant. The result was that the three of us, Lovat Cave-Chinn from Paramount, George Oswald from Universal and myself, straight from Moss Bros in uniform with black buttons, white shirt, black tie, set out from London for Scapa looking like three chauffeurs.

After a cold and rough passage across the Pentland Firth from Thurso we arrived at night at the depot ship, the *Dunluce Castle*, in Scapa Flow. Like so much at this time everything seemed unreal. Here I was in a rather dirty coal-burning depot ship with masses of equipment and no idea where I was going. However, in a way, it was quite exciting to be in such a new environment. I knew little about warships except that the sharp end was the front. Ever since I started work I seemed to have been thrust into situations about which I knew little. First publicity, then camera work and now the navy. I knew little about the sea either except one could paddle in it. After some searching through signals we learned that one of us was to be accommodated in a battle-cruiser, one in a battleship and one in a destroyer. It was up to us to arrange who went where. Cave-Chinn, more senior and more experienced than Oswald and myself immediately plumped for the destroyer. We did not object and tossed for the other two places. I won the battleship – it was HMS *Valiant*, and Oswald went to HMS *Repulse*. Then Cave-Chinn was told he would be billeted in the depot ship as, in harbour, there was no room for an extra body in a destroyer. He would be put aboard any one that was going to sea. That was a setback he had not expected. Destroyers went to sea more frequently than the other ships, which is why they had been his choice, but not having a permanent base in one was very unsettling. Boats were at a premium and distances between ships great so we had to spend the first night in the depot ship. When I awoke next morning and saw all the warships I was in a daze.

I felt some trepidation as the boat approached *Valiant* and came alongside the gangway, which seemed miles below the deck above. I was not sure what to do and did not wish to appear too gauche. I scrambled on to the gangway and on reaching the quarterdeck was greeted by a very smart lieutenant, telescope under his arm – pukka Royal Navy – an Honorable and Junior Carlton Club member I learned later. He saluted me and I gave a sort of wave back. Following me up the gangway came my gear as if I had just returned from safari. The officer looked at me incredulously and obviously had not seen the signal announcing my arrival. Eyeing some of the cases which had arrived on the deck but too polite to ask who I was, he conducted me to the wardroom and asked me to wait a moment. There was no one there and I felt very strange and alone. The low headroom, clanging doors and austere bulkheads seemed most odd to a cosseted landlubber. After a few minutes a youngish Church of England padre arrived with the officer who, as I recollect, introduced me in a rather mumbled way: 'This gentleman is to stay with us for a while, Padre' – and we were left together. Before we could say anything in marched another priest, this time a Roman Catholic, a jovial-looking fellow, older than his colleague. 'Have a gin,' he bellowed and three pink gins appeared. What an odd beginning. My sins must have travelled ahead. Small talk followed, none of us knowing quite what to say. Another gin arrived and the formal exchanges between us began to be less tense. I was asked how long I was to stay, where was my church and offered the facilities of both churches aboard. It was then I guessed the officer of the day, not having seen anything like me before and wearing black buttons and no dog-collar, had concluded I must be a Methodist minister of some kind – and this turned out to be the case. At least he had not taken me for a chauffeur. I enlightened my two hosts why I was in the ship. There were hoots of laughter, more gins were ordered and I thought I detected some degree of relief in both of them. I imagine even padres don't care for too much competition for the available souls and no doubt they had a fair distribution of the ship's company. Soon the officer, having discovered his mistake, came to apologise. More laughter and more gins. I was now something of a curiosity as the officers began to assemble for a quickie before eating. I received a message that the captain and commander wished to meet me. With so many gins I was a little tipsy and staggered along to the captain's cabin. He was a marvellous man, had heard about his new cleric and was very understanding about my unsteady arrival.

Connie Boyd

Commander Reid on the left and Captain Rawlings of HMS *Valiant* – my first ship.

He and the commander made me very welcome – with more gins. Captain Rawlings and Commander Reid both became admirals. I could not have been more fortunate in beginning my life with the navy by joining HMS *Valiant*. So began a period of intense interest and good pictures in this friendly and happy ship.

After my early debut in the wardroom and another session in the evening I slept soundly in spite of all the noises, the constant pipes calling men to duty and the many things necessary to run that mass of steel as a war weapon and a living community. Then came the awakening. I was woken at 4.30 a.m. by a messenger and it took me some while to realise where I was as I looked into the face of the sailor who was shaking me. One of the padres was leaving the ship at 5.30 a.m. to visit a cruiser just back from Norway and had suggested I should go with him as there should be an opportunity for some spectacular pictures. So at dawn I stepped into a naval cutter with the padre and set off across the cold, grey, choppy waters of Scapa Flow soon to be reminded that it was to war that I had come. The padre was silent in the boat and I could not begin to guess what was ahead. As we approached the ship I saw her superstructure had been badly damaged, the bridge and forepart of the ship torn and twisted metal. 'Bombing,' I heard as we clambered up the gangway. It still had not occurred to me why a padre was visiting the cruiser at this hour. I soon found out. The ship was unnaturally quiet as I stood on the deck wondering what I was supposed to be filming. 'I'll be back,' said the parson. Sailors passed by eyeing the camera curiously. 'In there,' the returning cleric pointed to a doorway.

Inside, in semi-darkness, were the bodies of many sailors not yet prepared for burial at sea. Now I knew why the padre was there. To this day I do not know what the object was in taking me on that macabre journey to the stricken ship. Whether he really thought they were the sort of pictures we actually wanted, whether he thought they would be useful archive film or whether he was wiser than he appeared and wanted to make me aware right at the start what war was really like – not all wardroom frolics. It certainly did the latter because I was not prepared for what I saw and have never forgotten it. Being so unexpected it vividly showed me what can happen when one leaves harbour. On the way back to *Valiant* I told the parson there was not enough light to film and I did not think it was a suitable subject to boost morale. He said nothing then or later and shortly afterwards was transferred to another ship before I had an opportunity to question him further. A most disturbing episode. Today, as I remember those cold, dead bodies in Scapa and the many occasions later when I saw so many souls perish, the awesome finality of death on this planet is constantly with me as it is for those left behind.

My first days were spent getting to know the geography of the ship; getting to know the sailors; getting to know about the guns – the fifteen-inch monsters, the six-inch and four-inch bombarding and anti-aircraft guns supported by the pom-poms, Bofors and Oerlikons. I had to learn which was which, how they worked and be guided by the gunnery people as to what kind of blast and noise to expect when they were fired. I also had to earmark a position for myself when at sea where I would not be in the way but would have the maximum view from the ship and in the ship if we were in any action. It was always a priority for any assignment to find a position from which everything that was happening could be seen. I could only make a temporary assessment before going to sea. As we had no admiral aboard I decided on the admiral's bridge, one deck above that of the captain. There were many other things to consider apart from viewpoints such as vibration, accessibility and personnel. It proved to be the right place.

In those early days of the war many of the old naval traditions were still carried on, particularly in big ships where discipline was more rigid. The ranks of the regulars had not been reduced by the influx of the volunteers, the conscripted and the merchant navy reserves. At first I had the feeling of being in a hotel. The cabins in long corridors were the hotel rooms. This feeling did not last long; it was much too noisy. Being in such a big ship was a bonus, for unless I had joined the navy and become an officer I would not have had the opportunity of seeing how this service operated in peacetime for both officers and men. I was able to take part in some of the traditional routines. There were board and card games in the evenings, particularly 'twenty-one', which was played with great gusto and a favourite throughout the ship. Sometimes there were film shows. There were guest-night dinners (I was lent a bow tie) and reciprocal visits to other ships. Afternoons were recreational with hobbies, sports, sailing or trips ashore. Mornings were spent cleaning, with general chores, drills and inspections. I kept to the afternoon routine. Services have a habit of applying nicknames to people. It was not long before I became known as 'Twister'. This arose partly from my association with the camera and the notion of turning the handle and partly from my skill – or perhaps luck – at the above card game. It was an unusual life for me with its regular hours, its rigid discipline, its saluting the quarterdeck, of being part of a community in a way I had not experienced since I left school. My life had been anything but regular. No telephones nagged, no tedious car journeys in fog and ice, no hunting for cafes or restaurants late in the evening. War did not seem such a bad thing. However changes had to come and key regulars were drafted into smaller units although *Valiant* was not affected much while I was there.

I was now ready for some sea time. I was grateful for this period in harbour to get to know the ship but I had not taken any pictures. Having now joined the fleet I had to get some film at sea. I did not know what my colleagues were doing. The spirit of private enterprise and competition was still alive. I knew where Oswald was, not far from *Valiant*, and his ship had not left the harbour either. I learned later he had set up a developing and printing business in his ship's darkroom and was doing very well – if not for the newsreel. Ships were frequently on the move, destroyers and cruisers, and I imagined Cave-Chinn grinning to himself as he sailed by to get historic pictures of wonderful sea battles. In fact, stuck in the depot ship, he found boats hard to get and when he did get the buzz to join a ship, due to the distances

My friends on HMS *Valiant*.

he often could not reach the destroyer before it sailed. I invited him to lunch in the *Valiant* and he told me he had thought of asking London to recall him. I think he got his wish for I did not see him again. He had been to sea several times but mostly they were on night patrols. If there was action during the day the destroyer was always going at speed, constantly turning, with the deck awash most of the time and thick spray presenting a further problem. The highest point in a destroyer is the captain's bridge and there was no room on that for an extra body when in action. Other than the bridge and gun positions there was no elevation, which meant that he had to work from deck level – almost an impossibility in the North Sea.

I liked the bleak environment of the Orkneys and Scapa Flow, closer to the Arctic Circle than to London. The *Valiant* was anchored about an hour's boat journey from Mainland, the largest of the eighteen or so inhabited islands that made up the seventy of the Orkneys. The messman used to go ashore early each morning to Kirkwall, the principal town in the Orkneys, to get provisions, post and any special things required by members of the crew. I would go with him sometimes as did some of the officers who had naval business. Kirkwall was fascinating. There was only a short time to look around as we could not be away from the ship too long. I would make for the old town, transported back to olden times. Its narrow streets, its ancient ruins, its cathedral of St Magnus built of sandstone in 1137, told the story of a history going back to the tenth century.

Sometimes in an afternoon a liberty boat would go to Hoy, the second largest island. Everyone off duty relaxed after lunch – some sailing, some playing ball games on the upper deck, and some like myself going ashore to walk. Hoy was a dream for me, my favourite escape, lonely and barren, although one could not completely relax for always at the back of one's mind was the thought that the ship might be ordered to sea before one could get back. The ship was always at four hours' notice which could be quickly shortened in an emergency. The island is hilly, the most mountainous of the islands, rising to some 1,500 feet, and was completely unspoiled at that time. There are lovely wonderful cliffs along the north-west coastline. The highest point of these is St John's Head, 1,000 feet above sea level and the highest perpendicular sea cliff in Great Britain. Those glorious walks were a real tonic, marvellous to stretch one's legs after the confines of the ship, large as she was. The temperature was fairly mild, rarely was there ice or snow, only strong, exhilarating winds. If it had not been for those sombre fellows in the distance, dressed in grey, I would have thought I was having a wonderful holiday.

These outings had to end of course. Events in Norway were not going well and at last, at the end of April, the battle fleet was ordered to sea to bombard the Norwegian coast somewhere between Narvik and Tromso to try to help our troops, which were under severe pressure. Apart from one or two day jaunts outside the harbour this was my first real journey to sea in a warship, and a very special one it turned out to be. It is difficult to describe how I felt as we steamed through the opened protective boom at the entrance to Scapa Flow and reached the open sea. It was dark and eerie as the ship began to feel the heavy swell. Nobody knew what was ahead. With harbour routines suspended most of the watertight doors below decks were shut and clipped, not to be opened; all the others had to be closed behind one when going through the ship. Everything movable was secured and made fast. Fiddles (small railings) were fitted round the tops of tables to prevent meals and objects from falling off during bad weather. We headed north towards the Arctic Circle and the Norwegian coast. With us were the aircraft carrier *Ark Royal*, which the Germans claimed to have sunk, and a force of screening destroyers and cruisers. I had been given the captain's sea cabin to put my head down and keep my things in while in harbour. It was a pleasant small room way up in the gods near the bridge. There were many noises and pipes all day and night with which I had to learn to live. I was becoming a sailor. Later I shared a cabin with one of the officers. Now, at sea, I was transferred to the admiral's day cabin, one deck below the upper deck, right aft. It was a vast, beautiful cabin, luxury indeed I thought, for Admiral Turner. It would have been wonderful in harbour but at sea, when I came to sleep I wondered what had hit me. The cabin was situated directly above the ship's screws and when the ship started to move the noise of the propellers turning below was thunderous and the vibration unbelievable. It was almost unbearable. There was a fair swell in the North Sea and as the stern of the ship rose and fell and we put on speed the screws revved mercilessly as they came almost out of the water. I had been allotted a camp-bed, unsecured, and when I came to doss down I was travelling all over the huge cabin. I had to wedge the bed between fixed pillars and spent an almost sleepless night on that first venture to sea. We had been told to expect air raids and I was up very early, without much difficulty, to be about as soon as it was light in case of an early attack. My position on the admiral's bridge fitted in well with everyone and I was not in the way of anyone needing access to the captain's bridge. With daylight I saw the *Ark Royal* steaming on our starboard side and quite close. I was joined by a petty officer, the ship's official photographer, who was operating a cine-camera under the direction of a very pompous lieutenant commander, the fleet photographic officer. I left the bridge to take some build-up shots, guns manned at the ready, signalmen and such-like. It being early in the war, pictures like this at sea had not been seen.

We had been at sea for a day when the air raid warning sounded and the ship went to action stations. As my routine was to be on the admiral's bridge during daylight hours I was in position when the alarm went. The petty officer and his boss joined me again. An air strike soon developed and planes came in from all directions. The target was primarily the *Ark Royal* and bombs exploded all round her sending up columns of water. I managed to stop jumping every time the guns fired and being close enough to the *Ark Royal* and at exactly the right angle I was able to use a medium-sized lens with the camera in the hand.

I filmed everything I could see, planes, guns firing, bomb splashes – a field day. During a lull I was on the captain's bridge to show the control activity, very different from today when the control is not on the bridge. Then all was in the open, orders given through speaking tubes to the engine room, loud speakers, as the Royal Navy had operated through the years. All good newsreel material. Then back on my bridge when another attack came. To film the *Ark Royal* and the bomb splashes all round it and us I used a two-inch lens, which, to the uninitiated, means a fairly wide-angle view – the kind of general picture you would get with the average still camera when you were taking a snapshot of Aunt Mabel. To film the aircraft I used a four-inch lens which gave a closer view, the longest lens one could safely hand-hold. With lenses, the higher in inches the closer the view, and a one-inch lens would be very wide. It was not possible to use a tripod due to the vibration of the ship at full speed, the wind and the constant altering of course to avoid being a sitting duck. It was possible to get away with a six-inch lens in the hand following a fast moving object like a plane at close range if it was the only way of getting a picture, but it would be a last resort. I was therefore very surprised when I saw the petty officer holding his heavy camera, similar to mine, using a twelve-inch lens, difficult enough to use on a tripod under reasonable conditions. He was also committing one of the worst filming crimes by using quick pans all over the sky trying to follow an aircraft, losing it, waving all over the place trying to find it again. I ventured to tell him a wider angle would give him a better result. His pompous officer heard me and told him to carry on as he was doing. It was not my business, of course, but I knew what the film would be like and so it proved to be. I said no more.

This was going to be a big story, I knew. We had shown the German claim to have sunk the *Ark Royal* to be false. Miraculously she was not hit and we and none of the other ships suffered any damage. With no further attacks appearing imminent I went for more build-up. I had filmed men at the guns at the ready. Now I wanted the guns being fired in close-up. I was allowed to take everything in the ship except the radar aerials, which were still on the secret list. I thoroughly enjoyed myself; I was determined the story would have everything.

We steamed on to the north and Norway. There were no more air attacks, as it seemed we had steamed out of the range of the enemy planes. It was now the turn of the big guns, the fifteen-inch giants, a formidable sight with their long, grey snouts housed in pairs in their turrets. As we neared the Norwegian coast to carry out our mission to try to assist our forces, everything on deck was battened down and no one was allowed on the upper deck except the bridge personnel and those manning guns who were protected from blast. In the gun turrets the huge shells, each weighing three-quarters of a ton, were brought up on lifts from the ammunition room deep down in the ship and rammed into the gun barrel, followed by the cordite pack which sent the shell on its murderous journey. I filmed all the activity in the gun turrets on the way back to Scapa. I was able to get enough light by using special high-density photoflood bulbs I had brought with me. Up on the admiral's bridge I was warned to watch out for the blast. The guns rose, moved sideways getting the range. Round after round was fired and the whole ship shuddered. The noise was dull and horrible and the blast significant. But it was not so devastatingly unpleasant as the four-inch anti-aircraft guns which produced a very nasty blast and a crack of a noise which was hard on the ears. Whether it was like that to everyone I do not know but that is how it was to me. As I filmed the recoil from the fifteen-inch guns I wondered where their shells were landing in the hazy distance. Our job done, we returned to Scapa without further action. I had experienced a full baptism of fire and had been very fortunate to obtain such pictures on my first encounter with the enemy at sea. And it gave me a good idea of what to expect in the future.

Back in London, Gaumont gave the story the full treatment and devoted a whole newsreel to it. My managing director and editor-in-chief, Castleton-Knight, sent me a copy to show to the ship and to present to the captain for the ship. Such gestures were typical of the film industry, for spontaneous and generous thoughts were one of its better sides. The captain arranged for a special showing of the film on the

Imperial War Museum

HMS *Valiant*.

quarterdeck, a gala evening, and most of the ship's company were assembled to see it. The sailors were thrilled at seeing themselves, although there were some ribald remarks and much laughter at close-ups of mates firing guns. It was a very good morale booster both for the ship and for relatives and friends. Letters arrived all telling of the joy of wives and daughters when they saw Tom's or Fred's face in close-up in the local cinema. It made me quite popular but more importantly it made the crew aware of the importance of newsreels in a war.

That evening had its embarrassing side, however. Unfortunately for the fleet photographic officer his film arrived on the ship from Portsmouth on the same day as mine and both films were shown, mine first, his afterwards. I felt extremely sorry for the petty officer. My film had the advantage of professional editing, sound effects and commentary. His arrived uncut, silent, just as it had been filmed, made worse by the use of wrong lenses as I had expected. However experienced one may be a percentage of film taken is wastage. There are camera starts and stops, sometimes unintentional errors in changing focus – no one is infallible. To have everything screened looking so much worse against the professional job was very difficult to explain away as being due to the prevailing conditions. My reel had been received with cheers to be followed by the other material – derision. It was very embarrassing and I wished it had not happened that way.

The *Ark Royal* had been an excellent start to my naval career but it was a very difficult story to follow. While I had made a good job of that occasion I realised I had not left myself very much else to film without repeating what I had already taken. I had to look for more action but to find another *Ark Royal* was a major problem, and so it proved to be. On the few occasions when we left Scapa we saw little and it was mostly at night. When there was an air-raid warning, and there were quite a number of them in and out of the harbour, it signalled a reconnaissance plane or a lone attacker on other ships too far away to film. I did make a short semi-documentary film of life aboard a battleship in a war but that had its limits. If one has lived an active life with plenty to do the claustrophobic conditions of living aboard a ship soon begin to tell, even with a good ship's company and a ship as big as the *Valiant*. It was really quite a strain having a job with no specific duties. I was aware, too, that there would be coverage coming in from the combined resources of the five newsreels, from many cameramen distributed throughout the world, and film from the service cameramen. London, I was sure, preferred to receive nothing than be sent a story just to justify one's existence with the consequent trouble of collection, processing, viewing and censoring which each hundred feet demanded. So eventually after several months I decided to ask the captain if he would enquire of the C-in-C if I could be transferred to a cruiser as I was there to work and had to try to find a way to get more film of the war at sea.

The answer came one evening at the end of August 1940 and was very different from that which I had envisaged. A signal from the C-in-C told me to proceed in all haste from Scapa and join HMAS *Australia* in Liverpool. This was it, thought I, there must be a big operation imminent. A boat was got ready, hurried farewells, signals sent to the depot ship to put me aboard the first boat to Thurso. With all my gear, bewildered, in a couple of hours I was packed and waving goodbye. I was sorry to be leaving Scapa and especially the *Valiant* with its friendly crew, its comparative comfort and its great captain and commander. She had been a lucky ship for me for pictures. Many months later she was again the platform for a very dramatic film.

Armed only with the commander-in-chief's signal and a travel warrant I began a long, cold, sleepless journey south in an unheated, restaurant-less train. I hadn't expected this. When I made my request for a transfer I thought it would entail a short boat journey across Scapa to another ship. As I sat in the dark I thought of the wardroom of *Valiant*; of a full stomach, of a sherry or two and cheerful company. I consoled myself with the signal – 'In all haste' – so it must be for something worthwhile.

After a change of trains, with all that meant, I arrived the following evening at Bootle, fifteen miles north of Liverpool. The few people who had been on the train had left earlier. Liverpool was under air attack and this was as far as we could get. So there I was on the empty, pitch-black platform of Bootle station, with all my equipment and no taxis, no cars, no porters. I had no idea where Liverpool was or whom to contact. I was to join HMAS *Australia* with all speed. She could have been a thousand miles away. Somehow I managed to find a telephone that worked. I was thankful I always carried a torch, a lesson I learned when on the road. The telephone operator was wonderful. I told her I had to contact naval HQ urgently. She got me through and again I was fortunate in finding a friendly and helpful duty officer, and this in the middle of an air raid. I lied that I was a naval officer with an urgent signal from the C-in-C Scapa to make contact with the *Australia* that night. He promised to send some transport but it would be a long while because of the air raid. And a long while it was, but he kept his promise. At last, out of the darkness of no man's land rumbled a large naval truck. Goodness knows how the driver, a naval rating, had found his way to Bootle. He told me it had been very unpleasant leaving Liverpool. But after all that he remained good-humoured. In my book he deserved the Victoria Cross. After we set off I shuddered, hearing my equipment bouncing about in the back of the truck. However, it survived without damage. The driver did not know where the ship was berthed. He said he hoped it was alongside and not in the stream as there would not be any boats that night. In the docks we had the greatest difficulty locating her and when we did, there she was – in dry dock. 'In all haste,' the signal had said! When I managed to make contact with those aboard I was told I would not be able to join her in Liverpool. The ship was due to be refloated the next day, would spend several days doing trials after her spell in dry dock and would then make for Greenock, where I was due to join her. Imagine my feelings, having just come all the way from Scotland, to have to return there next day. Luckily the naval truck had not been unloaded and I managed to find a small hotel for the night. The next day I made the trek to Greenock.

So in early September 1940 began a bizarre journey that in my wildest dreams I could never have imagined. When I joined the *Australia* in Greenock the Australians regarded me with as much amazement as the officer of the day had on my arrival on the *Valiant*. It was the so-called uniform I was wearing that surprised them, but this time they knew who I was. In their good-hearted, generous way they soon made me welcome and found me a decent cabin which I shared with the ship's pilot, the only naval Englishman aboard. I was in a happy ship again.

HMAS *Australia* was a cruiser so I had got my wish in that respect. At the time I had no idea why I was rushed from Scapa to Liverpool, and the captain professed not to know either. However I discovered recently that the Admiralty and War Cabinet had concluded in mid-August 1940 that Dakar in Senegal on the west coast of Africa could be a dangerous base in enemy hands. French ships were in the harbour and the Vichy French were not friendly to Britain. So it was decided to mount an operation to occupy the port, to install Free French there and get the French ships to surrender. Shortly before I left Scapa I had been up to the Arctic Circle and around Bear Island. Now in my new ship at the beginning of September we set sail heading south as part of an escort to a large convoy. It so happened, although I did not know of it at the time, that three groups of transports left Scapa, the Clyde and Liverpool for Freetown, with 4,000 British and 2,500 Free French troops aboard. They left at the same time as we did. With hindsight they could have been part of our convoy. Naval ships called Force M consisting of two battleships, the *Ark Royal*, cruisers and destroyers were also heading for the same destination. Again, with hindsight, I now believe that was why I was rushed to join HMAS *Australia* – to become part of that force to take Dakar. However, before we sailed from Greenock, a naval civilian, Trevor Evans, joined the ship. He told me he was destined for Egypt to take up the post of superintendent of Alexandria dockyard. We became great friends. He thought the ship would go round the Cape to Suez as the Mediterranean was too dangerous, depressing news for a war correspondent looking for action. I am certain that he too was not aware of the impending Dakar operation.

So there I was, accredited to the home fleet, steaming towards the Equator. I could not inform Gaumont where I was or even that I had left Scapa, and assumed the Admiralty would do that. They did not. I was quite unprepared for going out of home waters. My clothes were a thick uniform, balaclava helmets, duffel coats and similar, and no arrangements had been made for me to draw money as in Scapa. As we passed Gibraltar and got into hot weather I needed some tropical gear. The Aussies were a grand bunch and helped me in my predicament. The doctor offered to cash cheques for me so I was kitted out with light clothing from the ship's stores and a right charlie I looked with shorts too long and shoes too big. I took a few shots of the convoy in the distance in case there was an attack but the outlook for pictures was not very bright. We were bound for a long journey, the war was hotting up elsewhere and convoy film without action would not be very welcome.

We sailed into Freetown Harbour in Sierra Leone. It was, I think, 13 September. For me this was exciting. I had never been further afield than the Continent. Little boats came alongside the ship selling souvenirs offered by very black grinning faces. Freetown then was a shanty town. The locals, in the sweltering heat, walked through the unmade streets with great bunches of bananas on their heads to sell in the markets. It was poverty-stricken in the extreme, but for me so colourful, so tropical it demanded film – another side to the war.

Then I learned of the Dakar operation. It seemed at last I might get some war pictures. As a prelude to the forthcoming action some months earlier a number of French ships, having sought refuge in Mers-el-Kebir harbour at Oran, were ordered to surrender by the Royal Navy. They refused and reluctantly many were sunk or damaged and 2,000 men were killed. In July 1940 there were unsuccessful attempts at Dakar to put the French battleship *Richelieu* out of action. So with the intention of trying to take Dakar without more casualties and a repeat of Oran all the naval and transport ships were assembled in Freetown in mid-September. General de Gaulle had also arrived and made his headquarters in HMS *Barham* and I was transferred there for the action. Vice-Admiral J. Cunningham, flying his flag in the cruiser HMS *Devonshire*, and General de Gaulle were jointly in control of the proceedings.

Operation Menace, as the project was called, left Freetown to arrive off Dakar in dense fog on 23 September. Unfortunately we lost the element of surprise as it transpired that poor security in the UK and ambiguous orders between admirals and London had made the Dakar authorities aware of our approach. In addition a naval force from Gibraltar failed to prevent further French ships from entering Dakar harbour a few hours before we arrived. Not a good start. De Gaulle made a radio request to the governor of Dakar for the French ships to surrender and to allow a peaceful occupation of the harbour. The reply he got was a salvo of shells from the shore batteries and the nine-inch and sixteen-inch guns of the *Richelieu*. A cruiser and two destroyers were damaged and the remainder of the fleet straddled as they attempted to get our range. We returned the fire but only for a short time as the orders were to try to avoid confrontation and casualties. At midday the governor of Dakar sent a message that all attempts at landing would be opposed. The mist had got denser and observation from the *Ark Royal*'s aircraft difficult, and the action was suspended for the day. Late in the evening an ultimatum was sent to the governor saying that he must agree to prevent the enemy (the Germans) from occupying the port and that he must accept this demand by 6 a.m. the following morning – the 24th. Just before the deadline the refusal came. The mist had lifted a little, so *Barham*, *Resolution*, *Australia* and the *Devonshire* moved in closer to bombard. Aircraft from the *Ark Royal* took off to try to take the Dakar airfield, to attack *Richelieu* and to observe the bombardment. But poor visibility made the attacks abortive and prevented us from ascertaining where our shells were landing. *Resolution* received four hits but was not seriously damaged, and we were straddled frequently, so it was decided to withdraw for the night.

On the 25th the mist was gone and it was a clear day. Early in the morning torpedo tracks passed close down the side of the *Barham*, to be followed by a loud explosion, and a huge column of water rose up. *Resolution* was listing alarmingly, having been torpedoed by a French submarine. Sixty sailors were killed and 200 injured. It soon became apparent that the whole of our fleet was in a very dangerous situation. We were outgunned, the French ships were not going to surrender, and the shore establishment was not going to capitulate. Cunningham decided to end the action, a decision endorsed shortly afterwards by the War Cabinet in London, which had been monitoring the situation and now ordered the ships to return to Freetown. We managed to tow the *Resolution* back and learned later that the French had lost 100 dead and about 200 injured from our bombardments. I sent my film back from Freetown but I do not know whether it was used or passed the censor as the operation was a failure. I rejoined *Australia* and we continued our journey to round the Cape with the next stop to be Durban. I wonder now whether it was intended that I should continue on that journey, but with no directions from the Admiralty to return to England, I had little choice but to remain in the *Australia* as she was still part of the home fleet.

Sharing a cabin with Jackie Hoath, the pilot of the ship's Walrus aircraft, enabled me to discuss with him the possibility of getting film of our ship and the convoy from the air. We got on well and he obtained the captain's permission to take me up. A Walrus becomes airborne by being catapulted off the ship. Sitting in the cockpit, strapped in next to the pilot, and receiving directions shouted above the noise of the revving plane on how to release myself should we go in the drink was extremely nerve-wracking. The aircraft was shaking, pulling hard, anxious to go, but held back by the wires on the catapult. The ship steamed at full speed into the wind. Ahead stood a sailor with an upraised flag. When the conditions seemed right and full power was gained, the pilot raised his hand, the flag came down, the charge on the catapult was fired and with a terrific jolt we shot forward at 70 m.p.h. over the edge of the ship, dipped towards the sea and then rose gently into the air. So quiet it seemed after the noisy take-off and tension gone as we climbed into the sky and over the ships. After I had finished filming we landed on the sea and were hoisted back into the *Australia*. An experience indeed.

The voyage continued uneventfully. Here I was in the South Atlantic visiting places I never thought possible to see – and in a war which seemed somewhere else. No enemy aircraft came near us, no submarines attacked us, no fleet shelled us. I could not deny it was anything but pleasant sitting in the sun and air all day, camera at the ready, but a quiet life meant no pictures. We steamed on lazily round the Cape of Good Hope with me hopefully wishing for some action.

The Indian Ocean was magical. I would stand on the bows of the ship watching the flying fish winging along the surface of the water, some even reaching the deck, and the sun would disappear over the horizon in just a few seconds, leaving a wonderful sunset. The phosphorescence would twinkle in our wake in the warm, balmy evenings, my thoughts often miles away from the war. Sometimes, though, I would feel guilty as the obscenity of war intruded – people being bombed and killed, ships sunk, planes shot down, cities ruined. It was an unreal situation for a newsreel cameraman, a war correspondent. As we steamed through those calm waters I saw war as a mixture of good and bad memories, a desire to preserve some, erase others. By the end of the war I had accumulated experiences of both.

As we approached Durban (in mid-October 1940) the Southern Cross was bright in the heavens, reminding me that just before we crossed the Equator in the Atlantic I had seen both the pole star and the Southern Cross at the same time, a unique memory. Durban gave us an opportunity to stretch our legs and spend a few pleasant days with the local people. The doctor, a man of ample proportions, was the subject of an amusing incident. He was almost a teetotaller and returning to the quayside after a party, three sheets in the wind – probably for the first time – he emerged from a taxi huge beam first, a splendid sight. He was a very likeable man with a profound knowledge of music – classical, jazz – the lot. I spent some very happy evenings with him listening to some of his vast repertoire of records. And he continued to cash my cheques.

We left Durban, heading north, for the last leg of our journey to Suez, when we suddenly rejoined the war. A German raider had been reported in the Indian Ocean and we were ordered to leave the convoy with the destroyer screen and try to find the enemy ship. Someone must have been listening to my thoughts as we rounded the Cape. We called into Mauritius and my colleague, due to go to Alexandria, was off-loaded to find another ship to take him to Suez. After some days searching for the raider unsuccessfully we put into Colombo harbour in Ceylon, to refuel and take on stores. I watched the dhows, the catamarans and the many small boats as they hurried about their business or were tied to buoys with their owners nodding in the warm winds and the hot sun. This was the East, a touch of the Orient. When I asked the captain if I should try to return to England he told me there were still reports of the raider and advised me to stay with the ship as eventually she was to rejoin the home fleet. It was now well into November and getting on for three months since we left England, with only a failed action for pictures.

At sea again we continued the hunt for the raider but it could not be found, if it really was there. Soon there was an excited buzz around the ship that we were going to Fremantle, Perth. Such rumours usually proved to be true; this one was. Nearing Australia a line of Shelley came to mind: 'See how the mountains kiss high heaven and the moonbeams kiss the sea', for each evening the moon shone bright among the myriad of stars, casting its gentle light upon the undulating waters of the Indian Ocean. Romantic it was – but still no pictures and we were even further away from the war. A short stop in Fremantle brought the news that we were to proceed to Sydney where the ship would spend several weeks having an overhaul. Joy for the Australians but not for me. Again the captain, ever the optimist it seemed, advised me to remain with the ship as she would be going to New Zealand to become part of an escort for some of the biggest ships in the world due to take troops to Europe. How many more foreign countries would I visit, I wondered, before I got back into the real war. However, frustrating as it was, there was little I could do except take another few weeks of my enforced holiday and see what Sydney offered.

First I took the opportunity of getting processed what little film I had taken, other than at Dakar. Exposed film in hot climates can suffer from a very undesirable disease called reticulation, which brings it out in spots and forms a network pattern across the film making it useless. Everything I had taken was unusable. I had done my best to keep it in a constant temperature in sealed tins. As I sometimes had to keep it in refrigerators, sometimes of necessity in hot cabins, this meant it really did not have a chance of survival.

Untouched physically by the war, Sydney was a normal, fun city. With most of the ship's company in their home town I was offered a great deal of pleasant hospitality, was shown all the sights and taken swimming on Bondi beach, making me almost forget the war. When it was time to return to the ship I had to bring myself down to earth with a bang.

We left for New Zealand as the captain had predicted. Among the many great liners of the convoy we were to escort were our two giants, *Queen Elizabeth* and *Queen Mary*. I arranged with the Walrus pilot to fly me over the ships when we left New Zealand. I had become used to the aircraft as we had made several flights off the sea while in Sydney. I looked forward to some historic film. Such ships had never sailed together before and were never likely to again. But it was not to be. As we approached New Zealand the pilot was detailed to fly ahead to Wellington to make some arrangements for the ship. Then came tragedy. The Walrus was catapulted off the ship but the charge that fired the catapult was faulty. The aircraft failed to gain full speed, went off the edge of the ship and into the water. In a few moments it had disappeared and with it my friend Jackie Hoath. A most upsetting episode for everyone. It was a much subdued ship's company that entered Wellington harbour.

Christmas had passed and we were well into early 1941 as we steamed with the convoy to Sydney, back to Fremantle and into the Indian Ocean bound for the Cape, Cape Town and Europe. I had taken what I could of the liners but it needed air shots to show them properly. There seemed to be a jinx stopping me getting any useful film – even more so when HMAS *Australia* was told to leave the convoy and make again for Ceylon and Colombo. And here we learned the ship was to go to Singapore to be attached to South East Asia Command (SEAC), no longer part of the home fleet.

This time I had to part company from my Australian friends. Once again I was alone, ashore with all my gear, with no ship and miles from where I should have been. I spent another disheartening delay trying to get the naval authorities in Colombo to contact the Admiralty for directions. The wheels in the East turn slowly and so they did in London. I sat for days on the beach eating pineapples, brought to me each day by the locals, waiting for the reply. It came, telling me to return to England, but did not say how. Was I to fly back or was it to be another long sea journey? With all that equipment I realised, with a heavy heart, that it was going to be the sea.

Armed with an Admiralty signal I managed to get the naval office to act quickly. They fixed accommodation of a sort in the *Aquitania*, an old four-funneled liner which was leaving for Suez carrying Australian troops. I will not dwell on that journey. It certainly was not home from home but it was my only chance of getting back without further delays and at least I was going in the right direction. The troops played their favourite Australian gambling game of 'two-up' non-stop all the way to Suez. Two coins were spun and bets laid on their landing with the same face upwards. I joined in occasionally.

At Suez another message told me to join one of the Empress ships berthed there. It was to return to the UK via the Cape. Not even a warship, not even the Mediterranean. This prospect was depressing especially as the captain of the Empress ship was as mad as a hatter. He would not allow water aboard, preventing the ship from sailing. It was absolute hell in the boiling sun in Port Tewfik harbour. In the event I thought the captain wonderful, for a signal came from the shore instructing me to leave the ship and wait in Suez for further directions. It seemed at last someone had become fully aware of where I was. Fortunately the naval office ashore sent a boat for me or I doubt whether I would have got away from my mad saviour.

So there I was again with all that equipment, which I began to hate, this time by the Suez Canal watching ships coming and going. I was able to make friends with the owner of the French Club, who found me a room in a small hotel. I had no money but he trusted me with the cost of my accommodation and food on the strength of my association with the naval office. Since leaving England I had been living on goodwill – first the doctor in HMAS *Australia* and now the French Club owner. At last came specific instructions to proceed to Alexandria. Goodbye to the home fleet; I was to be attached to the Eastern Mediterranean Fleet.

At the end of March 1941, after what seemed years in the wilderness I walked into the Leroy Hotel in Alexandria and the first persons I saw at the bar were my colleague from the *Australia* – the superintendent of the dockyard – and Ben Hart, a cameraman from Paramount. I was among friends again and I was a war correspondent again. Everyone knew where l was. I would get mail and the Mediterranean was certainly a war zone. Now, with events out there at a critical stage, with vital Malta under siege, the opportunities for filming were considerable. Seven months after leaving England I felt born again.

Chapter Four

The Malta Convoys

The unrealities of the last months were now superseded by the realities of the situation in the Mediterranean. I was now in the real war. I have not found war an easy subject to write about. I felt I was very fortunate to be in a position to witness so much heroism and so be able to illustrate the difficulties and hazards that my service, the Royal Navy, had to face in those vital months when the battle could have gone either way. With so much happening I have thought it best to concentrate on those events which gave the best film, for that was what I was there for. In describing my experiences so close to those doing the fighting I am also recording the sailors' war.

Malta from the air was but a speck but it was large in the planning of naval operations. The main objective was to get supplies to Malta from east and west.

The four Marx brothers who shared a house in Alexandria; (L-R) Trevor Evans, Bill Smith, myself, and the naval paymaster commander.

These would enable ships, submarines and aircraft based there to protect incoming convoys, to attack those supplying Rommel in the desert and to help relieve the hardships of the people under siege. A second objective was to help the Eighth Army by harassing the enemy with bombardments and to aid in supplies when the lines of communications lengthened.

No longer having permanent accommodation on a ship I decided it would be advantageous and less costly to find somewhere to live other than a hotel. Although hotels had advantages as places to meet, it was difficult to relax when they became the headquarters of all the press in the area. To come back from the sea to the Leroy or the Cecil, the two main hotels in Alexandria, was far from restful. The Leroy, where I was staying, was very expensive and its bar always a potential danger. One had to pass through it to get to one's room, a clever arrangement. There was inevitably someone there whom I knew, and Jackie, the barman, an ace dice-thrower, was adept at stopping his customers en route to their rooms, and one was trapped. So Trevor Evans, my friend and colleague from HMAS *Australia*, and I decided to rent a house. Trevor, as dockyard superintendent, had a very important post. He was responsible for victualling all the ships, coping with survivors' needs and providing most of the other things ships required. He bought all the bread and a great deal of food for the navy from Mr Pastroudis, whose bar and restaurant was another main meeting place in Alexandria, and they became great friends. Mr Pastroudis, a Greek, was very rich and very charming. He was always beautifully dressed, had impeccable manners and also owned a nightclub which was well patronised by sailors when ashore. It was with his help that we found a marvellous house owned by a French woman in the best part of Alexandria. To make it a viable proposition we needed two more to join us. We enrolled two who were staying at the Leroy – Bill Smith, the manager of Gieves, and a paymaster-commander, an austere-looking officer whose looks belied his sense of fun and good nature. We were a good team. I was the youngest in age but all were young in spirit. When I was away my three colleagues kept the house going with the aid of two servants, one a cook, who came with the deal. All expenses were shared equally and we could invite whom we liked. With a bedroom each and no housework it was a very pleasant place to stay. When I returned from an assignment I would often bring back some of the chaps from the ship I had been in and this would usually result in quite a party. Pastroudis lived nearby and he would sometimes join us with his beautiful French wife. He would then organise all sorts of delicacies from his nightclub and restaurant and on occasions even a band. For the second time since joining the navy, the war did not seem too bad. Pastroudis owned a Packard car which he put at my disposal when I was ashore, sometimes to drive, sometimes with a chauffeur if I needed to get to the harbour quickly – a great help as the house was several miles from the centre of Alex. Bill Smith also had a car, so with that and the odd taxi it was reasonably easy to get to and from the town. The house had a lovely garden which bordered on a large area of grassland. Here, each morning, Egyptian ladies and gents would come to perform their natural functions. Such was the norm in this part of the world wherever there was a wall or an unoccupied open space. Not the most delightful of habits – it was just as well the garden was walled at the rear and the house some way from the goings-on beyond.

Having been so long without any permanent direction as to where to film or what to film, it was a pleasant change to find a proper set-up in Alexandria. There was a naval press office, the job of which was to assign cameramen, photographers and journalists to ships whenever they were going on operations. The office was generally casual and flexible, too much so on occasions when possible stories were missed, but mostly it worked well. We were free to initiate any venture that seemed to have picture possibilities providing we obtained permission before carrying out our ideas. This was sensible as we could easily have found ourselves covering a mission that had no hope of passing the censor. Most of us had our own sources of information apart from what came from the press office and generally I was ready for any call to arms when it came officially. Processing and the despatch of film to London was organised in Cairo, the centre for the receipt of all service material from navy and army.

Since I had been on my travels naval war correspondents had graduated from chauffeurs to semi-officers with regard to uniform. We were allowed brass buttons similar to the naval ones but without the crown. We could also have a cap badge and various ideas were tried for these. 'WC' for 'War Correspondent' woven above the anchor was one but this gave rise to obvious comment. Eventually most of us finished up with 'NC' for 'Naval Correspondent' – also somewhat doubtful, I thought. In place of stripes on the sleeves was 'NAVAL WAR CORRESPONDENT'. One enterprising cameraman, David Prosser, promoted himself to admiral with thick stripes on his sleeves; he was politely told to demote himself. Although these were certainly better than our original ones, this question of uniform was never really satisfactory because no two were exactly alike. Eventually, irrespective of service, all wore the only one which was officially recognised – the army job. This I adopted when I returned to England.

While I had been establishing my base and getting to know the general routines of working with the Eastern Mediterranean fleet there had been little opportunity of going to sea. Greece and Crete had been lost, any ships sunk, there was almost no air cover and Malta was under constant bombing. Although there was no change in the navy's objectives, there had to be a reassessment of resources in order to carry them out. Based in Alexandria there were three battleships: HMS *Valiant*, HMS *Queen Elizabeth* and HMS *Barham*. There was the 15th Cruiser Squadron: HMS *Naiad*, HMS *Dido* and HMS *Galatea,* to be joined later by HMS *Euryalus*. There were submarines, ancillary vessels and flotillas of destroyers, not a huge fleet for what had to be done. In Malta there were three cruisers, plus destroyers and submarines.

Over the next eighteen months, well into 1942, I was at sea on expeditions which had every ingredient for arousing all the emotions. I wanted action and I got it well and truly. Most of my journeys, sometimes in a battleship, occasionally in destroyers, and generally in cruisers were to show the efforts made by the navy to get food, fuel and ammunition to Malta – the Malta convoys. When we left Alexandria harbour we wondered whether we would see it again. Ships were sunk in front of me, behind me and on each side. Torpedoes passed close by, bombs fell all around, shells near-missed, yet any ship I was in suffered little damage apart from pieces of shrapnel from near misses. I was very lucky. Not all of these actions produced film, for many attacks were at night. However I was able to get dramatic, sometimes historic film, although too often of the wrong sort, for it was our own ships that were the targets. With virtually no air cover for much of the time and too few warships our convoys had heavy losses and too many of the escorts were sunk as well. In June 1941, with the troops evacuated from Crete, one of the navy's immediate priorities apart from re-equipping was to try to assist the Eighth Army. The desert war was not going well for us. With Malta being so heavily bombed Rommel got supplies into Benghazi almost unmolested and had pushed our troops

HMS *Valiant*; (R-L) myself, fellow cameraman David Prosser, American reporter Larry Allen, British reporter Desmond Tighe, and far left Captain Rawlings.

back to Sollum. In the middle of the month, however, Malta received a welcome addition of fighters and was able to resume raids on Rommel's supplies making for Libya. Meanwhile the navy bombarded his forces on the coast road.

During a lull between convoys, David Prosser, partly with the navy but not on convoys, and I decided to make a short documentary film around submarines to show what it was like below the surface in wartime. The submariners cooperated wonderfully, placing a submarine at our disposal during one of their rest periods. They were very enthusiastic and interested in the project. With the aid of photo-flood high-intensity bulbs which I always carried, we were able to film inside as the submarine submerged and show the conditions in which the sailors lived. Very grim in my opinion compared to a surface ship. We got one fantastic shot due to the pluck of David Prosser.

David volunteered to be tied to the conning tower with his feet on the deck to film the waters covering the submarine as it submerged. It was a very dicey operation depending on the skill of the officer in control of the submarine. He had to take the deck to just below the surface until it was covered in water but to stop it going down any further before the conning tower and Prosser disappeared below the waves. All went well and full marks to David. I would not have liked to do that. It would have been a superb shot but we never found out what happened to that epic.

On another occasion I went out in a Greek torpedo boat on a special mission to search for an enemy ship reported damaged and which we were unable to find. With the smell of fuel oil, cooking and the movement of the small vessel in a fairly rough sea I came the nearest I ever did to being seasick. Fortunately I had discovered right at the start in Scapa that I was a good sailor and apart from a little dizziness at first I was never troubled by rough seas. I managed not to succumb this time but I did not attempt any more trips of that kind.

I was in a destroyer accompanying some ships along the coast which did not result in anything worth filming but it gave me an interesting experience which I am glad was not repeated in the future. I was below writing some notes on a pull-down table. Across the page of my notepad marched a battalion of cockroaches. Line after line they came; I could almost see them wearing tin hats as they advanced in perfect formation. The females followed behind the army stopping to produce a myriad of babies on my pad. On the floor it became impossible to move without the squelchy sound of crushed bodies. For their lunch they were partial to the emulsion on pieces of discarded film, leaving the celluloid completely clear. For our lunch we had cockroach soup and the bread played host to many corpses. In bed there was the disturbing feeling of movement across my face. There are stories of explorers eating insects to survive. It was now possible to appreciate what it must have been like for them. The ship had to be fumigated when we returned to harbour.

In HMAS *Australia* with its Walrus aircraft I was able to get pictures of the ship I was in from the air. In the Mediterranean our cruisers did not have this facility and anyway, with constant air attacks, it would have been suicidal to attempt an air shot over those waters. In October returning to Alexandria after handing over a small convoy to the Malta escorts I was on the bridge of a cruiser, moaning to the captain what a pity it was that it was not possible to get a picture of the ship at sea. We had not had the usual plane trailing us and calling up the dive bombers, probably because the desert war was going in our favour. For once we were not at action stations. The captain agreed with me and said the only way to get the picture I wanted was from another ship and the only way to transfer from one ship to another on the move was by breeches buoy. If there were no air raids imminent he said he would ask permission to transfer me as it would be a good exercise for the ship.

Much to his surprise, as he had not been very hopeful of getting agreement, he was given the go-ahead, the decision to be his as to when he carried out the transfer. A destroyer was informed and brought closer to our cruiser. The two ships then took position on a parallel course and a line was fired across from our ship and secured on the destroyer. First I watched my camera and tripod go across, heart in mouth as they dipped towards the sea on their journey. Then it was my turn. The breeches buoy is a ring-shaped lifebuoy with a line round a pulley block and a support in the form of a pair of short breeches in which one is suspended. In this way one is pulled across from ship to ship, and it requires masterly handling of the ships as they are steaming very close to each other. As I was crossing and dipping down to the sea like my equipment had done I remember thinking, 'Why do I suggest such shots?' On arrival in the destroyer we had to steam further away as I was too close to get a full-length picture of the cruiser. Then the whole process had to he repeated for the return journey. It was worthwhile, for I got a very nice shot and I was very grateful to the two captains for their cooperation. It was one of the few days when I was at sea when there were no air attacks. Lucky me again.

Ships were leaving harbour but nothing came our way from the press office. When asked what they were doing the answer I got was, 'It's only a patrol.' I tried to point out that I only got pictures when at sea and not sitting in Alexandria and that even a patrol might encounter the unexpected. That did not result in being assigned to any ship. I then said I would look around and see if I could work out a story aboard one of the ships in the harbour. There was no objection, but I was told with some emphasis that no arrangements could be made for me to be accommodated in a sea-going ship in the harbour unless there was a worthwhile mission ahead.

As I went back to collect my gear in the afternoon I thought these were strange times. One minute I was wondering how cold the sea would be; the next there was nothing to do. It seemed odd also to be going to look for pictures to depict a war while in the town the people were going about their business as normal not caring, it seemed, that the Germans and the fighting in the desert was almost on their doorstep and the ships were going out to sea, some never to return. Little did I know what was ahead.

It was 24 November 1941 as I sailed round the harbour in my hired felucca. I did not have much hope of finding a story but it was worth a try. Then I noticed that some of the destroyers were making for the open sea. I was close to HMS *Queen Elizabeth* and HMS *Barham* and very close to HMS *Valiant*, my lucky ship from Scapa days. To my amazement I saw the battleships all weighing anchor and obviously going to follow the destroyers. I was too late to find out where they were going and wished I had been around earlier. The commander of the *Valiant* was on the quarterdeck, telescope under his arm. I saw him raise it to peer at my boat, which was very close to a ship about to move. He looked for quite a long time before he recognised me. A previous happy relationship and goodwill now worked wonders. The commander moved swiftly. A loud hailer was produced and he yelled at me asking if I wanted to go with them. I signalled that I did. He motioned me to come right alongside the ship, not easy to do in a felucca, but the boatman managed it although not at all keen to do so. I could not believe it would be possible to get aboard. There was no gangway and the propellers were already beginning to turn. Then a large net appeared over the side and was lowered alongside the felucca. The commander told me to jump in. I had visions of all the equipment and myself going into the water, but, hurriedly pressing some money on the boatman who was doing a marvellous job keeping his boat alongside, somehow I piled everything and myself into the net. In minutes I was landed in a heap on the quarterdeck as the battleship gathered speed, leaving the bewildered Egyptian boatman, now well astern, standing in the felucca no doubt wondering what it was all about and whether I had paid him enough. A laughing commander welcomed me aboard and as we reached the open sea and took station behind the other two battleships he took a slightly damp me up to the bridge to introduce me to Captain Morgan, who had replaced Captain Rawlings, my first captain in Scapa. It seemed I could not meet either captain in a normal way. In Scapa I was full of gin; this time it was water. It was good to be back in the *Valiant* and I was soon joined in the wardroom by many of my friends from those early days. The personnel had not changed much since Scapa. I was told we were going to try to intercept two enemy convoys making for Benghazi with supplies for Rommel, vital for him as he was trying to stop the advance of the Eighth Army. This was a story the press office should have known about, especially as they had told me ships were only going on patrol, whatever that meant.

The, next day, soon after dawn, I was back on my old position on the admiral's bridge. We were some 200 miles west of Alexandria between Sollum and Tobruk. We had not been trailed by any enemy planes and there were no air raids. Then, unluckily, by chance we were seen by a reconnaissance plane, probably near the Italian convoys we were seeking. Before long there was a signal saying the Italians had turned back. With this news the C-in-C in *Queen Elizabeth*, Admiral Cunningham, had no option but to abort our mission and return to Alexandria. This was disappointing both for our force and for me for we had been hoping for some action, this time as the aggressor.

The day was sunny and the sea calm for late November. The remainder of the morning went by uneventfully and passed into afternoon. Lunch had consisted of bully-beef sandwiches made with thick slices of bread and a mug of tea, brought round by those not on duty such as the doctor, enabling us not to have to leave our posts. In these waters, so far west, ships were normally at action stations and as we had been spotted it was a necessary precaution. We steamed in line astern, *Queen Elizabeth, Barham* and *Valiant* with the escorts way out on either beam. At intervals we would alter course according to the particular pattern of anti-submarine zig-zagging we were adopting. Towards teatime, when everything seemed particularly quiet and peaceful, I decided to take a chance and go down to get a mug of tea. I had just stepped on to the ladder leading down to the captain's bridge below when there was a very loud bang. I looked round and saw a column of water. Immediately I remembered Dakar and *Resolution.*

Torpedoes! I was back on my bridge within seconds to see *Barham* listing heavily to port and cursing myself for ignoring all my training that if you take a chance inevitably something happens. I was very lucky this time I was not further down in the ship. It transpired later that an Italian submarine had managed to get inside the escort and had fired a salvo of four torpedoes, three of which hit the *Barham* on her port side between the funnel and the after fifteen-inch gun turret. The *Valiant* turned violently to port to avoid the stricken ship, which had stopped in her tracks, and we took position parallel with her and quite close. I had a wide-angle lens on the camera, which gave a picture showing the full length of the *Barham,* and I started to film as the ship had turned over to an alarming degree. I was in a dilemma. A cameraman's nightmare. The camera held 200 feet – two minutes' continuous filming – and I had already shot some of it. I envisaged the battleship would turn right over, bottom up. To stop filming and put in a new roll would take at least a minute. To stop while she was turning would spoil the shot. To run out of film in the middle of the turn would be disastrous. The *Barham*'s funnel had almost reached the water so I decided to let the camera run and trust to luck there would be a moment when I could change rolls. As she turned on her side and the funnel touched the water, terrifying in its suddenness, there was a terrible, unforgettable explosion and, realising she had lost her last battle in twenty-seven dramatic years she died and blew up – her whole inside, turrets, machinery, pieces of ship flung high in the air. A huge pall of smoke, red glow in the centre, rose above the water, billowing out and mercifully covering the dreadful scene that must have been enacted in those dark, oily seas. As we began to move away I heard the ominous click that told me the camera was out of film. Had that explosion taken place fifteen seconds later I would have missed it. The gods were certainly with me on that day. The pom-poms had been firing. The force of the explosion had brought the

Imperial War Museum

A frame still from my film of HMS *Barham* as she was struck by torpedoes.

submarine to the surface and it had scraped along our starboard side and disappeared in seconds. It had been too close for the guns and for me to see it from the bridge. The destroyers came in to pick up survivors and I put in a new roll and filmed what I could as we left the area. Trembling with excitement at the picture I had just obtained I felt no immediate emotion. Everything had been so quick. My thoughts were, 'Was I in focus? Was the exposure properly set? Was the camera steady, hand-held (we were close enough for that)? Had I the right lens in the camera?' Yes, I believed I had done all the right things. As the *Queen Elizabeth* and *Valiant* headed far Alexandria I remember sitting on my camera case stunned, hardly believing what had happened, and only then did the enormity of the loss of a battleship and probably many of my friends hit me. Witnessing a major disaster like that produced a numbness akin to shock. I felt nothing, similar to someone when hit by a bullet feels no immediate pain. I had seen ships sunk before in those waters but they had been under constant air attack. This was so unexpected. It was just an incredible four and a half minutes from the time the torpedoes struck until the ship disappeared – four and a half minutes in which I thought most of the sailors had perished. Miraculously 405 survived, but 869 were lost.

After a while I went to the bridge to let Captain Morgan know what pictures I had of the sinking. He appeared as excited as I had been and said he would let Admiral

Cunningham know at once. He sent a signal to the *Queen Elizabeth* stating what I had obtained. The dramatic events must have affected our judgement. Back came a reply to the effect, 'Your Mr Turner should be aware it is not in the interests of the war effort or of the Royal Navy to show our own warships sinking.' A rebuff indeed, cutting us down to size and bringing us to our senses. It was certainly understandable to get such a reaction. The admiral had just lost a battleship and many men and did not want a reminder. However, the film was used in the enquiry to try to understand why the ship had sunk so quickly and eventually for training purposes. It was censored and not released to the newsreels until after the war ended although the directors of the newsreels were allowed to see it the following February. When we got back to Alexandria I took the film personally to Cairo far processing. It was too valuable to risk sending any other way and I was able to ascertain that it was all right. The *Barham* had had a full life in her twenty-seven years at sea. She had been at the Battle of Jutland, at the Sinn Fein troubles in Ireland, in West Africa, in the West Indies. She survived being torpedoed at the end of 1939. She was at Dakar, bombarding the Vichy French ships. In the Mediterranean she was at the battle of Cape Matapan and at Crete where she was damaged by a bomb and had to go to South Africa for repairs. On returning to the Mediterranean she made her last voyage. As far as I am aware there was only one other British ship that sank so quickly in this war. HMS *Hood*, struck by shells, also blew up and sank in about four minutes. In her case there were only three survivors. It was amazing so many were saved from *Barham* when one saw that awful explosion.

One other interesting thing with regard to the *Barham* was a curious case concerning a wartime spiritualist, Helen Duncan. She had claimed that the spirit of a dead sailor had told her during a seance, 'My ship has sunk,' and named the ship as HMS *Barham*. This was when the loss was still on the secret list and before the relatives of the dead sailors had been informed. It seems a bit unfair, but she was imprisoned under the Witchcraft Act of 1735, in case she revealed any further secrets concerning D-Day.

HMS *Euryalus* arrived in Alexandria in early November 1941 to join the 15th Cruiser Squadron. She was a new ship commissioned in June, fifth of that name, arriving in the Mediterranean via the Cape and Suez. She had ten five-and-a-quarter-inch dual-purpose guns, anti-aircraft and surface, pom-poms, Oerlikons and radar, which was still quite new. Her captain, Eric Bush, was a very experienced officer, and later we became great friends. For the next few months *Euryalus* was my ship. I was always made welcome, as they found out it was lucky to have me aboard. I hope that was not the only reason. Every ship had a different personality. All were run efficiently. All those I sailed in made me welcome, but most people have favourites be it a dog or a ship. For me my true love of the big ships was HMS *Valiant*. In the Mediterranean *Euryalus* was one of the best.

Imperial War Museum

Euralyus followed by *Galatea*, which was later torpedoed and sunk.

Before long, after returning from the *Barham* disaster I was at sea again, my first time in HMS *Euryalus*. We set out in company with the flagship HMS *Naiad*, Admiral Vian in command, and HMS *Galatea*, to intercept some Italian ships reported out of Taranto and just south of Italy. At that time the Italian fleet included five or six battleships, two eight-inch gun cruisers, eight six-inch gun cruisers, destroyers, submarines and torpedo boats. All we had at the start of December were two battleships, four cruisers, destroyers and submarines in Alexandria and three cruisers, a few destroyers and submarines in Malta. The odds were very much in favour of the Italians. In this critical period with very little air cover, sometimes none, we were constantly attacked by Stuka dive bombers and torpedo bombers. It was a bad time for the Royal Navy and with a more determined enemy than the Italians we could have lost every ship. I was in action with my camera as soon as we left harbour. Much depended on the situation in the desert. The fighting there was very fluid. When the Eighth Army was on the offensive and in possession of Tobruk and Cyrenaica the air attacks lessened; when it was pushed back we were attacked from dawn to dusk. As we steamed towards the Italians, who were no doubt aware of our approach from their bombers, they turned back in spite of their superiority. We were ordered back to Alexandria. Air attacks, submarine alarms, air attacks all the way until some fifty miles from Alex, late at night, just as I was thinking of bed, there were three explosions. I was up on deck in minutes to see that *Galatea*, close astern of us, had been torpedoed and she sank almost as quickly as the *Barham*. About half her crew were saved. There were two journalists in the ship – American Larry Allen of Associated Press and Massy Anderson of Reuters. Allen was rescued but Massy did not make it. He was a very nice man and a friend of mine. Coming so soon after *Barham* and several other smaller ships either sunk or damaged, this latest loss was a devastating blow, reducing our fighting strength to a level that made the Malta convoys even more hazardous. As we left this last disaster my memory of that dark night is of standing on the deck in the wind. Above the stars were very bright. The silhouette of guns pointed evilly seawards ready to add more deaths to the already ever-growing pool of blood and destruction that the Mediterranean was becoming. It was not a nice night. It was 14 December 1941.

The next day, after refuelling, we were at sea once more. With HMS *Naiad*, an anti-aircraft cruiser HMS *Carlisle* and several destroyers, we were escorting the merchant ship *Breconshire* bound for Malta. She was a veteran of the Malta run and this one was as difficult as ever. Our objective was to meet Force K from Malta, the cruisers HMS *Aurora*, *Neptune* and *Penelope*, which would then take *Breconshire* on to Malta. As soon as it was light the enemy planes were over us and the bombs dropped but we made our rendezvous without any serious damage. Just as we were

A heavy air attack on a Malta convoy.

Connie Boyd

preparing to part company a torpedo bomber came in almost at sea-level between the destroyers and ourselves, intent on a suicide run to get our merchant ship. It gave me a marvellous picture as it was shot down, bursting into flames and plunging into the sea. Once again I was aware, as on previous occasions, I was rejoicing in having got a good film when I had just seen some poor devil plunge to his death. In covering disasters in peacetime one emphasises the tragedy of the event. In wartime the picture glorifies the achievements of destruction either by one's own side or that of the enemy. One was only doing what one was there for of course, but my reaction brought into focus how evil war is. There were more disasters to follow, however. Force K in Malta, having safely escorted the *Breconshire* into Valletta harbour, attempted to intercept an enemy convoy making for Tobruk. They ran into a minefield, losing a destroyer and the cruiser HMS *Neptune* with the loss of all her crew except one seaman. Two other cruisers and a destroyer were damaged. That was not all. When we returned to Alexandria in the early hours of 19 December, three Italian human torpedos, each with two men aboard, launched from a U-boat lurking close to Alexandria, followed us through the open boom as we entered harbour. At daylight two Italians were found sitting on the buoy to which HMS *Valiant* was attached. They were taken aboard for questioning but would say nothing except to advise the captain to get everyone on the upper deck. Shortly afterwards there were three explosions in the harbour. An oil tanker was in trouble and it leaked its cargo into the waters; the bows and forecastle of the *Valiant* were well down with a list on the ship; the flagship *Queen Elizabeth*, with Admiral Cunningham still aboard, was badly damaged with a hole blown in her bottom and causing a number of casualties. Limpet mines with delayed-action timers had been attached to the three ships with the result that the two battleships were out of action for months. The C-in-C must have been at his wits' end. The Eastern Fleet now had no battleships and only the cruiser squadron of HMS *Naiad*, *Dido* and *Euryalus*, and the anti-aircraft cruiser *Carlisle* plus a few destroyers. In Malta all the surface ships had gone or were out of action apart from HMS *Penelope*, which had not been too badly damaged in the minefield disaster. I can only say I marvelled and admired the courage and audacity of our sailors and ships against such odds as they continued to carry out their vital tasks of trying to get convoys to Malta. It was a great privilege to film many of their endeavours as the year turned to 1942.

In January of that year the Eighth Army's new offensive had driven Rommel back to the Tripoli area, almost out of Libya. When Rommel counter-attacked at the end of the month the Eighth Army was forced to retreat. The Far East was in trouble. The Japanese had taken Singapore and were into Burma. To bolster that situation important units of the desert army and RAF squadrons had been withdrawn and sent to the East, leaving the Eighth Army much weakened. It must have been a difficult decision for the war chiefs to make for we could have lost the desert war, Egypt, Suez and more. The Germans and Italians got to the west of Tobruk where they were held and there Rommel stayed for some time, building up his forces for further advances which were to take him to El Alamein in June.

The weather became misty, raining, dreary, more like the North Sea than the Mediterranean. I managed to spend a few days at the house but it was back to sea in February. Our small force made a gallant attempt to get a convoy of three ships to Malta. With the desert situation now favouring the enemy, air attacks were increasing again. On the first day out one of the convoy was badly damaged but somehow managed to struggle into Tobruk, which we still held. On the following day the bombs fell relentlessly and we lost our other two merchant ships. Only the strong barrage of fire put up by the warships saved them from joining the convoy. We were well on the way to Malta when the last two ships were sunk, so some empty merchant ships including the *Breconshire*, which were returning to Egypt were able to rendezvous with us and we escorted them back to Alexandria without further mishap.

In early March our cruisers, only three now with the loss of *Galatea*, began a search to try to find an Italian cruiser reported damaged by a torpedo from one of our submarines, but we failed to locate it and hoped it had sunk. Well to the west again we were joined by the cruiser HMS *Cleopatra*, sent from the home fleet to make up the 15th Cruiser Squadron to four once more. As we were reasonably close she had left Malta where she had been refuelling to take up station with us on our way back to Alexandria. Led by the flagship HMS *Naiad,* the four cruisers steamed at full speed for home without further harassment from the air. As it got dark and we were thinking of food there was the sound we were hearing too often – a loud explosion. HMS *Naiad* had been torpedoed. She remained afloat for a time but was too badly damaged to save. Our squadron, so soon only three again, unable to help, sailed on, leaving the destroyers to pick up survivors. Admiral Vian and the captain were saved as was Jimmy Cooper of the *Daily Express*, but another ninety sailors were lost. It was truly a disastrous time for the Royal Navy.

Malta was by now in a desperate situation. Its food, oil and ammunition were at an all-time low and unless more supplies could be got there, it would be forced to surrender. However, whatever the cost, we could not afford to lose the island. By doing so we would probably have lost the desert battle as well since Rommel would have had almost unopposed access to his supplies. The Germans had planned an invasion of Malta but the problems on the Russian front caused them to abandon the idea. With the island now so vulnerable and with so many ships lost it was a frightening time but in the middle of March our small force of three cruisers left with a convoy of four ships, including the redoubtable *Breconshire*, and with Admiral Vian now flying his flag in HMS *Cleopatra*. Until just west of Tobruk we had air cover and almost unbelievably remained undetected. The day passed quietly with no attacks. Then we were unlucky. At dusk, an enemy transport plane flying to the north chanced to cross our path and would have certainly reported our position, for early next morning we received a signal from the C-in-C in Alexandria saying one of our submarines had seen a large force of the Italian fleet leaving Taranto on a southerly course. As we took up our positions at action station, at dawn HMS *Penelope* and a destroyer joined us from Malta to add strength to our tiny force. Before long a large number of torpedo bombers appeared low over the convoy. Out of the range of our own fighters, and with the bombers too far away from us to be able to use our guns, here we were in the frantic position of the convoy being sitting ducks. In an effort to give them some protection we steamed at full speed to get closer and in doing so seemed to upset the bombers. They split up. Some came near us and were shot down. Others made half-hearted attacks and no hits were scored. Some hovered around, uncertain what to do. By midday we were all still afloat and undamaged. Then high-level bombers arrived, but their bombing was just as inaccurate as their fellow attackers' and by early afternoon we continued on our way without losses. The sea was reasonably calm but the wind was getting stronger, and we were thinking we might get to nightfall without further trouble. Not so. The radar alerted us that ships were in the vicinity. Soon smoke was seen on the horizon and three Italian ships became visible well out of our range. Admiral Vian ordered the convoy, with destroyer escorts, to steam towards the Gulf of Sirte and signalled the cruisers and the remainder of the destroyers to make smoke, to split into

The smokescreen used by Admiral Vian during the action in the Gulf of Sirte.

Imperial War Museum

groups and advance towards the enemy. We paired – *Cleopatra* and *Euryalus*, *Penelope* and *Dido* – with the destroyers together in other groups. Thick black smoke from all the ships hid us from the Italians as we closed in to attack.

This was dramatic stuff, difficult to film, with sudden turns, strong winds and smoke, but it made wonderful pictures. I was really getting something different, a sea battle, and I completely forgot the danger we were in. When *Cleopatra* and *Euryalus* were within range we emerged through the smoke-screen, opened fire, made emergency turns and dashed back through the smoke before the surprised Italians could open fire on us. I believe the other ships were doing something similar. We repeated this operation and although we did not know whether we had had any success these sorties kept the Italians from adopting the same tactics. Their two eight-inch and one six-inch cruisers sent several salvoes through the smoke-screen, their shells falling quite close. Possibly they were guided by the bombers overhead that bombed us at the same time, but none of us was hit by either shell or bomb.

The battle was short; the Italians, unnerved by our sudden appearances through the smoke, withdrew to the north and out of range. It seemed we had driven them off and we proceeded to rejoin the convoy in the Gulf of Sirte. They had been heavily bombed but were still intact as we steamed north-west towards Malta. We had not gone far when the Italian fleet was spotted again, this time with the battleship *Littorio*, cruisers and destroyers, enough firepower to blow us all to the skies. The convoy was ordered to the south again and we resumed our former groups laying even thicker smoke-screens this time, adding white smoke from smoke-floats. I joined the commander at his action post on a platform at the after part of the ship where I had an uninterrupted view of whatever was ahead. Again it was tricky filming with the wind stronger, guns firing, constant change of course and vibration, but I continued to get good pictures. 'Blow up your lifebelt', said the commander cheerfully.

From time to time the smoke thinned in the high winds and shots were fired from both sides. The Italians did not attempt to come through the smoke so skilfully laid under Admiral Vian's direction and the destroyers were able to stop them getting closer for a while. Our problem was that the enemy could stay out of our range while we were always within theirs. It was too risky to repeat our earlier tactics. Suddenly, in the freshening wind *Euryalus* became exposed through the smoke and we were in the sights of the *Littorio*. Her fifteen-inch guns opened fire, straddling us, with huge columns of water rising up as the shells burst, shaking the ship violently. It was very frightening seeing those orange flashes from the battleship, knowing we were unlikely to survive a hit. Then the smoke-screen thickened again and we were hidden once more. The *Cleopatra* had been hit by a six-inch shell, suffered some casualties but continued in the battle. With the light fading and the situation looking grim our destroyers made a joint torpedo attack scoring a hit on the *Littorio* and damaging a cruiser, enough to frighten the Italians, and they turned away to disappear into the darkening evening. Two of our destroyers were damaged but undoubtedly their brave action saved us all. The Italians could have sunk all of us had they been as courageous as the Royal Navy. The resolution of Admiral Vian in facing the Italian fleet head-on and his masterly use of the smoke-screens was a brilliant achievement. Without doubt we won that battle – and I had film to show it. As the commander and I left our position we saw a large hole just below our platform made by a big piece of shrapnel from one of the near misses. It was fortunate it had not entered a couple of feet higher. 'Lucky us', murmured the commander.

With the night upon us our attention was directed to getting the convoy on its final leg to Malta. Each ship was told to proceed independently with a destroyer escort and with all the speed it could manage. As we left and headed east the high winds had reached gale force and the seas were uncomfortably stormy, causing us to slow down. We had several attacks by torpedo bombers the next day but were able to reach Alexandria without any further problems. News travels fast and there was a great welcome as we steamed into the harbour. Admiral Vian and his force received many congratulations on winning the battle against such odds.

The convoy was not so lucky. We heard the very disappointing news that one ship had been sunk in the early morning the day after leaving us. The *Breconshire* had made its last journey, bombed before it could get into the harbour and sunk shortly afterwards by further bombing as it neared Sliema. The other two ships did get into Grand Harbour and managed to unload part of their precious cargo before they too were sunk. These supplies helped to stave off the predicament Malta was in but they were very much short of the intended relief. It was a sad end to the heroic efforts the navy had made to get those ships safely to port. For me, I had another experience of naval warfare at its best, and had secured some very dramatic pictures. As I unloaded my five camera magazines to send the film to Cairo I thought how lucky I had been once again and, thank goodness, had brought that luck to the ship I was in.

In the following months Malta continued to be heavily bombed, reducing her capability to stop supplies getting to Rommel and making her own position vulnerable again. A desperate situation needed desperate measures and in June 1942 it was decided to try to relieve Malta by sending two convoys at the same time, one from the east and one from the west. Whenever she was at sea I was still in *Euryalus* and this time we left with a convoy of eleven ships, our squadron reinforced with a further cruiser, HMS *Hermione*, while from the west a large naval force including two aircraft carriers and a battleship escorted a convoy of six ships. With circumstances in the desert deteriorating we had no air cover at all for our convoy and endured extremely heavy bombing as concentrated as we had ever experienced. At night there were U-boats and E-boats operating, with the result that

Author's collection

The author during a quiet moment aboard HMS *Euralyus* in the Mediterranean.

before we had gone very far we had lost two of our merchant ships from the convoy, two escorting destroyers and the cruiser *Hermione,* with other ships damaged. Then a report was received that a large force of the Italian fleet had sailed from Taranto. The C-in-C in Alexandria, Admiral Harwood, who had taken over from Admiral Cunningham, decided that with the losses we had already sustained it was too risky to get involved with the Italians again and ordered us to return to Alexandria. The other convoy from the west was also heavily attacked and lost four ships and some of their escort, including an aircraft carrier. Two ships struggled into Malta badly damaged but with vital supplies of oil and fuel for their aircraft.

The position in the Mediterranean east of Malta was now becoming even more dangerous. At the end of June Rommel was able to resume the offensive from near Tobruk, where he had been held since January. Having received the supplies he needed, brought in to Benghazi and Tripoli while Malta was being heavily bombed, his Panzer divisions made rapid progress towards Egypt. Tobruk was recaptured and when only fifty miles from his objectives of Cairo, Alexandria and Suez the Eighth Army stopped him at El Alamein. In July, with the enemy now so close to Alexandria harbour, what was left of the Eastern Mediterranean fleet was evacuated to Haifa, Beirut and Port Said. It had now become time for me to say goodbye to *Euryalus* as she was leaving the Mediterranean temporarily for service and a clean-up. It was also goodbye to our nice house in Alexandria as I moved to Port Said, where most of the warships were. Our paymaster at the house was moved to another job and Evans, the superintendent of the dockyard, with Bill Smith of Gieves, thought it better to move back to a hotel with the Germans so close in the desert.

Port Said was certainly different from Alexandria. I had always imagined it as a romantic town standing at the entrance to the Suez Canal. I used to see it on colourful posters advertising cruises to the East. I found it to be a town of much interest and of many contrasts. The nights could be romantic but had their far-from-romantic side too. On a warm evening with the moonlight casting lovely shadows through the narrow streets, the silhouetted shapes of the ships, the soft murmur of the waters of the canal and the stronger call of the sea beyond all combined to produce a feeling that this was indeed a romantic place. Sometimes of an evening I would stand in my pyjamas on a verandah of the Eastern Exchange Hotel where I was staying. It was pleasant and amusing in the light, warm air. I would look down on the inverted rugs covering the open-air dance floor used in peacetime. I would hear a band announce the next tune and there would be a fanfare. Mme Mimi Thingamabob would enter and there would be roars of laughter from the spectators. After a few visits I was able to picture everything that was going on by the different tunes. Shake-a-Leg Sally to this tune, Languorous Lily to that, Doleful Dora, Russian Rudy and so on. And the nights could be sinister with the many vice-ridden dens, brothels in plenty with prostitutes of many nationalities, and the dark forms who approached with dirty postcards and would you like...? A town of many moods. There were the old houses, the Wild West structures. By day Port Said was equally fascinating. Sun and half-lights; rich and poor; soldier and sailor. Old taxis, new taxis, decrepit buses and donkeys and the clip-clop of the gharries. Vendors of bread, vendors of everything. Beggars with mutilated arms and legs. It was very cosmopolitan – Armenian, Jewish, French, Greek and Lebanese and the influx of English and Australians. There was the ironmonger's shop with a lavatory seat hanging next to pictures of the Crucifixion and a small hole in the wall to get into it. And of course there were the ghilly-ghilly young boys doing the three-card trick

Author's collection

Not my normal method of travel during my time in the Mediterranean.

with live chicks under tumblers. What would Egypt have done without its small boys? There was, too, the officers' club with its mixed crowd of nurses, merchant seamen, naval officers, army officers, civil staff and Wrens, called ship-women by the hotel waiters. Port Said in wartime.

I arrived in Port Said when there was a holiday, one of many. All the women and their children appeared in the town, each family dressed alike in their Sunday best. I imagined Mama had bought a long piece of material from which she had made each a dress. They all looked happy and were very conscious of their new attire. It was a day they were all determined to enjoy, celebrating some religious festival or other. The portly husbands bought dates, sweets and nuts and everyone had a good feed. Towards dusk the men decided it was time to leave and strutting ahead of their families, the women gathering together their bits and pieces, and taking hold of their children, they all marched off to their homes on the outskirts of the town. It was another very strange period in my war. Port Said more than fifty years ago.

After the hectic period I had just experienced there was now a vacuum which needed filling. There was little naval activity in the Mediterranean. It was very difficult to get up-to-date information as the press office had stayed in Alexandria, and I had to make several train journeys to Cairo and Alex to keep in touch. On one journey, in my carriage was an Egyptian accountant apparently of some standing,

Osman Pasha by name. His English was perfect as he spoke of economics, his ideas on culture and a wish to promote a better understanding between the English and the Egyptians, almost apologetic for his own people. I must confess I was not exactly on the same wavelength but it made one tedious journey more pleasant than usual.

With not much chance of going to sea for a while I decided to make a supply story based on the importance of the Suez Canal to the Eighth Army. Tanks, men, ammunition, everything for an offensive was coming through the canal and going up to Alamein. This was a comparatively short route for supplies. Rommel, attempting to do likewise, was disadvantaged by the longer distances his supplies now had to come. Benghazi and Tripoli were the main ports he was using, but as Malta was active again as a result of the June convoy not many ships were getting through. Special passes were required for filming in Port Said, but when shown to the police or Egyptian soldiers they were of no use as they did not understand what they meant or could not read them. On one occasion I left an army major and a police officer nearly killing each other. I had enquired if they would do me a favour by asking a tenant of a nearby house if I could use his verandah to take a shot of the canal as I had been unable to make him understand what I wanted. The policeman looked at my pass and thought I wanted a warrant to enter the house. That started an argument with the major and I left as it got heated and did not get my shot. This story would have reached London about the time of Alamein, which would have given it a topical edge, but I do not believe it was used. These build-up stories were not really worth doing when so much film must have been coming in from other fronts, but I made them with the thought they might be useful in the future if any kind of compilation film was made.

Although the ships remained in Port Said and Haifa the C-in-C returned to Alexandria in August. I made a brief visit to Haifa but that did not produce anything useful so with the difficulties of communication, in early September I too returned to Alexandria and this time checked in to the Cecil Hotel. Egypt's prime minister came to stay on a short visit causing quite a furore in the lobbies whenever he entered or left, all the tarbooshes bowing dutifully on each occasion. It became quite amusing with everyone saluting everyone and soldiers and sailors pushing pashas aside, not appreciating who they were. Frequently there were a number of bottoms parked seawards, devout foreheads hitting the dust as their owners bowed towards Mecca. I admired those disciples of Muhammad for observing their ritual no matter what the occasion or where they were. I cannot imagine followers of our churches kneeling down in the road to pray at a given time.

I had a friend, Weston Haynes, an American photographer for *Life* magazine. He came rushing into the Cecil Hotel in mid-September saying he had just fixed a passage in a ship going to Malta and there was a chance to beat the rest of the press in getting there first. Did I want to come? I do not know what made me accept, for he was full of crazy ideas. Maybe it was because I was having such a quiet time.

Anyway I agreed to go with him without advising the press office, as we had to leave that night. After a somewhat hilarious dinner we made for the dockyard. Haynes knew where the ship was berthed and after some shouting between him and those on the deck we went up the gangway. It was a merchant ship and there was a strong smell of petrol as we got aboard. I discovered to my horror we were in a ship loaded with petrol which was intending to make a fast run to Malta without an escort. I was off that ship just before they pulled up the gangway, followed by Haynes. He told me that he had only met the captain casually in a bar and had not known what the cargo was. I must have been as crazy as him for I was going to make that trip with the minimum of equipment, just what I could carry, and nothing else. We all have our moments when we do stupid things. I wondered afterwards whether the ship ever got to Malta and who would have given permission to make such a run. We would probably have discovered that we were going in the opposite direction. Maxim – always tell the press office where you are going.

It was still a bad time for the navy. Tobruk was attacked by some small naval units with the intention of landing Royal Marine commandos and retaking the town. It was not a success. Two destroyers were lost and the marines captured. Meanwhile, in Alexandria, the bars, restaurants, casinos, shops and offices carried on as normal, although everyone was aware that at any time they might be seeing German tanks

A chat with army personnel during my desert expedition to Tobruk (I am on the far left).

Author's collection

driving through their streets. Beneath the outward calm there was an underlying tension. Then everything changed. On 23 October 1942 the battle at El Alamein began. After some initial very heavy fighting the Eighth Army, having built up its strength well in excess of Rommel's, advanced rapidly, driving the Germans back to south of Benghazi in less than a month. Everyone became more relaxed and cheerful in Alexandria and even the Cecil's doorman, who had feared the worst, smiled again and tried to sell me flowers, as he did to all who entered the hotel.

It was becoming apparent that if the army could drive Rommel out of Libya we would soon be able to get to Malta. So, while waiting for such an opportunity my friend Haynes and I decided we would follow the army and make a flying visit to the desert, to show any activities of naval units ashore. The army correspondents had their own transport and were up with the advancing troops. We had none, but a great deal of gear. Apart from camera and sleeping equipment the American, a master cook and a gourmet of quality, insisted on taking cases of food. He said the promise of a good meal would help us in getting lifts. He proved to be right, but we certainly did things the hard way. We started off in an LCT (a landing craft) going to Sollum with water supplies. This took the best part of two days on a fairly calm sea – just as well for our cook. We saw transport – our transport – moving forward. There was some bombing in the distance but we were not disturbed. The sun shone and the chaps unloading the water from the LCT gave us something to film and picture, and as the LCT was going on to Bardia we stayed with it arriving the same evening. The weather had deteriorated. It was now rough and stormy and we were unable to get ashore until the following morning. Another night on the deck and a very uncomfortable one. In Bardia we found a naval truck that was going to Tobruk and that suited us well, for we were sure there would be plenty to picture in the town and harbour. It was not a nice journey. Having been warned when making our arrangements for the desert that the roads were likely to be mined on either side I was none too happy when our driver pulled off the road to pass slower vehicles. Seeing the aftermath of the advance – broken tanks, tyres, tins, rifles, clothes – I realised how fortunate I was to be accredited to the navy. As we bumped along those sandy roads I thought I would rather go down in the waters than be left behind among the sordid debris of a retreating army. When we reached Tobruk Haynes gave us all a splendid spaghetti supper cooked to perfection within the limits of desert facilities.

And Tobruk was as far as we got. We found somewhere not too badly damaged and moved in for the night with the floor our mattress. Soon I heard the buzzing, whining sound of mosquitoes and with my torch, the only source of light, I saw the walls were covered with them. The American shivered and brought out a bottle of quinine pills, telling me he had contracted malaria in the Belgian Congo. I was stirred by a moaning as it was getting light and on the floor my friend was boiling hot and slightly delirious. We both had been bitten by mosquitoes but his had brought on an attack of malaria and he obviously needed help. Eventually I found a doctor who was going straight back to Cairo, and on seeing Haynes, volunteered to get him back as quickly as possible. How often when one thinks one is in an impossible situation something comes along to resolve it. However, with the departure of Haynes, I was left with all his valuable cameras, all mine and all the food. There was quite a lot of activity in Tobruk and the harbour so I filmed what I could before considering how to get back. After a few days I discovered some very weird characters in the charge of a British officer with a large truck who was going back to Cairo. As most of the transport was going the other way that was indeed fortunate. The officer was part of an intelligence unit and had been picking up spies planted in various locations. He was returning by way of Bardia, Sollum and Mersa Matruh to pick up some more on the way to Cairo. He agreed to give me a lift. Huddled in the back of the lorry with his collection of individuals of several nationalities was interesting and fascinating. They were a tough lot but certainly not illiterate, as one might have thought by their appearance. They all spoke more than one language and were very entertaining in recounting some of their exploits, mostly unprintable. When we stopped at dusk it was mealtime. I had given the food away in Tobruk, some to the doctor who took Haynes and the rest to people who helped me in the harbour. How I regretted it now. The meals were ghastly. Chickens, which looked as if they had lived rough, were caught, strangled, and cooked almost before they were dead. In fact half-cooked over a makeshift fire they were hardly edible – awful. It was a wonder we were not all poisoned. The officer, who was quite young, was as tough as the assortment he was collecting and appeared to enjoy those repasts. I was pretty hungry by the time we reached Cairo and could not get to Alexandria quick enough. My desert journey had been rewarding as an experience but little of real value for the newsreels. There was no continuity in what I was able to film, the subjects being much more suitable for still photography. Again I was aware how fortunate I was to be with the navy. One might have to swim but it was generally a much better existence than having to face all the privations and discomfort the army faced. I booked into the Cecil Hotel again and found that Mr Haynes was staying there. He looked fit and well and blessed me for salvaging his cameras and typically took me for a celebratory meal. In the cool night air his temperature had dropped and by the time he got to Cairo he had fully recovered.

Malta was relieved in the middle of November. HMS *Euryalus*, back in the Mediterranean, left Port Said with a convoy of four and reached Malta unharmed. It would have been a very good story and I was sorry I missed it. Even if I had been in Port Said it was questionable whether I would have known about that convoy via the press office in Alexandria. If they had had the information I would have expected to have been informed in time to get to Port Said. However, it was time for me to leave Alexandria and move on up the line, to Malta. I took passage in the cruiser *Orion*. It was very different this time. Nothing happened, no air raids as we left harbour. We kept well into the coast until near Benghazi, a sign of the times because formerly when we left Alex we did not see land again until we returned to the harbour.

Entering Grand Harbour I felt I was seeing the finale of a grand opera. This was the island we had made so many dramatic attempts to reach; so many tragedies in those efforts; so many ships gone; so many sailors lost. Here before us lay the wreckage of so many ships which told the story of the terrible times the Maltese had endured and why our navy had striven so hard to relieve their distress. There would be a new production in which this little island would play a principal part, only this time as the aggressor. Sobering as it was I was so pleased to be able to see the curtain fall on the part the navy had played in this drama over so many months and that I had been given a role in its performance. On my way over in the *Orion*, standing alongside the silent guns with a clear sky above, I thought back to the many journeys made through those waters when the guns were not silent and the sky had been darkened by the attacking planes. I had been in every kind of vessel to try to get different angles on the navy's activities. Sometimes there had been much to film, other times nothing. As the war progressed it had become ever more difficult to get something different at sea. Wishing for action usually meant attacks on us, even if we were winning. As a naval war correspondent it was important to me to show through our newsreels as many different and difficult situations as possible which the navy had to face, and by doing so demonstrate how well it coped. So in coming to Malta it seemed likely this new location could offer new opportunities. It held a challenging, even exciting prospect.

After disembarking, before finding somewhere to stay, I parked all my gear and walked round the narrow streets to get the feel of that historic island. It was not new to war. In the 1500s, attacked by the Turks, the Knights of St John, a militant organisation, had saved Malta from invasion by holding out to win one of the most arduous sieges ever known. By restoring the harbour and the surrounding buildings to their former grandeur after the ruinous war, the Knights' grand master, Jean de la Vallette, was rewarded by having the town and harbour named after him. Centuries later the Knights, having become less militant, involved themselves in hospital projects and charities and during World War I created the St John's Ambulance brigade. Now, once more, echoing those early turbulent times, Malta had been under siege, had suffered terrible damage, but had not been invaded, saved this time by the courage and gallantry of the Royal Navy, the merchant navy and the RAF. I was charmed by its quaintness, its narrow streets and special atmosphere – almost a calm acceptance of all that had taken place as if its history would always be repeated through the centuries. In spite of the vandalism of its many fine buildings and the hardships suffered by its people somehow it seemed almost untouched.

The author in action with Newman Sinclair camera. From the 1943 documentary CAMERAMEN AT WAR.

Imperial War Museum

However it was still very much a war zone, ravaged and left with few of the fundamentals for normal living. I found accommodation in a small hotel – the Osborne – in a narrow road off the top of the main street in Valletta. No running water, no hot water, primitive toilets; bugs, fleas, mosquitoes and a shared room. What a change from Alexandria on life aboard a warship! It did not take me long to appreciate that up to that point I had had quite an easy life as far as creature comforts went.

A number of war correspondents arrived, as it was obvious this island was going to be a centre for further action and the Osborne Hotel became our headquarters. The press information set-up was poor, far too secretive, and when we did get information it came at the very last minute, particularly infuriating for the journalists. This meant we had to rely on unofficial sources, the grapevine, to keep ourselves up to date. The scribes were very helpful in this respect for they were well trained in finding out what was going on. It was early 1943 and it became a case of being patient and trying to find stories until the big objective, which, it was whispered in the corridors of the Osborne, would be Sicily. When I was unable to find anything to film I looked for other ways to spend my time. It was a good opportunity to replenish my film stock and to replace filters and light bulbs so I cabled London for what I required. Five thousand feet of film and the other things were soon on their way via the Admiralty and arrived safely. I was very pleased to get the film as I was down to a few hundred feet, not enough to cover a major event. I bought a few souvenirs at sky-high prices, there being a flourishing blackmarket. In company with Jimmy Cooper of the *Daily Express*, recovered from the sinking of HMS *Naiad*, I visited other parts of the island away from Valletta. The damage we saw was horrific. Hospitals, schools, theatres, churches had been destroyed and hundreds and hundreds of houses either made useless or demolished. Although London and other British cities were suffering likewise, in such a small area as Malta the devastation affected every single person.

I got an unexpected invitation from the Malta Information Office to see the film IN WHICH WE SERVE, which was to be screened in a Catholic hall. When I arrived it was to find the hall full of children, some priests and a number of elderly ladies. Boys and girls sat on my knees and stood on my feet; there was a strong smell of garlic and a great deal of chattering. They seemed to enjoy the film, particularly any action. In an interval there was a rush for the lavatory near the gangway in which I was sitting. There came to mind a ditty I had often heard in service circles, had often sung myself, which began – 'Three old ladies locked in the lavatory and nobody knew they were there,' only this time everyone knew they were there for little children kept opening the door to make sure. In spite of the noise and chaos it was a pleasant diversion and I quite enjoyed it. I was not worried about following the film. I had seen it twice before, once in a destroyer.

Somehow the days seemed to pass quickly. There was little social life. There was the Union Club, where, if one was lucky, one might get a beer in the early evening. With the islanders deprived of so much over such a long period it was obvious it would take a considerable time for their lives to become anything like normal again. In May there were signs of impending action. Ships and an assortment of craft were arriving in Grand Harbour and the adjoining Marsamxett Harbour by Sliema. In the desert Tunis and Bizerta had been captured and by the middle of the month the war in North Africa had ended.

It was decided the small island of Pantelleria, some 150 miles west of Malta and about 70 miles from Sicily, needed to be silenced as an enemy base. The destroyers *Paladin* and *Pakenham* from Malta fought a battle with two Italian destroyers near the island and sunk one of them. *Pakenham* was damaged and was sunk later from the air. I went on a bombardment of the harbour, which made a welcome break although what film I got was not very dramatic. After a strong resistance Pantelleria surrendered on 11 June. This operation plus the build-up of ships endorsed the buzz in Malta that the invasion of Sicily would not be long in coming. There were some attempts at air raids during this period, all fought off by our Spitfires.

On 20 June, a hot day, the cruiser HMS *Aurora* steamed into Grand Harbour with King George VI aboard. His arrival had been announced earlier over the rediffusion system and there were dense crowds to welcome him as he stood on the bridge in the early morning while the ship was berthed. The King was given a terrific welcome as he came ashore to be greeted by the governor, Lord Gort. The Maltese were genuinely thrilled and overjoyed to see him among them, a recognition of the vital part they had played by not surrendering. There were all the usual formalities that are part of a royal visit, but mostly it was informal and everywhere the King went the enthusiasm of the people made it a pleasant and happy day for all, although it must have been an arduous one for the King in his uniform in the heat and dust. We, the press, were only told officially of his programme a few hours ahead on the previous evening. This was too late to try to make arrangements between the numbers of cameramen for a coordinated coverage, a sort of voluntary rota, or to fix any special positions on the route of the King's progress. The result was all of us shooting almost the same shots. With hindsight it was probably just as well we did not band together. It would probably have caused all kinds of problems sorting out the various negatives and their sources. After the King left more ships and men filled the harbours to capacity.

Operation Husky – the invasion of Sicily – began on 10 July 1943. The Americans were to land on the south-west coast at Gela, the British on the eastern side just south of Syracuse. I was in the cruiser HMS *Uganda*, my mission to concentrate on naval support to the invasion, without going ashore. There were hundreds of boats of all kinds making towards the beaches as zero-hour approached. The weather had been very bad but in the early hours there was a change, and the sea became calm. Our planes were in continuous action during the night with very heavy bombing. The ships, too, had been heavily bombarding the shores. It was a noisy night. This was a different phase of war for me – invasion – the change I had been wishing for when I arrived in Malta. It was a night of changing silhouettes, of ships moving stealthily forward, of planes blotting out the stars as they passed overhead. Cocoa on the bridge. Silence. A glider was down. The commandos were at work. The bombardments ceased. More gliders were down in the sea. Not intended. The ships crept on to zero-hour. Machine gun bursts could be heard. Silence again. Eerie. Then Very lights, star shells, flares. Zero-hour. It was light. In went the landing craft. More boats, more ships arriving. Air raids and more air raids, near misses, some from the shore. I was on the bridge of the *Uganda*, and with daylight could show that awesome scene, with the navy in a very different role from the one they had in those torrid days trying to get ships to Malta. Now we were working from Malta where Allied headquarters had been established. The day passed and it was dark again, the only light coming from the hospital ship in the distance. Suddenly those lights went out. She had been bombed. I could only imagine the fearful scenes resulting from that wicked act. I was very tired and had bedded down on the deck unable to rid my mind of those poor sick people in their distress. The next day we heard good news; Syracuse was in our hands. The army was moving fast. By the end of the month half of the island had been overrun and our ship moved up to Augusta.

More transports, more landing craft as the troops advanced towards Catania. More air raids, too. We spent a day with the destroyers bombarding and then returned to Malta to refuel and re-ammunition. As we covered the sixty miles back to Sicily it was very hot in the ship. The perspiration was running in streams down my back and front. I was glad to get back on the bridge as we joined other ships a little further north this time. The sun rose into a clear blue sky and blew the early mist away, revealing villages on the hills and shore. The breeze gently teased and ruffled the smooth blue waters below. Until the war my thoughts of the sea had been that generally it was somewhere people went to for their holidays. Now I knew differently. That benign water I was looking at was deceptive. It hid many secrets. Embraced in its capacious bosom was the wreckage of ships and their men, torn and twisted by the vicissitudes of war or broken and engulfed by the waters themselves when the seas were in angry mood.

On the other side of the island the Americans were meeting strong resistance. Catania was ours on 5 August and after a few days I managed a short trip ashore to find the town very badly damaged. I picked some grapes and limes and returned to the ship. As I took up my position on the bridge I noticed the captain had a hole in his sock. Strange what one recalls. It was a big hole too. Now in the misty distance we could occasionally see massive Etna looking down on the battles all around it. The Allied troops entered Messina on 17 August and the battle was won. Sicily was ours but with heavy casualties on both sides. We returned to Malta where I sent off my film and waited for the attack on Italy. It was not long to wait.

In early September troops, including the Eighth Army, landed in southern Italy and the Italians, but not the Germans, surrendered. I was on my way to Salerno in a different ship, a cruiser. As we passed through the narrow Messina Straits between Sicily and Italy, less than two miles at the northern end, between the two countries we encountered the first attack from a guided missile from the air. No one was hit on this occasion but it was unnerving and unsettling for we felt extremely vulnerable thereafter. I was glad we got through the straits unharmed. I was mindful of the mythological monsters, the whirlpool Charybdis and Scylla opposite, the sea nymph waiting to drown sailors passing through. If you avoided one the other would get you. The modern version was the guided bomb, so we were lucky.

The attack on Salerno began on the 9 September. The approach to the beaches was similar to the invasion of Sicily but more dangerous. The landings were comparatively easy but the Germans were waiting a short way inland and for some days it was touch and go whether the operation would be successful. In the bay were a large number of warships including *Valiant*, *Warspite* and *Uganda*, the ship I had just left. We had all been pouring shells across the bay to try to soften up the Germans while in went the invasion barges holding for some soldiers their last few hours – for some honour, for all the unknown. Those first days of this invasion were high drama with the assault so much in the balance. Then came the guided bombs and once again my luck held as my ship did not appear to be a target. *Warspite* was hit, the bomb going right through the ship causing much damage and many casualties. *Uganda* was also hit. *Warspite* eventually managed to get back to Malta with the aid of tugs and *Uganda* made it under her own steam. We stayed offshore for some days until the army was in control and well inland. Then we left Salerno to return to Malta once more. On the way we heard the cheering news that the Italians had scuttled many of their warships and merchant ships and had surrendered the greater part of their fleet to the Royal Navy in Malta. After leaving Salerno there was an opportunity for me to go to Bari on the Adriatic coast to join a secret operation intending to cross the water to Yugoslavia with a special force. It promised exciting film, but at the very last minute as I arrived in Bari the project was cancelled and I never learned what the mission had hoped to achieve. I returned to Malta.

My time in the Mediterranean had come to an end and I was recalled to the UK. My plane for England was to leave from Egypt so I flew back to Alexandria and was able to say goodbye to those friends still there. My passport was endorsed 'government official', and I returned to London via Lisbon in a Dakota – a good reliable plane but not very comfortable as I sat on a hard bench encased in parachutes. I spent one or two pleasant days in Lisbon, at Estoril, before the final leg home. So three years and several months after my trek to Liverpool, having been half way round the world and seen much action, I returned to England to experience a very different way of life and a very different kind of war.

When I returned to England the war was about to enter a new phase, from the defensive to the offensive. I had come from many different situations where, in the privileged position of war correspondent, I had been able to witness the courage of the servicemen and servicewomen, accompanying them in actions in the front line. My association with the navy in the close environment of an overseas theatre of war, living in ships, the sea always on my doorstep, was now at an end, but I was still a naval war correspondent. There were still to be a number of important assignments ahead of me with that service. Meanwhile I was in the curious position of being part war correspondent and part civilian, but again, as a newsreel cameraman, in the privileged position of being able to witness the courage of the men and women on the home front line.

Gaumont-British News title design from 1940s.

Returning to the UK meant appreciable adjustments to my life and thinking, now so different from what I had just experienced. One of the most important things in gathering news, whether it be as journalist, photographer or newsreel cameraman is to keep situations and areas of coverage in perspective. Away from home, overseas especially, it was so easy to believe one was at the centre of everything, that it was the most important area to be in, that one's stories were number one. In London, with film coming in from all over the world, the same outlook obtained. War fed that attitude. Everyone had a war story. Everyone's experiences were as important to them as mine were to me and it was almost certain that others in similar situations would have different viewpoints. So when I returned to England with many tales to tell – some are here – I soon began to feel my time away was insignificant. I heard so many heroic tales of bombings, of fires in London, of fire-watching, of miraculous escapes, rationing, nights in tube stations and so on, that I soon shut up.

Rationing had started before I left to become a war correspondent, but now, three years later, the sudden return to it hit me like a bomb. It seemed almost unbelievable. Having lived in ships where food was reduced a little but was certainly very adequate, and ashore, wherever I was, there were no shortages and I had lived in relative luxury, I now had to exist on four ounces of butter, twelve ounces of sugar and one ounce of cheese for a week plus all the other things that were rationed. The only thing that was better in this field were the prices – butter at a shilling a pound; beef at a shilling a pound; sugar at three pence a pound, whereas overseas although we could get everything we had to pay a high price for it. It seemed a hard life at first and it most certainly had been for all my fellow countrymen who were fighting the war in Britain.

Talk of invasion was in the air. D-Day was imminent. All sorts of meetings were held and arrangements made so that we could be spirited away in secrecy when the time came. I was to join one of the invading naval forces. It was not too difficult for me to disappear unnoticed. I was undergoing yet another new experience – living in digs near Marble Arch. Before the war I had lived at home with my mother, brother and sister, my father having died young. At the start of the war my mother and sister moved to Devon and later my brother was reported missing. So I was on my own in a dingy establishment run by a typical stage landlady, a formidable-looking battleaxe – a Mrs Potts (not her real name). I would never have entertained such a place had not one of my colleagues recommended it to me. The location was certainly convenient for me to get to my office in Soho. Mrs Potts took all my rations for breakfast, which was the only meal I had there, but at least she did make it more than a snack. The furnishings were basic and the bed uncomfortable and she was not especially kind or understanding if I returned late in the evening. Although I had a key she was usually up, waiting to lock the door. I suspect her austerity was born of long dealings with people of all kinds in that area, and strong discipline was very necessary with most of her odd clients, some of whom no doubt tried to smuggle in girl-friends – or boy-friends. However, she had three special assets of which I definitely approved. She was clean, almost to excess; she did not intrude; she was trustworthy, not going through my things when I was out. I used to set little traps to test her but they were never disturbed. Having travelled so much before the war and during the three previous war years I was hardened to sleeping rough in odd places, so although I had been raised with very good food and essential comforts, I was not unduly put out by Mrs Potts' establishment.

From this hideout while waiting for D-Day, I sallied forth to film air raids and the occasional peacetime story which the newsreel covered to lighten the emphasis on the war. It was a time, in the current stage jargon, of 'resting' between engagements. The government continued to give us petrol for our professional needs, so in an old Ford I acquired I was able to get about reasonably well. This was particularly useful for events outside London, although driving in the blackout took some getting used to again.

When the call for D-Day came I entrained for Portsmouth. In great secrecy (in the best traditions of the 'Silent Service'), in company with a still photographer and a journalist, we were embarked in a destroyer lying out in the harbour. Safely incarcerated, we were briefed on the plans, shown maps, told everything except the date. It was very exciting. Then there occurred one of those situations which could not have been foreseen by the most expert planner. Inexplicably the three of us were allowed to leave the ship. I cannot remember why we wanted to go ashore, possibly in my case to try to get an extra piece of equipment I thought I might require in the light of what we had been told, but away we went with all that vital, secret information in our possession, most of it not known even to the ship's company. Had we been irresponsible, got drunk, or been types that talked I dread to think what might have happened. As it was I had an uneasy feeling as we landed. There were few people about and common sense told me we ought to return to the ship quickly.

The ship could have sailed, for it was at less than the normal four hours' notice, which was usual for warships in harbour in wartime. As luck would have it we were soon spotted by a senior officer who had been involved in our embarkation and wanted to know what we were doing off the ship. He was horrified to see us and told us to get back aboard immediately. It was as well he did not know what we knew for I am certain we would have been locked up and the captain court-martialled. We were fortunate in getting a lift quickly in a boat which dropped us off on its way to another ship and nothing more was heard of that bizarre incident. That same evening we moved away from our anchorage to the south of the Isle of Wight. It was the 4th of June.

Operation Overlord – the invasion – had been planned for 5 June but due to poor weather it was postponed for a day. On the afternoon of the 5th the great fleet of all

Connie Boyd

A typical royal navy LCT that carried troops to Normandy on D-Day and to Walcheren Island during the assault to free the Scheldt.

kinds of ships and craft began to move across the Channel. The sea had eased but was still very choppy and for the smaller vessels must have been very uncomfortable. Having experienced the landings in Sicily, a big operation, with around three thousand invading force, and Salerno, a difficult one, I knew the type of coverage I might expect. This was *the* big one, and I was all keyed up with thoughts of something tremendous to film the following morning. I did have some misgivings about being in a destroyer whose duty appeared to be to protect the little ships on their way over, but I believed we would be close enough in to see the landings. When it got dark nothing could be seen as no ship showed any lights; there were occasional glimpses of that mass of advancing vessels when the moon came out from behind the clouds. I remained awake all night prepared for any sudden attack until, at daylight, when some distance from the French coast, everything passed us and we remained a long way off the beaches. There were worthwhile pictures, of course, as the armada sailed on but we were too far away to witness any of the scenes on the shores. Nothing happened to us or around us; no action of any kind. We could hear the distant firing from ships bombarding, we could see the great number of aircraft flying overhead and we knew what was going on ahead of us. It was very frustrating. We cruised round until the beachheads had been established and then returned to Portsmouth. From my point of view D-Day turned out to be a disappointing flop, one of the biggest anticlimaxes I had ever experienced. It was difficult to understand why we had been assigned to a ship that was destined to stay in the wings. Admittedly with such a massive attack anything could have happened but the odds were against my colleagues and me from the start. I returned to London.

After the initial D-Day landings it was vital to follow up with supplies – guns, tanks, transport, and so on. Until a port was captured everything would have to be landed on the beaches, a particularly difficult operation if the weather was unfavourable. This problem had been foreseen and a prefabricated, artificial harbour had been devised, named Mulberry. It was actually a floating dock constructed from large steel structures and concrete caissons called bombardons, and old ships sunk in line. The harbour was positioned some way off the shore in deep water where ships could unload. Their cargoes were transported by heavy lorries along a specially constructed floating causeway to the beach. It was to this imaginative project that I was assigned soon after returning to London after D-Day. My warship this time was a tug towing a huge concrete block with tall piles sticking up from it, the whole to be sunk into the seabed on arrival. There were two of these harbours, one at the American beach, Omaha, and one at Arromanches-les-Bains, which was our destination. Although it was summer the sea was rough, and the living was rough also. There were days of rolling from side to side as we inched our way across the Channel at what seemed like one knot an hour. There was little opportunity for sleep – there were no spare berths. Meals consisted mainly of doorstep bully-beef sandwiches and mugs of stew-up tea consumed at perilous angles as we lurched from port to starboard and back again. It was just as well I was a good sailor with that treacherous swell and the continual erratic movement of the boat. Although not a spectacular picture it showed the difficulties, the problems and the efforts and seamanship required in getting the sections of the harbour into position. The finished job was a tribute to whoever dreamed up what at first must have seemed an impossible task of towing a harbour across the Channel to the beaches. It was very interesting to see our small section fit into the jigsaw of the harbour.

And so back to London again and to Mrs Potts, whose room I had retained. The flying bombs were coming over in large numbers followed by the V1s. The thought of spending nights in a cellar with Mrs Potts in her nightie, upright lady though she was, caused me real fear and a fatalistic attitude to the raids. I remained in my bed on the top floor. Sudden death seemed preferable to a night with the madam of the house – unkind thoughts I suppose, in retrospect. There were uncomfortable moments when the wretched things seemed to cut off directly overhead and sometimes there would be an explosion without any warning when the V1s made their appearance. I had guilty feelings that I ought to dash out to see if there was anything to film but it was dark and that seemed as good an excuse as any to stay in bed. Again I had to adjust to filming 'shore' stories after having been so long at sea.

The flying bombs increased in numbers as did the V1s, causing much damage and many casualties. In mid-July 1944 a special anti-aircraft unit, consisting of almost 1,600 guns and under the command of General Sir Frederick Pile, was sent to the south coast and based itself in fields in the vicinity of Rye in East Sussex, an area over which the majority of these bombs made their entry into Britain. The sole task of the unit was to try to stop the bombs from getting further inland by shooting them down. They did an excellent job bringing down very many and eased the pressure on London. In company with Ted Candy, one of Gaumont's cameramen, I was sent to Rye to make a documentary film around that unit. We were there for several weeks and it was very exciting whenever they made a kill. I believe our coverage was incorporated into a film – THE SECOND BATTLE OF LONDON – dedicated to the men and women of Anti-Aircraft Command, and produced by Castleton-Knight. Ted Candy had been in a convoy in the Mediterranean sailing from Gibraltar to Malta when the ship he was in was sunk off Algiers. He was rescued and taken prisoner of war and freed when we retook North Africa at the end of the desert war. It was great to see him back.

The V2s made their appearance in September and were deadly. Flying at 3,600 m.p.h. at a height of sixty miles and a range of 200 miles it was impossible to get any warnings of their approach. One of these fell in a side street near Selfridge's. I went to the scene as the emergency services were sorting out the injured and dead. An unpleasant cove, seeing the camera, approached me and said if I wanted pictures what about this and proffered me a thumb he had picked up from some unfortunate casualty. My response was two words beginning with 'f'. It was an unpleasant incident and I have referred to it because it surprised me. Those dealing with disasters, in peacetime as well as in war, I had always seen as the most understanding and compassionate of people even if sometimes they had to adopt almost a disinterested and hard attitude. In this instance the enormity of that tragedy by a V2, seeing what seemed an intrusion with a camera, could have tipped the balance of that individual. It is sad that, as well as the courage and heroics of people in a war, there is that other side which can release the less attractive areas in our make-up.

Following this I covered various routine events during the next month until one morning in late October I was told by my production manager to be ready for a special mission – that same evening. The naval liaison officer had phoned with a rendevous time for me to report at the Admiralty. I was to travel light. There was no further information. It seemed I was back in the war again. I arrived at the appointed hour to find a colleague from Fleet Street and a reporter from the BBC also waiting to go on the mystery tour. Our guide, Anthony Kimmins, told us nothing other than that we were going to the south coast. We arrived at Dover in the early evening of 31 October and were embarked in a small fast boat and headed for Ostend, still with no idea what was afoot. At Ostend we were transferred to a depot ship alongside a quay. It was very dark. After a short wait and a cup of coffee, one by one we were whisked away. I was guided along a narrow jetty, travelling light, but laden like a coolie with all my camera equipment and very cold in that eerie atmosphere. There was a whispered 'here' from my guide, then he said good night and wished me luck. Such secrecy made me nervous as I stepped into the boat alongside. It was some minutes before I realised I was in a landing craft and almost immediately we were moving away from the jetty. A bitter wind chilled me still further as I tried to make out what I was supposed to be doing. As I became accustomed to the dark I saw the craft was filled to capacity with men. One or two stared at me. 'You coming with us?' said one. 'It seems so,' I answered. 'Where are we going?' 'You don't know?' he queried incredulously, and added, 'Walcheren.' I remember those initial exchanges because everything seemed so weird and his answer did not enlighten me. I had no idea what Walcheren was, or if it was a place where that was. I explained to my questioner why I was with them and he and the others became very friendly, asked about filming, said I should get some good pictures and jokingly hoped I was a good swimmer. I then saw from their uniform that they were commandos but I still did not know what it was all about until I had a talk with the young naval lieutenant in charge of the landing craft. He told me that Walcheren was one of three islands at the mouth of the Scheldt estuary, the gateway to Antwerp. The port had been captured by the army early in September but was unable to be of use until we were in control of Walcheren so that our ships could sail down the Scheldt with the essential supplies the army required. The operation had been planned in the greatest secrecy as the capture of the island was absolutely vital to enable our armies to advance, and it was going to be rough. Walcheren had been very heavily fortified by the Germans and could only be assaulted either by a land attack across the promontory at South Beveland, halfway down the Scheldt, or troops attacking Flushing, the port at the southern end of Walcheren, or by a frontal assault from the sea, which we were about to undertake. Flushing was to be attacked by Canadians some hours before our landings. The sea attack was to be mounted by Royal Marine Special Service Brigade – Royal Marine commandos who were to land from landing craft (LCTs), landing vehicles tracked (LVTs) and various other amphibious vehicles. Our LCT was packed tight with Royal Marine commandos. The river flowed each side of Walcheren and we were approaching the north-west side of the estuary making for Westkapelle, one of the most heavily fortified areas. I learned later there were ten batteries with forty guns from three inches to eight inches covering the beaches, and capable of reaching all the advancing craft.

As the sky lightened on the morning of 1 November – the day of the attack – with zero hour, or H-hour as it was called on this operation, at 09.45, I could make out more of what was happening and see the size of the attack. The sea was alive with every kind of landing craft as the naval lieutenant had outlined to me earlier, an assortment of about two hundred vessels. We were to land our troops, part of the first of the assault forces, and then return to Ostend. There was no hanging about – we went straight in. It was cold and I felt cold, unusual for me, probably caused by the occasion. This was the first time I had actually gone in with an attacking force on to a beach. My previous filming of landings had been from the comparative safety of the deck of a warship. I had difficult decisions to make. In such a small craft a tripod was impractical both for space and unsteady movement and there was very little elevation. This precluded the use of telephoto lenses so it had to be a hand-held camera, resting on rails or whatever according to the immediate situation, if events in the distance made it worthwhile to try to attempt to use a longer lens. I had to show the approach to the beach so I joined the lieutenant on the small bridge. When the firing started everyone was ordered to keep out of sight. This was readily obeyed; no one, however brave, had any desire to be shot at sooner than he had to be. I certainly was not brave, in fact I was almost jelly, but I had no alternative but to remain standing. I thought I had done well to survive the war up to that point and wondered whether I would continue to be lucky. The odds seemed short this time. My only consolation in this unenviable position was that I did not have the unpleasant task ahead of having to leave the protection of the landing craft, such as it was, to go ashore into the hell that was building up on the beaches. Such were the thoughts of the untrained.

Fighter aircraft and low-level planes strafed the area just before we arrived. The weather was not good, with the sea very choppy with a heavy swell. The shore batteries fired at the incoming armada with devastating effect. Shell bursts were everywhere, the screaming whine of the shells almost continuous as they made their deadly journeys towards our forces. A landing craft ahead of us was hit and stopped. I took pictures of our marines in the drab morning light, crouching in the well of the boat. They were in good spirits, anxious to go. H-hour was a minute or two away as with extreme skill and coolness our young commanding officer urged and coaxed our craft forward, the engines groaning miserably as they did their best to cope with the extra-heavy load thrust upon them. A supreme effort carried us on to the beach, the drawbridge licked the sand and I filmed the men rushing ashore for cover. Suddenly we were empty, alone, just the four crew and me. Alone indeed but not quiet. The navy's job was to get the men ashore; what happened after that was secondary. Bullets streamed all around us but miraculously no gun seemed able to depress sufficiently to hit us. A change in position would have revealed their whereabouts to the troops now racing across the beach. Whatever the reason, perhaps my charmed life, they could not hit us. However I expected to be blown to bits at any moment for the drawbridge had sunk deep into the beach as the men rushed over it and the sand was reluctant to let us go. We looked doomed, for it could be only a matter of time before someone got us. Then we moved, the sand lost its grip and we backed away. The next ten minutes were very, very frightening and unpleasant as we struggled to get out of the range of the shore batteries. We were all wet from the water thrown up by the near misses. We were some of the lucky ones. There were many casualties, many losses of tanks, bulldozers and vehicles and less than ten of the landing force remained undamaged. Later I was told there were 8,000 casualties, the commandos losing almost half of their troop leaders. Brave men indeed those commandos. Walcheren eventually surrendered eight days after our landings and was said to be one of the most formidable and difficult of any assaults from the sea during the war. I was very glad to see Ostend again and to return to London. But not for long.

Two months later, in January 1945, I found myself at Port Said again, leaning over the side of a ship haggling with the Egyptians in their feluccas offering bargains in souvenirs and leather goods. Just when I had been thinking that perhaps Walcheren was my final stint on active service here I was going overseas again, still a naval war correspondent, assigned to the South East Asia Command (SEAC) under the command of Lord Louis Mountbatten. Events in Europe were going well and attention was now concentrated on defeating the Japanese.

I was going for an indefinite period which, as always, meant taking a great deal of equipment and hundreds of feet of film stock. That meant another sea journey because such a load going by air was impractical at that time. I left England in a Dutch cargo ship bound for Ceylon where the headquarters of SEAC was based. As the shores of Britain vanished in the evening haze I wondered how long I was going to be away this time and whether there would be more to film than on my first long sea journey. The war in Europe had still to be won and in the Far East just then it looked as if it would take long and unpleasant efforts to defeat the Japanese. However, on this transit journey to Ceylon there was unlikely to be anything to film, and on that first day out as we steamed to the south, the flying bombs, V2s, landing craft, and shattered buildings seemed to be in another world. The ship was very comfortable and took twelve passengers, a mixture of men and women, some service, some civilian. The Dutch were good hosts, everyone was friendly, we feasted well and looked to be set for a cruise in the style of a luxury yacht owned by a Greek millionaire.

Although it was winter the sun shone pleasantly on our little ship as we passed lazily through the Straits of Gibraltar to begin to cross the 2,500 miles of the Mediterranean to Port Said. I was anxious to know how I would feel back on those waters. I was amazed to find that Malta, Italy, Sicily, Greece and Crete were already just memories, perhaps more vivid than most, but only memories. It was difficult to take on board what had happened not so long before, with all those ships and men lying deep in that sea, in some instances almost 16,000 feet down. And now, unbelievably it seemed, I was heading for war again. The mind can play funny tricks or perhaps it was the Bols gin that the Dutch plied us with so liberally that made me let go those days in the Mediterranean.

The Suez Canal had fascinated me when I saw it for the first time on landing at

Fort Tewfik at its southern end when on my way to Alexandria. I had driven alongside it a number of times during my stay in Egypt but now, as we left Port Said to proceed along its 100 miles through the desert to Suez, I was thrilled to be actually sailing on it for the first time. We passed another very narrow canal which ran alongside the Suez Canal and which was used mainly for irrigation – the Sweet Water Canal – a misnomer if ever there was. It was dirty and the source of bilharzia, an often fatal blood disease, endemic in Egypt and particularly so to the locals who worked and lived in that area. Leaving Suez and into the Red Sea, past Aden and there once more was the Indian Ocean. Hot days, fantastic sunsets as the sun dipped at speed into the shiny waters with the 'green flash' momentarily visible if one was lucky. There again were the flying fish and warm balmy nights with the dancing phosphorescence ahead and astern as we disturbed the waters. I had not expected to be on those seas again. The navy and my office seemed determined to bestow upon me dreamlike travelogues. Once across the Equator the enchantment faded and the war began to creep back again. The last time I had been in that area war had not wiped its dirty boots on the magic carpets of the East. Then I had sailed from war to places still enjoying a peaceful existence. Now I was sailing through the same waters in the opposite direction, but into war. A paradox not expected. The lurking submarines were again a reality but, some three weeks after leaving England, we arrived in Colombo unharmed. The harbour had not changed since I was last there. It was as busy as ever with perhaps more warships, and its dhows with their large triangular sails and the little boats – an unmistakable touch of the Orient.

My assignment on arrival was to report to SEAC headquarters in the hills of Ceylon, at Kandy. We climbed through densely tree-lined roads on the drive up, passing elephants working on moving felled trees into piles by the roadside, until we opened up into the SEAC camp. It was four miles from Kandy, the ancient capital of Ceylon, and set in the Peridynia Botanic Gardens – the largest and most beautiful of the gardens on the island. A royal residence had been built in Queen Victoria's reign in case the Queen visited Ceylon. In normal times it had become the summer residence of the Governor-General. Now, in wartime, it had become the headquarters of Lord Mountbatten. The camp had been laid out in an informal way with thatched living quarters for the SEAC staff and canteens, messes and a clubhouse situated on the banks of a loop of the River Mahawoli, which ran through the gardens. There were avenues of palms and orchids, and buildings were linked by roads named Fleet Street, Ludgate Circus, Times Square and Broadway. With forest all around it must have been one of the most romantic and beautiful wartime headquarters ever – a paradise of a place. I presented my credentials accrediting me to the navy, an unreal assignment it seemed in that marvellous place miles from the sea. I based myself in Colombo, relying on the naval authorities there to keep me informed as they were in regular contact with SEAC HQ. It had been decided by the

Newsreel Association in London, to which all the newsreels belonged, that the senior cameraman of Paramount, Jim Wright, would coordinate the coverage of those of us in SEAC, Alec Tozer of Movietone and Ronnie Noble of Universal with the army in Burma and me with the navy, and he would act as liaison between the association and ourselves.

The prospect of getting to sea on worthwhile operations did not seem good. There was quite a lot of naval activity around the coasts of Burma but to be on the spot for any action of that kind one needed to be in a ship full-time. The area covered by SEAC was vast – India, Ceylon, Burma and Malay. Much of the time that goes into the making of a newsreel is unproductive, even in peacetime. In wartime more so; it was very much the waiting game. Unless one went on a specific operation it was a gamble to go to sea. One had to do so sometimes but gambles rarely paid off. In peacetime chancy stories were more of a calculated risk because we could usually make some kind of story. So it was very frustrating sitting in Colombo. I went on a number of those speculative sorties, which all turned out to be night operations with little to film. After playing the waiting game for a reasonable period I returned to Kandy on its quaint little train with other ideas – to tackle the navy from the land. I asked if I could be transferred to work with the army in Burma and perhaps pick up some naval activity on the coasts or on the Irrawaddy river on the way to Rangoon. The Fourteenth Army under General Slim was making good progress. Mandalay and Meiktila had been captured, and although my ideas were certainly speculative they seemed better than watching the flying fish in the Indian Ocean. I am somewhat hazy now, so many years after, exactly how I persuaded the navy to agree to my going but they gave me permission to go for a limited period and I was soon heading by air for Calcutta, clad in green kit, on the first stage to join the army in Meiktila.

I have often wondered whether it is best to leave things to take their course or whether to force a change when nothing seems to be moving. By some unkind twist of life whenever I have made a very serious effort in my business life to move things along, to change my natural course, I seemed to have come unstuck. Perhaps my judgement was not all that good. When I asked to go to Burma I thought at least I had a good chance of getting some good pictures. I knew the army correspondents were there, but, egotistically, I thought perhaps, apart from anything naval, I could take a fresh look at the army, almost from a layman's viewpoint. I thought if I stayed glued to the navy the only thing I was likely to get was cirrhosis of the liver. I could not have been more wrong. As I said earlier, with the navy it was the waiting game.

Calcutta offered its sweaty greeting in the lounge of the questionably-named Grand Hotel. The place was lively and cheerful when I arrived, for most of the occupants were chaps generally in transit, back from jungle areas, savouring civilised life once more. I suppose 'civilised' at that time depended on each person's particular circumstances. To me six beds in a room with one shower and one lavatory was far from civilised but then I had not come from a jungle life. After a trek through Burma the Grand Hotel would no doubt have seemed like a maharajah's palace. Firewater called Carew's gin, the local brew, was the only alcoholic beverage. The water was deadly, never to be recommended in those parts, and was undrinkable. The only other drink was bottled or tinned fruit juices. Although I am certain the Carew's burned holes in whatever it came in contact with I feel sure now that a generous intake of the stuff saved my life. I had not been two days on my road to Burma when cholera broke out in the hotel. In no time the hotel population was decimated and everyone and everything was put out of bounds. I was condemned to the lounge and Carew's and in company with the more enlightened I lapped it up. No germ could stand up to it. Nevertheless it was very worrying as unfortunates were carried out in scores, many at their journey's end. It looked at one time that Calcutta was as far as I was going to get on my new project but after some weeks of misery, hardly daring to wash in the rationed water, let alone drink it, sweaty and hungry, at last I was allowed on my way and from Calcutta's DUM-DUM airport I joined other travellers en route for Meiktila in an overloaded Wellington. We sat on hard benches on each side of the aircraft – no parachutes and no seat belts. A colonel sat opposite me very lovingly nursing a lavatory seat, a refinement of taste unexpected in that kind of war. I sympathised with his outlook, however, because 'going to nature' privately or even comfortably in the latrines of a battlefield or desert was far from easy, but I did wonder how he could use his seat. Perhaps colonels had special toilets. We had a Canadian pilot who brought the plane in to land on the narrow and short airstrip at breakneck speed. He had to do this because of the weight we carried; otherwise if he had tried normal speed we could have dropped like a stone. At least that is what he told us later. As it was the result was nearly as bad. We could not stop and shot straight off the runway and bumped and bounced to finish at an angle in a field. Apart from bruises no one was hurt. The colonel was on the floor still clutching his seat. The pilot ordered us to get out quickly. We did not need his advice; there was a smell of petrol all over the plane. So I had two near misses for survival so far on this expedition. I hoped there would not be a third. They say things go in threes.

Weeks followed of living rough, at least for me. I met Tozer and Noble, the army correspondents, who were curious to know what I was doing on their territory. When I told them I was looking for a naval angle they roared with laughter. To them the army life had become second nature. They knew how to conserve water and how to acquire it – from me at first while I remained as green as my battledress. Although I was not green, I was turning yellow from the mepacrine tablets we had to take to avoid getting malaria. My imagination ran riot. Every tiny noise I heard at night was a Japanese stealing up on me to stick a knife in my back. In all the time I spent at sea I never slept in a hammock yet here I was in the jungle with a hammock as my bed. I did not feel too happy with that and did not make it a regular bed. The ground offered no more comfort. Every movement was a python, although I did not see a snake until I reached Rangoon when I saw one hanging on a tree outside my bedroom window. Every shadow was the enemy, every tree concealed a sniper (later I learned some of them did). Whenever I opened my camera case I expected to find a nest of tarantulas. Not many days had passed before I thought a life on the ocean waves seemed wonderful. Once before, in the Libyan desert I had similar feelings but this was a very different war. There had been little cover in the desert; here there was too much. Pictures were few – the routine, or what was filmically routine, had been filmed again and again. Men struggling through jungle, plodding, camping, firing guns – unpleasant as it may sound – and was – it was necessary to search for a new twist or for real action. My arrogant assumption that I might bring a fresh look to the army coverage soon disappeared. The army cameramen knew what they were doing much better than I. My one main hope had been to find some naval angle. There was none that could be found in that area of conflict. I had not realised how far away was the sea from the route the army was following to Rangoon. It was possible to fake some front-line activity and I suppose in some circumstances it was permissible to re-enact an actual occasion as authentically as possible. It can be overdone and sometimes was but to the credit of cinema newsreels generally there was very little 'stunted' material included. I did not attempt to fake shots even in peacetime. It was so easy to see someone who could not keep his eyes off the camera giving away many a good shot.

On this journey we were out on little sorties but nothing big developed. Weather held us up. The monsoon was approaching. Bridges that had been destroyed slowed us down as we gradually worked our way south to Rangoon, which was our objective. Eventually, in April 1945, we were close to the city and I looked forward to being part of a team filming the army streaming in. It was an exciting anticipation for me. Previously all I had seen of a takeover was the shoreline from the sea. There would be some action of course, but now I would be with the first to liberate a capital city and there would surely be some naval angle there. There would be smiles on people's faces instead of tears and misery. Flowers would appear miraculously. Girls might even kiss me. The smell and decay of human flesh would be banished. I would share a sense of achievement. The weeks of discomfort would all be worth those scenes. Wrong once more. All my thoughts, no doubt, dreamt up from films I had seen, were dashed when on 1 May a combined operation, fairly small-scale, was parachuted along the coast south of Rangoon and the next day an Indian division was landed in Rangoon by the navy to find the city evacuated by the Japanese and there had been no opposition. On 5 May the city was secure. This operation virtually ended the battle to free Burma. When we arrived some days later it was in pouring rain. The monsoon had broken, and Rangoon was getting back to normal. The army cameramen went off with the army, which turned inland again to clear up the re-capture of Burma. Leaving the navy had done nothing for me in the way of pictures. While I fed back to London film in Rangoon and some useful material taken during those long weeks on the way down to the city such coverage could have only made minor items in the newsreels, if used at all. All footage of that kind, not used, usually went into the archives or libraries. Some, no doubt, found its way into the bin, that is, the cutting room bin which received the offcuts of film used. They served the save purpose as dustbins for anything that went into them was rarely seen again. Most newsreel cameramen will assert that fifty per cent of their best material went that way. Cutters and cameramen do not always agree about the finished product. When a cutter has been peering at hundreds of feet, sometimes thousands, it is not surprising that a cameraman's favourite shot is often missing on the screen. Time is always the decider in getting out the newsreel and personal feelings do not count but let no cameraman think I am supporting the cutting room!

To return to my story, in most Burmese towns and cities there were many temples and one of the most beautiful was the great Schedagon Pagoda in Rangoon with its lofty gilded dome and spires, which glowed orange in the evening light and gold by day. To be able to visit that famous shrine to Buddha was an opportunity not to be missed both for possible film and for my own interest. I walked, barefoot, up the wide steps, past beggars and sellers of paper flowers, paper umbrellas, images of Buddha and incense sticks. It was very dirty with excreta everywhere. However as I reached the main door, through which Brahmin priests and monks in their orange or brown robes were entering and leaving, there stood a large figure – half lion, half griffin – a foretaste of what was inside. Entering, the massive images of Buddha in every kind of posture engendered a very distinct atmosphere, a sense of immortality, bewitching, bewildering, but disappointingly I had no feeling of reverence for such a deity. But it was definitely a very unusual experience. As I walked between those huge Buddhas I thought maybe I should have whispered in the ear of one that I was going to Kandy where it is said repose the original relics, in particular the tooth, in its own temple. Perhaps then he would have told me how to get back there. I doubt whether I would have got any response; cold eyes only stared at me, and like the Sphinx, in inscrutable silence.

Having reached Rangoon there was nowhere else for me to go in Burma. I had learned a lesson; if I had played the waiting game I would have been with the landing forces that entered Rangoon. Now I was desirous of and determined to return to the navy. With the Japanese almost ousted from Burma the situation in SEAC had changed. Our ships would certainly be involved in any forward moves and I wanted to be sure I was with them. However, getting back to Kandy was not as simple as leaving it. The newsreels had to pay the total cost for any journey undertaken that was purely transit, such as the one from England to Ceylon. We had to pay mess bills in warships, too, although of course there was no other charge when going on an operation. Getting back to Ceylon was a transit situation. I did not want to travel on any private civilian aircraft or ship; the newsreels would not have thanked me for large additional costs especially as my venture away from the navy had not produced very much. It took me many days of circuitous air travel in service planes before I was able to march into the SEAC press headquarters.

At the beginning of August 1945 the atomic bombs were dropped on Hiroshima and Nagasaki and on 14 August the Japanese surrendered. Shortly after that I embarked in the cruiser HMS *Sussex* en route for Singapore. A massive amphibious and air attack had been planned to retake the island but with the surrender of the Japanese the operation was called off and on 9 September Singapore was re-occupied without any opposition. The official signing of the documents handing Singapore back to Britain had taken place in the admiral's cabin in HMS *Sussex* a

Gaumont British News.
Cameraman J. Turner.   600-ft.   September 4th,1945.

HANDING OVER OF PORT OF SINGAPORE BY JAPANESE ABOARD H.M.S. SUSSEX

Preliminary shots prior to Conference - Destroyer H.M.S. Vigilant
draws near to H.M.S. Sussex to receive official documents to take
to Convoy of troops bound for Singapore - probably one of the last
convoys of the war.
Shot of documents going over.
Shots of General Mansergh (G.O.C. 5th Division - occupiers of Singapore
coming aboard Sussex to be present at Conference with Japanese.
Shots of General Christison coming aboard (G.O.C.
Shot of Convoy - general distant view.
Shots of General Itagaki - C.inC. Southern Army of Japanese at the
Conference table signing the documents handing over Singapore - the
Japs responsible for carrying out order of document.
Shot of General Itagaki and Vice-Admiral Fukutome.
After signing the Japanese leave the Conference Room - bow -
A shot of the document - close-up with signatures.

_____

H.M.S. Cleopatria lays off whilst C.-in-C. comes to Sussex to discuss
Conference on the Quarter Deck - with Admiral Holland C.-in-C. two
                                                              generals.
Japanese Ship passes flying a black flag - as ordered.
Motor Boats with General Itagaki, Vice-Admiral Fukutome & Staffs
General Itagaki steps aboard H.M.S. Sussex (approach gangway)
Vice-Admiral Fukutome comes aboard.

Part of my dope sheet for the return of Singapore story.

BUFVC/ITN Archive/Reuters

few days earlier on 4 September. General Mansbergh, GOC Fifth Division, General Christisson and Admiral Holland were the British delegation and Admiral Fukutomi and General Itagaki were the Japanese representatives. With the war in the West ended a number of cameramen had descended on SEAC, each representing individual companies. They all tried to get aboard *Sussex* but as I was the only official naval war correspondent they were unsuccessful, so I had that historic signing as an exclusive – some recompense for my earlier failures.

The official surrender of the Japanese to the commander-in-chief Admiral Lord Louis Mountbatten, took place in a splendid ceremony in Singapore on 12 September. HMS *Sussex* was by then berthed alongside. In the harbour were over fifty warships, destroyers, cruisers, HMS *Nelson* and the French battleship *Richelieu* among them. Admiral Mountbatten drove up in an open car to be greeted by the three commanders of the navy, army and air force of SEAC. After an inspection of a guard of honour and a fly-past of Mosquitoes, Sunderlands and Dakotas flying low, the signing ceremony took place inside Singapore's municipal building. Twelve allied representatives sat at two long tables facing seven Japanese in the large council chamber, with Admiral Mountbatten splendid in white naval uniform and the dejected Japanese sitting impassively in khaki. Press, photographers and cameramen, including me, pushed and shoved, endeavouring to

British Pathe

General Itagaki and Vice-Admiral Fukutomi signing the surrender documents on board HMS *Sussex*. From the newsreel.

record the signings and particularly the signatures. It was a bit of a shambles but that was what we were there for. It became a little easier when it was seen how many documents had to be signed. After the formalities Mountbatten went out on to the steps of the municipal muildings and announced to the waiting crowds and assembled representatives of the three forces that he had accepted the surrender of the Japanese. There were three cheers for the King and the formal hoisting of the Union Jack, a very worn flag which had been kept hidden in Changi gaol. Altogether a very impressive ceremony, and plenty of film for the newsreels. The official documents had been signed by General ltagaki standing in for the supreme commander of the Japanese forces, Field Marshal Count Terauchi, who was ill. He had been ordered to hand over his sword in person to Lord Mountbatten as soon as he was better and this took place in Saigon on 30 November 1945. I had to get my film ready for despatch to London so I did not have much opportunity to look at Singapore with its small hills surrounding the city. From what I saw it did not appear to have suffered too badly in terms of damage. There were wrecks in the harbour and a fair number of buildings demolished but overall it had come through the occupation reasonably well. I had wanted to see the Raffles Hotel but did not have time to get there or see whether it had been damaged. It was hot and sticky and I was glad to be returning to the *Sussex*. I received an unexpected greeting.

HMS *Sussex* was a County Class cruiser, high out of the water. As I arrived at the ship the captain had just gone up the gangway. The bar would be open in the wardroom and in the muggy, sweaty heat I was looking forward to a drink and a bath. I got both sooner than I had expected. The gangway was at a steep angle to the quay. Over my shoulder I had a haversack containing exposed magazines of film – a magazine being the container that fits into or on to the camera. In one hand was my camera as I struggled up the gangway, and at the top, before stepping on to the ship I handed my camera and the haversack to a sailor. As I did so there was a loud cracking noise and I felt the ground slipping away from me – or so it seemed. The next few seconds were hazy. I know I was on my side. I know I plunged downwards between the side of the ship and the quay, head first into the murky waters. I know I seemed to be years beneath the surface and I know I could not understand why I could not see. I know hands were pulling me out of the water. I could breathe but I could not see. I was certainly confused and thought that in the fall I had lost my eyesight. Then someone removed my naval cap, which I had always thought too big, and I realised that it had been rammed over my eyes and ears when I hit the water. I must have looked a pretty sight as I came groping to the surface, the bridge of my nose bleeding profusely from the only damage I sustained. I was lucky, as was the sailor who was lower down the gangway when it slid off the ship. We both fell off it, he on to the concrete jetty and me into the water, but neither of us was hurt. I must have fallen some twenty feet and if I had fallen on to the jetty instead of into the water goodness knows what would have happened. Fortunately, too, the gangway got wedged or it could have easily come down on top of us. The sailor failing on to concrete was especially fortunate only sustaining a few bruises. And of course it was extremely lucky that I had handed my camera and film to the sailor at the top of the gangway before the accident.

With the war now ended on all fronts, clearing up processes were of no real interest to our editors so the time had come for me to return to England. War was out; peace was in. Victory parades were in the office diaries and many of the old favourites were due to appear in the reels again. Rebuilding projects were news; babies were news. I returned to Britain to take up normal duties again.

Looking back over those war years I realised my war overall had not been too bad compared to so many at home and abroad. I was after all a civilian in the privileged position of war correspondent, and I was sometimes in the front line but I did not have to kill. I had kept my profession so I did not have to start again at the end of the war. I had been able to see many places overseas in good circumstances as well as bad. I had generally lived very well with plenty to eat and drink. And I had been fortunate in my assignments, which enabled me to obtain some historic films. So, although scary at times, I consider I was very lucky to have been made a war correspondent. However, I do not wish and hope never to be involved in a war again. Back once more on British soil I was to discover more very interesting and challenging assignments ahead, but this time without the Grim Reaper banging on the door.

Chapter Six
Early Post-War Years

I put away my chauffeur's uniform with brass buttons; I put away my khaki job; I put away my uncomfortable peaked cap. My days as a naval war correspondent were over with the surrender of the Japanese in Singapore and I was back in Britain at the end of 1945 to resume my job as a peacetime newsreel cameramen. Although I had been back in the UK several times during the war they had only been temporary visits, but now that I was back permanently I had some rethinking to do once again. At first I was concerned I might not like switching from the five long years of independence I had enjoyed during the war to the competitive disciplines of business life under the eye of my London office and always at the end of a telephone. I even contemplated changing jobs to look for a new career. That phase soon passed. I could not think of another occupation which would give me the entree to so many places or enable me to be at the centre of domestic and world events. Journalism perhaps, but I had no qualifications for that. So when I walked into the camera room of Gaumont-British at Film House, Wardour Street in Soho, on my return and saw the familiar scene of chaps playing cards, camera equipment all over the place, the same locker in which to keep my things, everything, in fact, so normal as if I had never been away, I was very grateful I was not starting a new job. And I was glad to learn that some of my colleagues had similar feelings when they returned from their war commitments. It was also marvellous to know that all our cameramen and soundmen based in London had survived the war. I set out my trusty camera and equipment on a table to check it over, to see what needed replacing and to give it a good clean after five years of very little maintenance, and then I was away to take some leave.

Pre-war I had been filming nearly every day, as had my colleagues. During the war there were often quite long periods between operations and most of these were generally at a distance from the camera. Consequently my reactions to camera settings had become slower. For someone like me who was so often using a hand-camera and involved in getting close-ups of people it was extremely important to get back to those pre-war days, when with a hand-camera, distances and exposures had to be guessed. We could judge three, four or five yards almost to an inch. There was no time to focus or take exposure settings when, for instance, in Downing Street a Cabinet meeting broke up and ministers came out of Number Ten in quick succession. Settings had to be judged. There could be half a dozen changes in as many minutes, from a few feet to someone yards away in a doorway, from a dark corner to strong sunlight. While there was a certain amount of latitude if one was not always spot on, the changes on the camera had to become almost automatic. It took me a lot of private practice to get back to a satisfactory speed of action. Improvements were soon made to equipment. I had a turret fitted to the front of my camera containing three lenses which could be swung over avoiding having to stop the camera to change lenses. The viewfinder system changed, too. We were able to see directly through the lens so there was no adjustment of parallax from a viewfinder that had been either on the side or above the camera requiring a change with each change of lens. By being able to see the picture through the lens also meant we could focus as we filmed. But for most of us those were changes still to come. Immediately post-war I was still using my old faithful unchanged Newman Sinclair, which had served me so well during the war and continued to do so for some time afterwards.

In July 1945 there had been a general election while I was overseas and a new Labour government had replaced Winston Churchill and the Tories. This meant getting to know new ministers and a new set of faces and for a while even the prospect of a penance in Downing Street seemed acceptable. The Nuremberg trials had also started in 1945 and cameramen were despatched to cover those dramatic days.

I was soon back on the road for what looked to be a busy time ahead. While I filmed most of the stories I am writing about, sometimes as part of a team, there were of course many other events that went into the newsreels, for there was no shortage of stories and we all had plenty to do. It was a difficult time for everyone so soon after the war, not least for the many people who had lost their homes, their families, wives and husbands. There was so much damage everywhere, so much had been destroyed in so many cities and towns, so much to be cleared before any rebuilding could be undertaken. All this formed part of our early coverage. Housing was a priority and the immediate solution for many of the homeless was the provision of prefabricated houses, 'prefabs' as they came to be known. We filmed lorries leaving factories piled high with these and showed them being erected wherever sites had been cleared, sometimes in areas where the recipients had once lived. Most of these people put on a brave face and appreciated having somewhere to live, but I found it quite distressing talking to some who had lost everything and had to restart their lives, perhaps with children and no partner, in accommodation which although well designed was really very basic.

At the beginning of 1946 the newly formed United Nations Organisation (UNO) held its first meeting in Central Hall, Westminster. On the opening day of the UNO we had a field day in Central Hall trying to film as many representatives as we could in the limited time allocated for pictures. There were photographers and cameramen from all over the world and it became quite a battle as we were all going for the same personalities from the more important countries. This was an occasion when my decision to get back to automatic camera settings paid off, for moving from face to face, sometimes in the front row of seating, sometimes further back or elsewhere meant constant changes on the camera. In the evening I took arrivals at St James's Palace where a banquet was given to the delegates by the King. These were always difficult occasions for filming. One worked with an electrician with portable hand-lights and there was very little room on the pavement when a car drew up, a flunkey opened the door and the individual disappeared through the door opposite in seconds. Sometimes they did pose for a picture but it was the lesser-known nationals who were more cooperative and usually the most colourful in their dress.

The weather did not help at the start of the year with 70 m.p.h. gales over most of the country. Those brave men who dealt with unexploded bombs and mines were in constant demand. A bomb had fallen in St James's Park in London and proved difficult to deal with, and in the English Channel the gales had loosened many mines. One was washed up at Brighton and another on to the beach near the pier at Hastings, a job for the mine-disposal men to remove the detonator. I had to rush down there after the UNO meeting but arrived too late to show the mine being made safe. It was still on the beach with people round it so there was a picture. The high winds had caused huge seas to lash against the sea walls and Hastings was a particularly good place to show the seas high in the air as tons of water fell on the promenade. This made dramatic pictures and resulted in my journey being worthwhile.

Early in February we covered two thousand wives of American servicemen, 'GI brides', some with children, leaving London for Southampton to embark in the liner *Queen Mary* to join their husbands in America. Quite a tear-jerker story as they sobbed farewells to their families.

Another February story was the reopening of the Royal Opera House, Covent Garden, with the Sadler's Wells Ballet performing *The Sleeping Beauty*. It was a gala occasion attended by the King and Queen, Queen Mary and the Princesses Elizabeth and Margaret. I was very pleased when I was given this assignment because I have always liked anything to do with the theatre. Maybe this was because in my young days I was taken to film studios and absorbed the magnetism that prevailed in such surroundings. I like the atmosphere of the theatre – there is an intangible romance about it – I mean behind the scenes, not as part of an audience. Being on the stage amid the scenery and the lights and the general chaos that precedes a performance just before it opens and being with the actors and actresses is to be in another world, one of unreality with no one being themselves. I like music and I like ballet and *The Sleeping Beauty* was one of my favourites. So there I was on the stage of the Royal Opera House with the dancers in their dainty costumes and next to the great ballerina Margot Fonteyn. I was in my element.

However I was there to do a job and it was a tricky one. I had to film the royal family in the royal box from the stage during the national anthem before the show started. I was not to be visible from the front and had to film by pointing my camera through the safety curtains which would be opened, pulled sideways, as soon as the anthem ended and the royals were seated. In order to get as much footage as possible it meant remaining to the last second to try to get a general picture as well as close-ups. As soon as the curtains moved I moved behind them, praying I would not trip up or that the curtains would beat me to the side. I only just made it as the curtains opened very quickly. We were not allowed to take any close shots of the performance but I stayed for a while in the wings and watched the start of the dancing, rubbing shoulders with the Wicked Fairy and the Lilac Fairy and that made my day – or rather my night. I then went to the front of the house with the audience to get a general shot of the stage and see some more of the show. We were not supposed to get too involved or too interested personally in our stories but this was a one-off – or so I decided. This was a story which relied on the skill of the laboratory technicians for, with the poor lighting, most of the film was underexposed.

The Covent Garden market then was very different from that of today. Coming out of the opera house late in the evening there were already signs of produce arriving for the early morning sales. The open-fronted shops of the wholesalers would soon be stacked with fruit, vegetables and flowers, porters would be hurrying through the streets, tiers of baskets on their heads, and the pubs would be open to welcome buyers and sellers at all hours. Those old markets were full of interest with an ambience which would be hard to find in that area nowadays. Bananas, which had disappeared during the war, were again in the market shortly after the opera house reopened and we deemed that worthy of some footage too.

It was not long before we were back on the sporting scene. To start my season I was on the Thames towpath near Hammersmith Bridge to get crowd reactions at the Boat Race. Most of those lining the banks of the river sported tokens such as celluloid dolls adorned in dark-blue or light-blue colours or little cloth oars in similar colours and sold by vendors with their hoards of attractive novelties, doing a brisk trade among the partisan supporters of both crews. A cool March day brought forth flasks from overcoat pockets. Young children sat astride the shoulders of their dads and waved enthusiastically when the Oxford and Cambridge boats came through the bridge with Oxford leading and going on to win. But few minded who really won; it was a pleasant day out away from post-war cares.

The end of the war saw a change in policy among the newsreels in filming most major sports stories. Generally no company was prepared any longer to carry the high costs involved in securing exclusive coverage of an event. Where practical each company had its own cameramen at a story. Sometimes only one firm was allowed to film on a pool or rota basis, supplying all, and when charges were made all the costs were shared. We were at Aintree again for the Grand National. The owners of the course always charged a tidy sum for the right to film whether it was for exclusive rights or if all were there. This was an occasion where we had agreed earlier that post-war we would cover the race jointly. As described in another chapter, because of the number of jumps each reel filmed a section of the course and supplied the others with that section. There was some doubt in that first post-war year whether the racecourse could be returned to a fit enough state for the Aintree meeting but it was just in time.

It was very pleasant after so many years of war to meet up again with our colleagues from the other reels and the Cup Final at the end of April between Derby County and Charlton at Wembley Stadium, with all the reels present, provided a great opportunity for a convivial get-together. The central position was high up under the eaves of one of the main stands. This position was on a specially constructed platform on steel girders, long enough to take the five newsreels. My position was usually on the touchline by the side of one of the goals, but I remember before the war being on that platform as an assistant. A number of long ladders, roped together, was the only means of getting up there. The equipment had to be hauled up on ropes over a pulley. We had to be in position before the gates were opened and stay marooned under the eaves until after the match as the ladders were removed before the people came into the stands and were not put up again until the ground was cleared. Film was lowered at half-time and immediately after the match for early despatch to the laboratories. So, cut off from the world below for several hours, it was important not to be too convivial before going up as calls of nature were not encouraged. There was not much room for buckets or tins and loose objects were kept to a minimum for fear of their dropping on the crowds below. I do not think the fans would have been too happy had they known what might have descended from above. However, at this convivial 1946 Cup Final I was on the touchline alongside one of the goals. I remember that match especially because one of the Charlton players had the same surname as me and shortly before the end of full-time with the score at 0–0 he achieved the remarkable feat of scoring at both ends. First he was responsible for an own goal for Derby and then scored a goal for Charlton at the other end, making the score 1-1 and causing the game to go into extra time. Derby scored three more goals in extra time, winning the match 4-1. Apart from my stint by the goal I had to film close-ups before the match when the players were presented to the King. I was also at the foot of the steps leading up to the royal box when Derby went up to receive the Cup from the King. It was a memorable occasion apart from my namesake's achievements. It was the first proper opportunity to meet up with the other reels, to experience again a major occasion with vast crowds – Wembley then held almost 100,000 fans before seating was introduced – and to get a feeling that this was a further step towards normality again.

The ninety-foot tower which we built to film the Derby at Epsom.

Another venue where a main camera position was reached by ladders was at Epsom for the Derby. Here Gaumont erected a ninety-foot rostrum on the downs near Tattenham Corner, from which most of the race could be filmed. To get to the top there were several platforms, each reached by ladders. It helped to be able to cope with heights on these high positions for it could be quite dicey sometimes; if it was windy the rostrum tended to sway and often the ladders seemed loosely roped. I was on that Derby tower pre-war, again as an assistant. While waiting for the racing we amused ourselves by looking through our long lenses to observe many interesting goings-on among the crowd below. In those early days too there were many bookies who welshed after the big race and we would watch them packing up and disappearing over the Downs, sometimes pursued unsuccessfully by punters with winning tickets. The Derby, pre-war and post-war, was always run on the first Wednesday in June and was unlike any other race meeting. The Downs provided a marvellous backdrop and playground for everyone, rich and poor, young and old, to have a good day out. There were all the furnishings of a racecourse – the bookies, the tic-tac men, the tipsters, the con-men, the jockeys and of course the horses. On the Downs were fairs, roundabouts, fortune-tellers, picnic parties, and lined up against the rails not far from the finishing post were the open-topped buses with their champagne parties. Just outside the paddock was my old friend from my publicity days at Ideal Films – Prince Monolulu. Shouting his catch-phrase 'I got a 'orse' he was giving out his tips at a shilling a time with plenty of customers – a great character. My job was to show all this atmosphere leading up to the excitement on the rails when the racing started. Roaming all over the place to get my pictures was hard work, but I enjoyed it for it was lovely to see so many people enjoying themselves, particularly so soon after the war.

It was not all fun, however. Over the years there have been a number of bad accidents at football grounds when fans have been crushed to death, such as the major one at Hillsborough when ninety people lost their lives. The first one I encountered happened in that first post-war year in March at a Bolton v. Stoke cup-tie at Bolton Wanderers' ground at Burden Park. Fans broke down fences to get into the ground, which was already full, steel barriers on the terraces gave way and thirty-three died with 500 injured, many badly. Only prompt action by officials in tearing down fences at the front avoided many more deaths.

The railways did not appear to be too safe either. There were a number of accidents in this period. At the beginning of the year the London, Midland and Scottish station at Lichfield in Staffordshire was the scene of a bad smash as a fish train ran into the back of a train standing at the LMS station as passengers were alighting on to the platform, piling the coaches on top of each other and killing fifteen passengers with many injured. Covering this story meant as fast a journey as possible in the evening up the old A5 road, itself quite a dangerous journey for there were no dual carriageways, lighting was poor and passing in the dark against oncoming headlights could be very hazardous. It was as well there were not too many cars on the roads just then.

Referring back to heights and ladders I had a very unpleasant experience at Portsmouth. I was on my own to film a ceremony on board the *Victory*. I decided I would be able to get a good general view of the proceedings from the crow's nest if I did it right at the start. I watched a sailor go up the ladder and into the nest and it did not look too difficult. I wanted to be up there before the ceremony started so that I could be down again quickly in order not to miss too much on the deck. So without thinking, forgetting it was a rope ladder, I started climbing, my camera slung over my shoulder which, with accessories and a strong leather case, weighed almost thirty pounds. Let me advise anyone who is contemplating climbing up a rope ladder not to carry any weight on their shoulder. As I climbed the weight of the camera kept pulling me backwards as the ladder moved away from me – an unnerving experience. By the time I got to the crow's nest I was exhausted and then discovered that the ladder was glued to the underside of the nest, giving very little room on which to put my feet. I did not have the strength to pull myself into the nest and if that sailor I had seen go up had not been there I do not know what I would have done. Without him I might have fallen off, or dropped the camera – or both. He leaned over and managed to take the camera and then pull me in. After I had taken my shot I got the sailor to lower my camera although this delayed my coverage below as he had to go down to get a rope. Feeling light as a feather I managed to get down without mishap. I do not think my subsequent filming of that story was all it should have been. Actually I was not a stranger to rope ladders. There had been occasions during the war when in order to get aboard a ship it had been necessary to jump from a boat on to one – but not with a camera over my shoulder. It was not always fun being a newsreel cameraman!

There were quite a few fires during the year but they were not a priority as so many had been filmed during the war in very dramatic circumstances. If we were present and an important building was on fire, but not burning strongly on the outside, it was sometimes necessary to slow the camera in order to get an exposure. It was difficult to judge how much to reduce the camera speed, for if one ran too slowly the result was to speed up the movements in the picture and there would be firemen dashing madly across the road lifting hose-pipes with the ease of weightlifters and running up ladders like fairies, rather like some of the old silent-film comedies. The speed of the camera is something a cameraman had to constantly watch, especially when using a battery-driven one. Also when the weather was very cold it caused the camera oil and grease to stiffen. Fluctuations in speed caused havoc with sound recordings when recorded direct on to the negative. Speed became easier to control later when all sound was recorded on to tape in machines linked to the camera.

Perhaps the most important government project soon after the war was the National Health Service which was founded in November 1946 and came into being two years later. There were sound interviews for that story. The cinemas were booming with long queues and full houses for most evening performances. We boosted this by filming some show people. Margaret Lockwood, who made her name in the film THE WICKED LADY, was one and I went to her home for some informal pictures. She was charming. In the following year she and James Mason were voted the two best actors of the year. I filmed another young lady, informally, in a bedroom in what was the Mount Royal Hotel over Marble Arch tube station – not far from my former digs with Mrs Potts. The girl was a friend of a big-band leader who came in while I was filming and who had somehow arranged for her to be filmed – I think with an eye to getting her recognised as an actress and probably to improve his friendship. It may have done that but I do not think it got into a newsreel. An interesting assignment. With so many houses damaged and unoccupied some were soon taken over by individuals who became known as squatters – people who were to become skilled in an art of occupation which has survived to this day. My first encounter with them was in Kensington in London. That 1,000 pound bomb which had fallen in St James's Park was finally exploded in April. Buckingham Palace had to open all its windows to avoid possible damage from the force of the explosion. And there was an experimental bus put into service – 'pay as you enter'. It hardly seems possible today, when we get on a bus to credit that such an idea was thought of so long ago. With few television sets in homes it was the job of the newsreels to show such innovations and changes and to reflect the mood of the country as it moved from old ways to new and struggled to return to a normal way of life.

8 June 1946 was V-Day, the day of the victory parade, which was the tribute to those who won the war, and it was a very busy day for all the newsreels. Two main columns, one mechanised, one marching, formed the basis of the parade, which passed a saluting base in The Mall where the King took the salute. He arrived there in a series of processions through the London streets accompanied by most of the royal family, Churchill and the Chiefs of Staff. The first column to pass the King was the mechanised one comprising every type of fighting vehicle, with tanks, mobile guns and boats, all manned by service personnel. The marching column followed – men and women from the navy, army and air force, workers from the factories, police, air-raid wardens, firemen and ambulancemen and women and those who had dug to rescue the bombed. No one who had had a part in winning the war had been forgotten. From overseas had come representatives of the Commonwealth and the allied countries who had served this island so well. And there were very large crowds along the processional routes and in The Mall – the people whose courage and spirit had contributed so much to make that day a victory parade. Only the weather misbehaved. It poured with rain during the day, only relaxing for a short

while to allow an impressive fly-past of some 300 aircraft until it finally relented in the evening. The day ended with extensive floodlighting and a big firework display along the Thames, after which everyone made for Buckingham Palace where the royal family appeared on the balcony three times to acknowledge the cheers of the vast crowd. We had cameras in all areas during the day and evening. I had a roving commission, showing crowds early in the day, picnics in spite of the weather, and later I was in the vicinity of the saluting base and outside Buckingham Palace in the evening. It was a very long, tiring, wet day for all of us but an occasion we are unlikely to see again.

Now that I was back in Britain getting used to filming domestic stories I had certainly not expected to be packing my bags again so soon, getting out my passport, having the necessary jabs in my arm and preparing to leave the country once more. Shortly after the victory parade in June I was on loan to the Anglo-Iranian Oil Company to make a documentary centred on the discovery of oil in Kuwait, with the climax to be the ceremonial opening of the country's first oil pipeline. Oil was discovered in 1938 but World War II meant development and production had to be postponed until after the war.

So I returned to the Middle East, to this tiny desert state with its almost Arabian nights background. There was no large airport in Kuwait so I flew to Basra and then onward in a small private plane of the Anglo-Iranian Oil Company. To build up the film to the grand opening ceremony meant days in the sandy, pebbly desert to show wells being constructed and all the accompanying activity. I was told that the climate was mild compared to other Arab countries, but I found it extremely hot, with temperatures of 90°F (32°C) during the day which posed problems for filming. It meant I had to restrict my operations in the mornings from 6.00 a.m. to 10.00 a.m. and from 4.00 p.m. to dusk in the afternoons. It was impractical to film between those times as the film emulsion became soft and it stuck to the camera gate. I was fortunate in being accommodated a few miles into the desert with an American engineer who had a hut fitted with air-conditioning run off a generator. This helped in keeping my unused film at a reasonable temperature. Knowing it would be hot the film stock had been pre-packed into special metal boxes, the tins of film encased in silicone crystals. But loading and unloading the film into and from the camera magazines in the desert during the day was difficult. There was no darkroom and it had to be done in a changing bag as it was too time-consuming to keep returning to the air-conditioned hut. The changing bag is a large black cloth bag of double thickness with a zip opening on one side. Into this is put a tin of unexposed film, an empty tin, the camera magazine containing the exposed film and black paper in which to wrap the exposed film before putting it into the empty tin. The whole lot is then zipped up. There are two sleeves, one for each arm, which fitted tight on the arms by elastic bands on the tops of the sleeves thus making the interior of the bag light-proof. After putting the exposed film into the empty tin, the unexposed film is taken from its tin and threaded into the now empty camera magazine. The bag is opened, the exposed film tin taped up and the camera magazine is ready for the camera. In normal temperatures this operation was comparatively simple but in the desert heat it was difficult, for the bag became very hot, hands became sticky and it was vital not to touch the film emulsion especially when threading it into the camera magazine. Of course I had several magazines ready for use which could be reloaded at night in the air-conditioned hut. However the exposed film had to be despatched as soon as possible. The air service was irregular and I had to take the opportunity of putting it on a plane whenever there was one going to Basra, where it was transferred to a London plane. This meant a frequent use of the changing bag. It was a miracle it all got back unharmed and without loss. It was a constant battle labelling and packing up the film and writing dope sheets, often against time.

The big day arrived – the day of the opening ceremony, timed to take place at 6.00 a.m. on 30 June 1946 at the Mina Al Ahmadi oil terminal, the official opening of the first pipeline to carry oil from a well direct to a tanker moored offshore in Kuwait's harbour. There was a large marquee for the VIP guests while they waited for the arrival of the Emir, one of the Sabah family who had ruled the country for many years. The sheik, Ahmad al Jabir, greeted his guests, then guided by the chief engineer, turned the ceremonial wheel to start the oil flowing and in doing so turned his country from a medieval kingdom into a very modern state. From that small beginning when that first oil flowed to the tanker, Kuwait has grown to be the third largest producer of oil, immensely rich, with over 900 wells, and at least enough oil below its desert to last for an estimated 150 years. After addressing the assembly the Emir was presented with a golden casket containing a scroll commemorating the occasion, a gift from the Anglo-Iranian Oil Company. (I was told the casket was valued at £5,000, a great deal of money then, and it had been entrusted into my care on my going from London to Kuwait.)

In the evening after the opening ceremony there was a great banquet in the old city, to which I was invited. In 1946 Kuwait town was still a walled city. The wall, made of mud, had been built about 1710 and was strong enough to withstand raids by the Bedouin. It was a true Middle-Eastern Arabic town, quite large, with a variety of buildings, some very primitive, some more sturdily built, such as the emir's palace. It made good pictures. I was glad I was able to see it in those early days, for that epitomised the Arabia of my imagination. The long 'table' for the feast was laid out on the ground with places allocated on each side. I am not very flexible so I was not too happy sitting cross-legged and upright without support and dreading getting cramp during the lengthy meal. Before us were large joints of lamb, whole chickens, spices, olives, dates, fruit and nuts and sheep's eyes gazing at us reproachfully. With no utensils I had been advised that it was etiquette to eat with only one hand – I forget which one it was. Tearing pieces of lamb from a joint or pulling a chicken apart with one hand was not easy and an Arab sitting next to me helped me overcome my initial difficulties in tugging at the lamb. Everything was well-cooked and very tasty if sometimes somewhat messy. Old Kuwait was the right setting for such a meal. Nothing was wasted. When we had finished the servants were allowed to feed and when they had their fill those more lowly came and so on down to the poorest. The Sabahs had instituted this custom many years ago and I thought it a wonderful idea for there was so much remaining when we left. I liked the Kuwait people. They were good-humoured and always helpful and friendly.

For the remainder of the year we continued to film 'getting back to normal' stories. There were the service personnel just demobilised, meeting their families again; air-raid shelters being removed; people coping with the prefabs. It was a slow process particularly as so many things were still rationed, in some cases there was less than in the war, and for the first time bread was rationed. Our coverage tried to look on the best side of such things and when there was a relaxation of anything we were there. I went down to Southampton in October to see the liner *Queen Elizabeth* leave on her first commercial sailing since being a troop-ship. That was a cheerful occasion with those on board lining the side of the ship as she left. Bands played. Large ships on the move always made good pictures. 11 November was Armistice Day – the second since the war. There were large crowds at all the services throughout the country in those days. In London workers streamed out of offices and filled Whitehall. Everywhere everybody observed the two minutes' silence. I was on the roof of Richmond Terrace, a building directly in line with the Cenotaph. Coming so shortly after the war the proceedings were very moving. One could guess that many of those below, in Whitehall and beyond, had lost someone. To add to the poignancy there was the devastation and havoc of the last five awful years.

Christmas passed and we were into 1947. The start of the year did nothing to make the difficult times easier. They began on 6 January with a transport strike and atrocious weather at the same time. Heavy snowfalls in freezing conditions caused electricity cuts, adding to the general chaos brought about by thousands of London lorry drivers stopping work in the dockland and market areas. The sole concession they made was to deliver essential supplies to hospitals. Otherwise nothing moved. The most seriously affected commodity was food. A temporary rise in temperature made the situation even worse with pavements becoming slushy and muddy everywhere. We were very busy covering all aspects of the strike and weather – lorries idle in large numbers in car parks, ships in the docks with cargoes only partly unloaded, pickets, meetings of union and government officials and unhappy people battling to work in the snow and messy pavements. Admirably there was a desperate effort to keep going. After a week of the strike the government was forced to put into operation emergency plans and brought in troops to drive the lorries. This move made the Smithfield and Billingsgate market workers join the strike and it spread into other areas in the country such as Liverpool, Leeds and Southampton. In London a large very deep wartime underground air-raid shelter was the army headquarters and the barracks for the troops. At nearby Clapham Common toilets and large marquees were erected in the mud, the latter equipped as kitchens and places for meals. The troops were soon moving over 600 lorries with food to the markets where they sorted and distributed it to the retailers. Fortunately the strike ended after a fortnight with agreement to the drivers' principal demands of a forty-four-hour week, an eight-hour day and two weeks' paid holiday. However the weather did not relent; it continued to get worse.

I was diverted from the strike to Stowting in Kent, about ten miles east of Ashford, where a BOAC Dakota had hit a hillside on a Saturday night. There were sixteen people on board and the dead and injured had to be extricated from the wreckage by the light of torches. The aftermath in the early morning mists was a sorry sight. We have to try to keep emotion out of such jobs but it is always difficult to remain completely detached. Personal belongings strewn haphazardly everywhere told the story in graphic detail and the awful weather made it that much worse. There were not many people involved in this crash, which made it almost more distressing for I imagined they would probably have become friendly with one another, unlikely in a larger disaster.

Following this, at Portsmouth, there was another sad story, at least sad for me. That gallant veteran of the war, the battleship HMS *Warspite*, arrived to be broken up. The last time I had seen her in action was at Salerno where she was badly damaged by a guided bomb from an aircraft.

And then it was back to be faced with the weather, which by the end of January became the main story for us for a long while ahead. The snow earlier in the month had melted but now severe snowstorms hit the whole of the country and were especially bad in the South and South East. Roads became impassable with snowdrifts more than ten feet deep in many places. Freezing temperatures compounded the misery falling as low as 17°F (–10°C) at night in London. It is difficult to appreciate today how things were, how we lived in those early post-war days. Trams and trolleybuses were the main form of public transport. Tram-lines ran down the centre of the streets, the extreme cold causing the trams and buses to stop frequently when the connecting rods to the live wires overhead snapped. Many miles of London's streets were lit by gaslight. The Gas, Light and Coke Company of the day was unable to meet the demand and turned off all the street lights, and hurricane lamps had to be placed at strategic points to aid the traffic. London obviously provided us with plenty of film but getting pictures in the country was extremely difficult. Even with chains on our tyres we could not reach most places by road. Although long-distance trains managed to get through, albeit with very long delays, for shorter journeys movements were practically at a standstill. We managed to get some general pictures from the air but getting off the ground in our small plane was sometimes a risky operation. Helicopters were in their infancy and not available to us and experiments with autogyros were still in the planning stages.

They would have been ideal for us. So we had to use freelance cameramen further afield for some country shots and film in those areas we could reach by either road or rail. The Thames froze at Windsor as did the sea at Folkestone, and at Eastbourne the snow fell for ten hours without ceasing. Electricity cuts were widespread. And two million sheep perished in that big freeze. It was a ghastly period lasting into March and for some of our technicians a really bad time. I have good circulation which enables me to cope with cold and heat without distress, but for some this was not the case. Peter Cannon, a small dark-haired man, an excellent sound cameraman, suffered terribly from the cold. He worked principally from the top of a truck and I do not know how he ever managed to film anything. However many clothes he wore he was always chilled to the bone in the icy conditions. Even in normal times, perhaps at Newmarket where it was usually windy and cold, he was perished. In the freezing temperatures of 1947 it was a miserable time for him and quite a number of bottles of whisky found their way into his truck.

The snow continued in the North but, inevitably, came the thaw. The whole country being covered in white, this meant floods everywhere and for us a new set of pictures and new problems getting around, often by boat. Rivers overflowed, houses were ruined. Collieries were unable to work; either the miners could not get to the pits or floods made them too dangerous. Coal was an essential fuel. The coalman with his sacks of coal was part of life. The Labour government had nationalised the coal industry at the start of the year, the first of its nationalisation programme of electricity, iron, steel, road haulage, ports and gas. They could not have been too pleased to have to face the coal problems so soon after taking charge.

At the beginning of 1947 India was becoming of great concern to the government. In 1946 there had been serious rioting between Hindus and Muslims in Calcutta with many killed. Clement Attlee was determined to bring about the independence of the country as quickly as possible and in February 1947 he appointed a reluctant Lord Mountbatten to replace Lord Wavell as viceroy with a mandate to achieve independence by June 1948. Lord Mountbatten had other ideas, as I shall tell in the next chapter.

Chapter Seven
India

Through the years, through the centuries, India's long history has been such that it has always been a country that has been 'news'. So many pictures come to mind – Clive of India, the East India Company, the Indian Mutiny, Gandhi, the Black Hole of Calcutta, the Himalayas, viceroys, Kipling, maharajas – and more and more. Ever since history lessons in my schooldays India had fascinated me. So when I was called into my managing director's office at the end of July 1947 and told that I had been unanimously chosen by all the newsreels to go to India on my own to cover the transfer of power for India to become independent, and that I would be accredited to the viceroy, Lord Mountbatten, I did not know what to think. It was such a tremendous assignment that I was quite bewildered. Naturally it was great to be the one selected for such a prestigious, interesting and exciting job in a country with such a colourful, volatile history. There had been a great deal in the press and on the radio of unrest in India and of the forthcoming moves to independence but there had been no hint of talk of India in newsreel circles, which made my appointment so much of a surprise. Perhaps, therefore, I should go back to the period that led to the establishment of the Raj and give some of the background to events which resulted in Independence Day and to the point when the newsreels became involved. I am not attempting to tell a political story, of the many feuds, intrigues and wars that made up Indian history although, of course, they do have a bearing on what followed independence during my stay in that incredible, almost unreal, country.

In the early 1600s the East India Company began to trade in India, gradually establishing itself until it had acquired great power and influence. By 1773 corruption by its merchants resulted in the British government having to help it financially. This, however, was conditional on the setting up of a Governor-General in Calcutta, paid for by the company but appointed by the British government. The first of these was Warren Hastings, who ended corruption, reorganised the tax system and laid the foundations for the way the country was to be governed. Throughout the next eighty years a great deal of territory was gained by Britain during which time there were many periods of fighting and unrest, ending with the Indian Mutiny in 1857, centred principally in Lucknow, Cawnpore and Delhi. When order was restored in mid-1858 the British government decided to end the influence and power of the East India Company. The India Act of 1858 established a Secretary of State for India and the appointment of the Governor-General Lord Canning as the first viceroy, to be the direct representative of Queen Victoria in India. The Queen later became Empress of India in 1877. By such moves events in India became of increasing interest to Britain. In the First World War India provided over a million soldiers to fight for the British and suffered very heavy casualties. Everywhere the war had made nations restless and the colonies began to strengthen their campaigns for freedom. In 1919 a British general – Henry Dyer – massacred many Indian men, women and children at a festival gathering in Amritsar in a mistaken attempt to quell riots in the city. Fuelled by the Amritsar massacres and war losses, the Indian struggle for independence mounted and continued to grow until World War II. The Congress party, the Hindus, were opposed to this war and because of an active and defiant attitude their leaders, Pandit Nehru and Mahatma Gandhi and many politicians were imprisoned by the British. With this situation, and beset with decades of religious feuds generally between Hindus and Muslims, it was decided soon after the war that India should receive independence as quickly as possible. Terrible riots in Calcutta in 1946, when thousands were killed, made it the more urgent.

Clement Attlee, the new Labour Prime Minister, had always been well-disposed towards India. His original thought was for a united independent country but he failed to get agreement on the basic issue on how to reconcile Muslim and Hindu. He then planned a Union of India consisting of all the British territory combined with the states of the princes and passed this idea to Lord Mountbatten in February 1947 when he appointed him to be the last viceroy, with the requirement that the transfer of power had to accomplished by June 1948. Lord Mountbatten arrived in Delhi at the end of March 1947 and in meetings with all the principals of the parties soon realised that Attlee's plans for a united India were not going to be possible. Jinnah, the leader of the Muslims, would not compromise and insisted on partition. Having been given complete authority to act without reference to London, Mountbatten decided he had no alternative but to accept that the country had to be divided into two states – India and Pakistan – and that the transfer of power had to be more immediate than June 1948. He announced in June 1947 that the date of independence would be 15 August 1947.

This set the scene for what was obviously going to be a major story and with such a history it seems incredible that the newsreels had shown little interest. Paramount and Movietone had two Indian stringers (freelance cameramen) in Delhi and that seemed to be the only coverage envisaged. Gaumont, Pathe and Universal had nothing arranged, nor had made any effort for a tie-up with Paramount and Movietone. Lord Mountbatten, aware that the newsreels were the primary source for Britain and the world to see this all-important event, was appalled at their indifference, seemingly content to leave the story to Indians, both working for American-financed companies. He instructed his press secretary, Allan Campbell

Johnson, who had to return to London on another matter, to try to sort out the newsreel situation and in earlier correspondence with my managing director, Castleton-Knight, he had suggested that a British cameraman should be sent to India on rota. As a result, at the end of July 1947, made aware of Mountbatten's wishes in talks with Allan Campbell Johnson, the Newsreel Association decided to send a man to India and that I should be that person and I should get there as soon as possible. So it came about that I was in Castleton-Knight's office being given this decision with barely three weeks to prepare for an indefinite stay in a foreign country, get out to India and make arrangements to film a world story. Camera equipment had to be checked, filters and film stock ordered, passport checked, inoculations where necessary, an air passage booked in a holiday period, personal affairs sorted out – all the many things that had to be done for such an assignment. I arrived in India on 10 August 1947, which gave me just four days to organise an event which normally would have been planned months ahead and covered with a full staff.

When I landed at Delhi airport little did I know what lay ahead of me. Any of my thoughts of pictures I might get were generally so different from those I did get. What I can say was that if my romantic notions of India were not always as glossy as books and stories made it sometimes seem, nonetheless I could not have had a more interesting year; it was the fabulous country I had imagined it might be. I arrived at an exceptional time. The India of the Raj was no more – a new India was emerging. So much happened during those incredible months I spent there. From the first moments when I was overwhelmed by the huge crowds that thronged the streets on Independence Day I was involved in a kaleidoscope of events and situations almost beyond belief. The unforgettable vision of wild-eyed Sikhs, hair flowing, with their deadly kirpans, waiting to race across fields to murder all the passengers in a waylaid train; the bodies lying in the wide streets of New Delhi; the long queues of refugees and their camps; the quiet Gandhi ending a fast by sipping orange juice and the forever silent Gandhi after his assassination. Were there ever such places as the splendid palaces of the princes, the magnificent temples, the Taj Mahal and the mighty Himalayas? There were the cows taking their holy walks along the roads and pavements of the towns; the smells; the beggars, evidence of the dreadful poverty and hunger of huge masses of the people; the contrast of the elegant women in their saris; the craftsmen; the burning ghats of Calcutta; the murky, dirty waters of the holy River Ganges; the energy and enthusiasm of Lord and Lady Mountbatten; and Bombay and Poona which conjured up imperial India – the dying Raj. That was the India that I faced as I stepped off that plane at Delhi airport in August 1947.

I remember feeling rather lonely as I travelled into Delhi. I was in an unknown country with a population three times that of the United States of America but crowded into an area only one third the size of the States; a country which had numerous languages with two hundred dialects; a country with tigers, lions, monkeys, elephants, cheetahs and hyenas. It was not surprising I felt rather a small being entering such a nation. But there I was with the responsibility of sending back film of this first and most important of the forthcoming declarations of independence to all the UK newsreels and their associates worldwide. It was quite frightening when I realised I had actually arrived and what I had to do.

The first thing was to show my face at the Viceroy's House and establish good relations with Mounbatten's press secretary, Allen Campbell Johnson, and to obtain an official programme of events planned for Independence Day and the days to follow. Then I had to find somewhere to live. I had been booked into the Imperial Hotel in New Delhi for I needed to be central for the initial celebrations, so that took care of that immediate problem, but as Delhi was going to be my base for a long while I wanted somewhere less expensive and less formal. I subsequently found a delightful friendly hotel in Old Delhi, the Cecil, which had all the facilities I needed and being in Old Delhi I felt I was in India and not a tourist in a five-star hotel of the guide books. After meeting the press secretary and a brief 'hello' from Mountbatten the next most important thing was to make contact with the Paramount and Movietone cameramen. I had never met either but Campbell Johnson had the phone number of Paramount's man, Ved Parkash, and we met at my hotel early on that first evening. He had not worked for Gaumont but turned out to be a tower of strength, very likeable, and he was very friendly to that intruder on his territory just when a very big story had come his way. His knowledge of the city was invaluable in the short time I had to make arrangements for coverage. The task ahead seemed formidable. I had to go over the processional routes to the various ceremonies, establish vantage points and where possible arrange for stands to be built or elevated positions to be acquired. With the aid of Parkash I spent that first evening getting to know key places, watched flags and bunting going up, and felt fortunate to have found an agreeable and helpful associate. We arranged for another session the following morning. After that I sat down with Parkash and his brother Mohan, the Movietone man, to decide the positions for each of us to cover, with three men, a story with the importance of a coronation. Unlike England where such events were worked out to the nth degree, overseas there was a certain amount of unpredictability. Crowds were more excitable, routes could be changed, flagpoles could grow up overnight, possibly in front of positions I had chosen. I knew I would have to go over the routes very early on Independence Day to check our positions, to see that stands had not been moved and somewhat hopefully to advise people who occupied them that they would have to move later. Then there was the problem of transport. With roads closed, barriers erected, massive crowds and the three of us needing to get to more than one position the only answer was a good pair of shoes. And as important as anything we had to arrange a rendezvous at the end of the day to collect the negatives, and fix with the customs and airline for the dispatch of everything to London without delay.

With the basic arrangements under way I had to think about clothes. Although I was used to upheavals and finding myself in new situations overnight there had been no time to think about clothes before I left England. It was very hot in Delhi and the transition from the cool British summer to the British twilight in India meant I had to acquire a 'thin' wardrobe very quickly. I had to be prepared to go anywhere. Apart from working situations I knew there would be invitations to parties and social occasions. There always were on foreign assignments and there was still much of the pukka sahib around. Even during the war I found this to be so. With the camera there would be formal pictures of Viceroy's House, and formal pictures at the Congress Assembly parliament, and I would be hurrying from one place to another in Delhi's heat. Although I do not perspire very easily, I knew I would be wet through and then probably have to appear before a group of VIPs who had managed to change. I could arrive in a scruffy state and no doubt everyone would understand why, but a sweaty cameraman is not the best way of getting the best pictures, whatever the justification. I knew there would be occasions when I would have no choice, but I had been entrusted with a special privilege and I felt it was up to me to present as reasonable an appearance as possible. I have always made an effort, sometimes a super-effort, in that respect, the top layer often hiding a very different underneath. This may seem rather prissy but on every story I have ever covered I have always tried not to look scruffy. The Imperial Hotel in the centre of Delhi helped a lot on Independence Day. With all these thoughts I decided I needed a white dinner jacket, a light suit and casual wear. The Indians mostly wore very casual clothes but on official or formal occasions were very correctly attired. Fortunately in Eastern countries it was possible to get clothes made overnight. This I was able to do.

There was one other thing I had to do at once. A journalist friend of mine in London, well used to overseas assignments, had advised me to establish a tie-up with a news agency if possible. They would help to keep me informed of anything that might happen unexpectedly and generally keep me in the picture. It was good advice. I learned from Parkash that Associated Press of America had an office in Delhi. I was able to arrange good relations with them, my accreditation with Mountbatten no doubt helping initially. They had an American press photographer in their set-up, Max Desfor, and we became great friends and covered several stories together.

With the preliminaries taken care of I was ready to start work and did not have long to wait. I was told by Campbell Johnson to be ready to fly to Karachi with Lord and Lady Mountbatten during the day of 13 August. On the following morning Muhammad Ali Jinnah, the Muslim leader, was to be installed as the first Governor-General of Pakistan. On arrival the Mountbattens went to Government

House and I went to a hotel which had been booked for me. The rest of the day I spent finding out where the ceremonies were to take place and sorting out possible positions. I arranged for an assistant to carry a pair of high steps which seemed the most practical way of getting film with no time to build any set positions. The next morning I filmed Jinnah's arrival at the Parliament building, the viceroy's arrival, and shots as Jinnah was installed as Governor-General by Mountbatten, followed by the beginning of the state drive back to Government House. There had been threats that Sikhs would throw bombs on the return journey but it passed without incident. A rather worrying hour for me as I was only able to cover the early part of the drive. Then it was a dash back to the airport to return to Delhi for the Independence Day programme which began at midnight the same day – 14 August. There was to be no sleep that night. I began with shots at the Congress Assembly where the transfer of power took place as midnight struck, followed by Pandit Nehru departing for the Viceroy's House to ask Mountbatten to be the first Governor-General.

After a short rest I was out to check our positions among the crowds, which were already quite dense. As I had anticipated, our rostrums made good vantage points for some watchers but they got off without any trouble when we came to take up our positions. It was very different later on. As soon as it was daylight there were build-up shots to be filmed – general views, names of roads, sellers of souvenirs, faces in the crowd, decorations, anything to set the scene. Parkash and his brother were in their places early on and they had managed to find assistants to support them. I took up my position on a stand outside the Assembly where Lord and Lady Mountbatten were due to arrive, with Lord Louis to address the Congress after he had been sworn in as Governor-General. First came Nehru and other leaders in their cars, with the crowds trying to grab them by the hand. Then came the state drive, similar in style to one in England with outriders, guards, etc. The Mountbattens, in an open carriage, were surrounded by crowds who had broken through the police cordons and were insisting on shaking hands with the new Governor-General and his wife. They and the rest of the procession had the greatest difficulty in reaching the Assembly hall. After the arrivals I had problems in trying to prevent some Indians from climbing on my rostrum. It had been constructed in a hurry, just wooden planks nailed together without any strengthening supports and I feared it would collapse. When the return journey was about to start the mass of people went wild with excitement and swarms of them clambered on to my stand, which started to shake alarmingly. I was completely overwhelmed, neither able to move nor see anything and was unable to film the departure from the Assembly – so much for plans! Fortunately the other two fared better and between us we managed a reasonable coverage of the morning's events. It was impossible to get upset by the crowds. They were so good-natured and pleasant when I told them to get off the stand but such were the masses of people below that they were unable to get down. Having got good pictures of the arrivals I was not too concerned about missing the departure. I could not help but be infected by everyone's cheerful spirits on this, their Independence Day. It was good to see Indians of all religions getting together without animosity. This was the day, too, when the leaders of the Indian government and their Prime Minister, Harrow-educated Pandit Nehru, saw come to fruition their ambitions for their people and their country after enduring many hardships over many years. The first difficult goal had been reached. Friday, 15 August 1947, was a memorable day in Indian history as Indians prepared to assume control of their own destiny. Independence had been achieved even though it had meant partition. Only Gandhi had not taken part in the celebrations. He had spent the day fasting in Calcutta, where there were jubilant scenes as Hindu and Muslim fraternised in unprecedented accord. Alas, the euphoria of the day was short-lived for in a few days a very different story emerged with the beginning of a mass exodus of Hindus and Muslims fleeing from India to Pakistan and from Pakistan to India. However 15 August was Independence Day and everyone was determined to enjoy it.

In the afternoon the Mountbattens and their daughter Pamela, who had also been at the morning ceremonies, went informally to a children's playground where thousands of children were being entertained with roundabouts, dancing bears and snake-charmers, with the climax to be a distribution of sweets. When the Mountbattens arrived there was chaos with screaming, pushing youngsters anxious to see them and get their share of the goodies. This mean good pictures but hot work for me. The day finished at Prince's Park, near to the Victory Arch in Delhi. There was to have been a march past, an inspection of the various Indian forces by the Governor-General and a ceremonial hoisting of the new national flag. Again the vast crowds, said to have been anything up to 20,000, broke loose and invaded the parade ground. Mountbatten had difficulty in getting out of his carriage and most of the programme was impossible to fulfil, but they did manage to unfurl the flag. I covered the afternoon session on my own but arranged for the three of us to film the evening events and allocated positions for each of us. As the morning had illustrated, the best of plans do not always work out. We were pushed everywhere by the excited crowd, our vantage points overrun, but somehow between us we managed to get a good coverage. Thank goodness it was still daylight although generally the lighting was none too good for film. We rendezvoused at my hotel to pack up our day's efforts for dispatch to London, write what dope sheets we could, enclose programmes and then go to the airport with everything – to make sure there were no delays or planes missed. Rupees were very useful. So ended an exhausting but unforgettable day. All the material got back safely and the story appeared in the newsreels in their issues of 21 August. As a footnote to that day I quote from a letter from Lord Mountbatten to Castleton-Knight which showed that my efforts with those of my assistants had been worthwhile and had made a successful start to my stay in India:

I have just seen the copy of the Gaumont-British newsreel which you were kind enough to send out. It seems to be excellent and the general coverage which you mentioned in your cable to Campbell Johnson has certainly justified the Rota arrangements. Turner has undoubtedly got off to a good start and his presence here should lead to a great improvement in the hitherto meagre film material on India ... the newsreel of the transfer ceremonies in Delhi arrived very expeditiously in time to be shown at the Sunday evening show on the 24th August. This was seen by a large audience who were much impressed by the excellence of the photography and the competence of the commentary.

It is over fifty years since that letter was written and only now have I seen it!

The next day, 16 August, I was told that I was to fly in the plane again with the Governor-General to Bombay when he would be reviewing British troops the following day before they left for England. That was a historic occasion, for their departure marked the end of British rule in India. Whenever possible Lord Louis did all he could to help me to get good coverage and an incident happened on this event which was a case in point. There was a big parade and a very impressive guard of honour which he inspected. I was confined with some local still photographers some distance from the end of the ranks, not a good position to get close-ups, so I moved forward and a horrified officer stopped me. Lord Louis saw this and indicated that it was in order for me to move, and I was actually able to get in between the ranks, something I had never been able to do in England! The astonished officer in charge of the press was only partially able to stop the other photographers from following me. After this the occasion became more informal. Mountbatten addressed the troops on the quayside, bands played and the first ship to repatriate troops since independence, decked out with flags and bunting, sailed away into the sunset. On the morrow we returned to Delhi. On the way Lord Louis showed an interest in my equipment. He knew all about film-making, for he had undergone a course in America run by top Hollywood technicians. Knowing this I made no attempt to blind him with science but it was pleasant to show him what could be done with a quite unsophisticated hand-camera.

After those first busy days I thought maybe I could relax for a while. Mountbatten was going to be tied up in numerous meetings or making short journeys not suitable for filming. However, a different situation was developing. There had been trouble in the Punjab prior to independence but now, with partition, just a few days later it had become the centre for the most horrific acts of violence and killing. The mass exodus of Muslims from India to Pakistan and Hindus the other way had begun. My friends in Associated Press told me of massacres in and around Lahore and Amritsar and it was obvious there would be no relaxation, for I had to show what was happening. Lady Mountbatten was already in the Punjab near Amritsar so I started in that area filming her visiting refugee camps. Events were moving at a frightening pace. I filmed refugees trudging along the roads, pitiful men and women and their families with their pathetic bundles of belongings, sometimes on carts with bullocks, and terrified of attacks by marauding Muslim, Hindu or Sikh bands, depending on which way they were going. It was made worse by the approach of the monsoon, which made it very wet with many roads flooded. Some scenes were unbelievable. There was looting, arson, whole villages destroyed and the most horrible mutilation of victims on both sides. Some pictures had no chance of being screened. There were groups of Sikhs with their evil kirpans stopping trains and butchering the passengers. Although I did not see any of these attacks I did witness wild-eyed bands gathered together waiting to rush across the fields with murderous intent. History repeats itself. Almost a hundred years before when the Raj was facing killings during the Indian Mutiny, the Sikhs took advantage of the situation and indulged in massacres and horrors similar to the present ones. In that sorry exodus of populations from each side there were no firm figures of the numbers killed but it could have been as many as a million. They made the journeys by rail, motor transport, some by air, but mostly on foot, risking the attacks and massacres that occurred every day. It was many months before the transfer of the populations was complete. I returned to Delhi to despatch my film at the end of August just as Lord Mountbatten had decided he needed a rest and chose to go to Simla for a ten-day break.

Although there were to be no official pictures in Simla I decided to go up there too. With the country in the state it was and the killings as bad as ever I thought it wise to be reasonably close to Mountbatten. Also I was looking for a different kind of picture from the awful scenes l had just witnessed. It was very hot and humid in Delhi with the rains beginning so it was good to get up 5,000 feet into the Himalayas in the cool for a while. There was a fine hotel and restaurants and although it was pleasantly picturesque with red-roofed houses, many similar to English styles, it had too many signs of the Raj, which was not the story – we were post-Raj. However, it was a short stay. Mountbatten got an urgent call to return to Delhi. Some thousands of displaced Hindus and Sikhs were pouring in from the Punjab and it was feared that the many Muslims in Delhi would try to take over the city. So it was back to be greeted with an alarming situation.

This was not the first time there had been trouble in Delhi. It had a history of wars, violence and brutality from Mogul times to the terrible atrocities during the Indian Mutiny in 1857. Much of this had been centred round the great mosque, Jama Masjid, the Red Fort and the renowned Chandni Chowk, a wide street of shops, silversmiths, clothes stores, fruit and vegetable markets, bangle shops, sweet shops, fortune tellers, shoemakers and beggars, always crowded with people of all religions and castes and with the all-pervading smells of India – spices, herbs, incense sticks and flowers – and dust and flies and betel juice everywhere. This was once again the scene for violence and terror in 1947 where more of the shopkeepers

GAUMONT DOPE-SHEET

NEW DELHI. INDIA.

Curfew imposed. Shots showing empty Streets.
Close up of Bolted Doors.
Shot of a closed door of shop.
Looting in the heart of New Delhi.
Shot showing looted shop in Connaught Place.
Close up of Street name of Connaught Place.
Shot showing a section of Connaught Place, chief shopping
    centre of New Delhi.
Shot of Indian troops in the streets ready to fire at the
    first sign of rioters, looters or curfew breakers, semi-
    close-up.
Close-up of same.
Car is stopped for examination of curfew pass.
Sacred Cow walks by.
Soldier walks through the Street at the Ready.
Shots of looters at work showing 5 in the street and looters
    bringing things from the shops to throw on the fires.
General Shot and Semi-close-up of looters and rioters attacking
    Moslem shops in a side road.
Stream of refugees leaving an attacked area.
Shot of three knifed bodies lying on the pavement.
Shot looking down of a group of dead bodies which had been
    very brutally treated. One person's head being half
    missing.
Shot of refugee old man struggling through the litter and
    debris and dead, with an old lady on his back.
Shot of refugee with wounded colleague passing the bodies.
Smoke in the distance over the town.
Shots of a fire started by rioters in Connaught Circus being
    got under control by Fire Brigade.
Close shots of smoke pouring from burning cemetery.
Shots inside of JAMA MASJID MOSQUE, showing Moslems at prayers
    the day before the riots. (This Mosque is third largest
    in the world).

REFUGEES MOVED OUT OF THE CITY

General Shot of PURANA QILA. Shots of encamped individuals
    families.
The Water Queue. Lines of girls, women, boys and men. Close-
    up of individuals at the Water Queue.
Close-up of various types of containers being used to collect
    water. There is only one water point in the camp at present.
Cave-dweller refugee washing hair.
General Shot of the camp. Shots of refugees on their way through
    Old Delhi to PURANA QILA. Shots of refugees in the same
    Mosque. (These shots may contrast with those showing the
    Prayer meeting there just before the trouble started. All
    refugees in these pictures are Moslem.
NOTES: Delhi authorities are doing their best to cope with the
    situation, there are at least 10,000 refugees within the
    PURANA QILA Camp - known in New Delhi as the Old Fort,
    which was built in 1541, and is one of the best preserved
    ruins in New Delhi. The Camp lies two miles South of the
    City.

The dope sheet for my film of the riots in Delhi.

were Muslims. This would have been familiar to Old Delhi. For New Delhi it was something new.

In 1911 Calcutta had been the seat of government but it was decided in that year that Delhi should be the capital city as it had been many years before. Sir Edwin Lutyens was commissioned to design a new city. The work began immediately and splendid government buildings grew up around wide avenues and Connaught Place became the main shopping and administrative area, although the magnificent Viceroy's House was not completed until 1929. Now, unlike the old town, New Delhi was to experience for the first time communal hatred and strife. It seemed a lifetime since 15 August and the rejoicing on that day.

With the Muslims outnumbered by the resident Hindus, reinforced by the incoming Sikh and Hindu refugees, events deteriorated rapidly. Rioting broke out all over the city. Fires lit the streets at night. Looters fed the flames with goods brought from the shops and shopkeepers were decapitated mercilessly by Sikhs. Much of this took place around Chandni Chowk, not far from my hotel. A curfew was imposed from 10.00 p.m. to 5.00 a.m. To contrast with what had been happening earlier I filmed empty streets with soldiers everywhere at the ready to deal with anyone breaking the ban. I was not too happy in those unstable circumstances and took the precaution of attaching myself to a soldier. In the daytime the looters were busy again carrying out their insane acts, stripping Muslim shops, slaying every Muslim they encountered and lighting fires in the main streets, with the fire brigade having difficulty coping with all the outbreaks. In New Delhi in the early mornings there were bodies lying in the streets in Connaught Place and Connaught Circus near the Imperial Hotel, some brutally butchered and mutilated. Grenades exploded, shots were fired by the police, but the riots continued unabated. There were lines of refugees in New Delhi waiting to register for official evacuation and every so often there would be a dash across the road and one of the queue would be fatally stabbed. The Hindu police, there to guard the refugees, turned a blind eye to this. There were poignant pictures such as the old man who made his way through the litter and the dead with an old woman on his back. I was very wary filming much of this, for although there had not been any attacks on the British such was the frenzy and determination of the Hindus to exact revenge for the treatment of their people in Pakistan that they were half-crazed and could well have taken exception to being filmed. However, they did not seem to notice the camera. And through the smoke and chaos the sacred cows wandered unharmed and unperturbed oblivious to the mayhem around them.

Refugee camps were set up. Many Muslims took refuge in the huge Jama Masjid mosque for safety until moving to one of the larger camps. At Purana Qila (Old Fort), two miles south of Delhi, over 10,000 Muslims were incarcerated in the most appalling conditions of mud and filth. There was only one water point and men, women and children lined up to collect water in any container they could find. Then there was the problem of feeding everyone. Cereals were loaded into sacks from the godowns (warehouses) or unloaded from trains and transported to Old Delhi to be sorted in ration shops, the fronts of which were piled high with filth. Some cereals were taken to flour mills, tipped into machines and refilled into the sacks as flour. These too went to the ration shops. After sorting into batches the food was carried to the various camps. At the Old Fort very meagre rations were distributed to the refugees next to open latrines, filth and mud. I filmed at this camp and a sickening sight it was. Little wonder there were many cases of cholera.

Back from Simla, Mountbatten set up an emergency committee and was fully occupied dealing with the situations in Delhi and the Punjab. Having concentrated on events in India I decided this was an opportunity to show the other side in Pakistan. In the Amritsar area and in Delhi I had only been able to film small attacks and killings and I thought the other side of the border might offer the chance of a more major attack. I had been told there was much unrest in villages north of Lahore where there had been terrible violence and slaughter just after Independence Day. Now most of the Hindus had gone and the rioters had moved on to other places. So I gathered together some camping equipment and with my camera gear flew from Delhi to Lahore which then seemed the likely place to establish a base. All was quiet when I arrived, the town almost dead. The Hindus had been the clerks in the banks, the postal services and the railways and many of the shops had been owned by them. Most of the banks were closed and the other services only just managed to keep going. I made my headquarters in a hotel in the centre of the town and tried to find out exactly where trouble was likely to occur. It was sometimes possible to get an indication of imminent trouble from army intelligence but it was extremely difficult to be on the spot when anything happened. Army sources suggested a village some 100 miles northwest of Lahore might be worth a visit. Everything was chance. One could do the journey for nothing. And they warned that filming a mass attack could be hazardous as most massacres of that type were spontaneous and one had to be sure not to get caught up directly in them. Having arrived by air my immediate problem was to find transport. There was no official car to spare and no army unit was going to the suggested area. Frustration indeed. I needed to act quickly and as I sipped a John Collins in the hotel bar, I wondered what the chances were of hiring a car. I did not feel very hopeful. The answer came unexpectedly.

Two Hindus were sitting at a nearby table and were talking in English and rather louder than was wise. I listened with interest. They had a car – a Plymouth, I believe it was an American make – and were desperate to leave Pakistan and get to India before someone attacked and killed them. It was extremely hazardous living on the wrong side of the border. Their problem was that to attempt to drive the 300 miles from Lahore to Delhi was almost certain suicide. They would never make it past the bands of marauders waiting for such travellers. If they went by air they would lose their car; this seemed a better bet to me than losing your life. They were in a no-win situation for if they stayed as Hindus in Muslim country they were in constant danger. I had just seen the other side of the picture in Delhi – Muslims cut down in the streets in broad daylight. I moved over to their table and told them I had overheard their dilemma and had a possible solution. I was in need of transport. If they would lend me their car I would drive it to Delhi after I had completed my mission. I must confess I did not enlighten them as to exactly why I wanted the car. We struck a deal. I arranged to pick up the car the next morning and they set off happily to fix a flight to Delhi. Next day when I saw the car I wondered whether I had been so clever. Like so many vehicles in that country then, this was in the banger class. However it had four wheels and moved. It was a large car, thirsty on petrol – my next problem, as this was rationed due to the unrest. I managed to persuade the army to let me have enough to get to the troubled area and back to Delhi. So, loaded up with all my equipment and cans of petrol I set off from what now seemed a city haven into the unknown countryside of Pakistan. The clutch slipped, there was rain and the narrow roads were very lonely. I knew there were men wandering the country looking for victims and although they rarely attacked foreigners, I proceeded with not a little unease.

I came to a stretch of road with a high banking on one side and stopped to relieve myself. As I returned to the car I saw a movement on top of the banking and a man appeared, waving me to get away, to move on. He was armed and I left. It was not the time to question why or what. Some miles further on I came upon a ragged column of Hindu refugees heading towards that high banking down the road I had just come up. I realised they were probably walking into an ambush and that was why the man on the banking was so anxious to get rid of me. It was a guess on my part, of course, but I thought I ought to try to warn them. I tried but they smiled at me and did not understand. I wondered whether I should follow them and, if I was right, perhaps obtain a film of what I feared would transpire. Then I reasoned that if I had guessed wrongly I would have used valuable petrol for nothing. I took some pictures of the column and decided to press on as I wanted to get to my destination before dark. I did not fancy a night in that hostile area. Then came a frightening mishap. The road surface was poor, just a track. The rain had made it very muddy. The car was difficult to drive with its slipping clutch. Suddenly I went down to the hubs in a muddy hole. I stopped. I sat in the car for a while wondering what to do. I had no hope of moving the car out of the hole myself. The chances of anyone else coming along that road were minimal.

It was well on in the afternoon and the thought of being stuck there in the dark was not attractive. I had no means of communication nor any idea how far I was from a village or town. I had covered about eighty miles and was in open country. My imagination became very active. Although I did not think I would be personally assaulted, who knew what could happen to a solitary traveller in those volatile times? There was a case for robbery – my camera, my camping equipment and petrol. No one would know what had happened if I was found with throat cut, or stabbed or bludgeoned to death. I went through the full range of possibilities as I tried to rationalise what to do. It was impossible to walk and, indeed, that was just plain foolish – like setting out into the Sahara without water. And what about all that camera equipment? I surveyed the car and the surrounding countryside to see if there was any way I could move the wretched vehicle. But there was none. It was too far down in the mud. Well, miracles do happen, and I was about to witness one. Suddenly I was aware of faces, dozens of faces, smiling and making their way towards me. This is it, I thought. Put on a good show. Do not try to run. Then with amazement, I realised the faces were friendly. They advanced to the car, surrounded it and lifted it out of the hole and on to the road. I could not believe what was happening. I waved money at them but they were not interested. They spoke no English and once the job was done, placed their hands together in the Indian fashion of greeting and vanished into the fields as silently as they had come. I wondered if they had been watching me for some time to see if I was an enemy. I got into the car. Would it start? It did. I was away on my journey again.

The rest of this story is mostly anticlimax. I could not find the troubled area. Maybe the anticipated fighting did not materialise. On my return journey as I passed the high banking on the road where I had feared an ambush it seemed the worst had happened. The road was strewn with the sad relics of the refugees' belongings and there were other signs that the Hindus had got no further. Although I would have had some film to show for my journey I was glad I had not turned round and followed the ragged column. It sounds hard but that was not good thinking for a newsman. I drove without mishap to Delhi and made for the address where I had agreed to return the car to its owners. They would be pleased, I thought. There was no one there and I was unable to find the two Hindus. What had happened to them? I never found out. Their old banger was no use to me now. I left it near the address without regret but I gave it a pat as I said goodbye to it.

After that abortive journey to Pakistan I thought, in addition to the official ones, I should look for stories other than riots. The killings were continuing and although there were outbreaks in other parts of the country the Punjab remained the main centre of conflict. The Sikhs were very unhappy with the division of their area by the boundary commission which had left many of their sacred temples on the wrong side of the border. The murders and rapes had become less frenetic as so many villages had been destroyed leaving fewer targets for the marauders. But there were still the lone vulnerable columns of refugees – some estimates being as many as five million in each direction. The emergency committee managed to defend them to some degree but there were too many to provide complete protection. However with Delhi having quietened down and Mountbatten still very much occupied with the emergency committee I decided to make a quick journey to Agra, some 130 miles from Delhi. With no troubles there at that time it seemed a good opportunity to get some library pictures of the marvellous Taj Mahal. I had managed to get agreement from the Newsreel Association for me to buy a car to enable me to move about more easily in Delhi without having to rely on costly taxis. It enabled me to get further afield than the immediate environs of the city for stories other than the official ones with Mountbatten. As I travelled the road to Agra in my new car my mind went back to many years before, when I was six. Our family was living in the Isle of Wight, in Ventnor. I remembered a telegram arriving, my mother opening it and bursting into tears. Her sister had been on holiday in India, was in an open car on this same road on her way to see the Taj Mahal and was killed in an accident. How vivid was that memory even though the event had occurred so many years before. I will not attempt to describe the beauty of that marble tomb. Suffice to say it was every bit as perfect as so many others have said in books and poems.

Returning to Delhi it was off to Jaipur for the festival of Dasshera, which, like so many such occasions, was extremely colourful. There was a durbar and in this instance the added spectacle of a military show. I was accommodated in a splendid guest house with every possible convenience. There were servants for everything. It was like staying in a ten-star hotel with all the fittings of the very best quality, some even gold. Lady Pamela Mountbatten and General Auchinleck had been invited by the maharaja and were his honoured guests at his luxurious Amber Palace, the scene for the first of the military ceremonies. The proceedings began with the blessing of the colours; the state, the regimental and the maharaja's standard. The colours were marched up to the parade ground at the Amber Palace, which was at the top of a hill, handed over to a priest and taken into the private temple. There followed a gruesome sacrifice of a goat for each colour, which I filmed from the top of a building. Each goat was beheaded with a sword on the parade ground and the three heads taken into the temple. After the blessing the colours were ceremoniously returned to the army. Then followed the durbar with horses, elephants, camels and bullocks, all in their finery, parading through the streets. At the durbar hall the maharaja sat on a golden throne to receive the homage of rich nobles. l flew over Jaipur – a city of pink sandstone – and showed its wide streets, its walled surround and the Amber Palace, which made a spectacular picture from the air. The next day there was trooping the colour, which followed almost exactly the London one in Horse Guards Parade. Here the salute was taken by the maharani of Jaipur, the first time she had appeared so conspicuously in public as she was still in semi-purdah. The whole visit was a very grand event unlike what was happening not so many miles away in the north. Later in the year it was the maharaja's silver jubilee and the Mountbattens visited both Bikaner and Jaipur for the celebrations. There were duck shooting, fabulous parades and similar opulent surroundings, meals and accommodation.

In spite of the lavish entertaining those must have been worrying days for the rulers of the 562 princely states. They had been forced to accede to either India or Pakistan, and although at first they were able to keep their riches, they had lost their independence with the transfer of power from the Raj. Despite promises made, they were very vulnerable to change as indeed they discovered a few years later. The two largest states, Hyderabad and Kashmir, in fact did not accede before independence. Hyderabad held out for a year but then there was still no agreement. A short military action forced the miserly Nizam to join India. Kashmir, with a Hindu maharaja but a mostly Muslim population, eventually acceded to India, but the disputes between India and Pakistan over that decision are a major cause of trouble between the two dominions even today.

In November Princess Elizabeth and the Duke of Edinburgh were married and the Mountbattens flew to London for the wedding, with Pamela Mountbatten a bridesmaid. Because my assignment in India was chiefly a specific one to cover the move to independence and the follow-up during the period Lord Louis was Governor-General I kept close to Government House, but I did have a free hand to find other stories when there was a quiet period. I had been to Agra for library material – now I looked for something that showed a way of life of the local people but which would be of general interest elsewhere. Such stories were always useful as fillers in the newsreel when news was short. One did not normally provide items of this kind when on a rota appointment but I thought some extra coverage was legitimate in the exceptional circumstances and length of stay of that job. The skills of the craftsmen such as the silversmiths and tailors made attractive pictures. And building made a story. Here was a country which had constructed magnificient temples and places like the Taj Mahal and the palaces of the princes but could also, at that time, build by the most primitive methods and the contrast suggested a fascinating story.

The Mountbattens returned and became busy with official duties and gave garden parties as a way of saying farewell to many people. I filmed some of these. The Governor-General still had to cope with unrest and massacres and while he was thus occupied I took advantage of this to go to Calcutta. This was the city in which Gandhi had made his headquarters during the independence celebrations and I went there with the idea of trying to get some pictures of him. There had been some terrible riots and killings after Independence Day and he began a fast which he threatened to continue until the fighting stopped even if he died by doing so. It worked and the city became calm again. I went to Calcutta by train and that was an experience. Everywhere in the East the trains carried people on top and on the sides of the carriages in large numbers. All the long train journeys followed the same pattern, as I found out later when I went to Bombay by train. Periodically we stopped for meals at stations when there was time, and there usually was. Otherwise, when there was a short stop, the char-wallahs would board the train and for a few annas would produce an egg roll and tea – chancey but welcome. Hawkers would appear with phoney gold watches and rings and souvenirs of all kinds and sometimes they would offer exotic fruits. In the overcrowded conditions and among the general shambles and chaos they did their best to cater for our wants.

Calcutta was a mixture of wealth and extreme poverty like most of the large Indian cities. It was a city of diverse history from the days when it was the headquarters of the East India Company, from grim times like the legendary Black Hole in 1756 when a number of British were shut up in an underground shelter and suffocated, to 1858 when Government House, a splendid building, became the Viceroy's House on Lord Canning's appointment as the first viceroy. The seat of government remained in Calcutta until New Delhi became the capital in 1911. In the busy streets with their open-fronted shops traders carried goods on their heads and others had yokes across their shoulders with buckets at either end. Rickshaws weaved among the crowds, pulled by weary, thin men, or the grander bicycle rickshaws pedalled recklessly along the streets with bells ringing loudly. Chowringhee with its hotels was a fashionable residential area and a centre of entertainment, cinemas, restaurants, bars and clubs. Everywhere one heard the wail of 'backsheesh' from the hundreds of pitiful beggars, many devoid of arms or legs or both, or from young children who ran by with outstretched palms. Government House stood near to the Maiden, a huge park, peaceful and very pleasant by the Hooghly river which ran alongside the city. Here, in sight of the long bridge which crossed the river, the dhobi-wallahs washed their clothes in the dirty waters; coolies washed their hair, cleaned their dishes and urinated in the passing stream; others bathed or washed themselves unconcerned as corpses sometimes floated by, for the burning ghats ran down to the water's edge, some of the pyres still with gruesome remains of bodies not completely consumed by the fires when perhaps their folks had not had quite enough money for wood to finish the job. Nearby a barber wiped his razor on his leg. And always the cows wandered where they pleased, as though well aware of their sacred status and indifferent to their contributions to the filth that lay in many side-streets. Scenes that contrasted dramatically with the opulence of Government House within sight on the other side of the Maiden. Interesting film.

Before leaving Delhi I booked into the Grand Hotel where I had stayed during the war on my way to Burma. I had not seen Calcutta then for I had been confined to the hotel by an outbreak of cholera. Then there were six or more to a room. Now I had a spacious apartment with a noisy punkah in the ceiling. A net covered the bed to protect one from the mosquitoes, flies and other insects which flew around. Calcutta was very hot and humid – an unpleasant climate. I decided I would try to fix a meeting with Gandhi as soon as I could and return to Delhi as quickly as possible. Mountbatten had gone to Assam, however, and late one evening he telephoned me. He told me there was a marvellous festival beginning and he had arranged for me to go there the next day, partly by air and then by car up the steep, winding mountainous roads to the capital, Gawahati. I did not enjoy that journey by road. The Indian driver drove at speed round the many bends and insisted that I sat in the back of the car. I enjoy driving but I am not a good passenger and I was almost carsick as we twisted and turned. On arrival, as Lord Louis had said, there was a spectacular show – dancing in wonderful costumes, singing, elephants, everything. It emphasised how aware Mountbatten was of the importance of showing the other side of the country apart from political stories. Assam produced sixty per cent of India's tea but I did not have an opportunity to film at a tea plantation, nor did I get my pictures of Gandhi as I returned to Delhi in the official plane.

Mahatma Gandhi, having done all he could to bring a peaceful solution to the troubles in Calcutta, turned his attention to the Punjab. He decided to go there by way of Delhi, where although the killings had eased, there was still an underlying tension. He was there in early January and stayed at Birla House, the large lavish residence belonging to his great friend, G.D. Birla, a rich industrialist and politician who had financed many of his ventures since they first met in 1915. There was a large garden where he was able to hold his prayer meetings each evening. He had always been opposed to partition and on 12 January he saw Lord Mountbatten to tell him he was about to begin a fast to try to promote better relations between Hindus and Muslims. He started his fast the following day. By the third day he had become so weak he was forced to take his prayer meetings at his bedside, causing the greatest concern among the public and political leaders of India and Pakistan, who feared he might die. He was given immediate assurances from both dominions that they would make every effort to encourage understanding between the two countries. With these undertakings, on 18 January Gandhi broke his fast and I filmed him sipping a glass of orange juice, so I got the pictures I had tried to obtain in Calcutta. Two days later a bomb exploded at his prayer meeting. It did little damage and injured no one, but it reinforced the rumours about possible attempts on the lives of prominent politicians including Gandhi.

Prior to Gandhi's fast I had been attending his prayer meetings each day with a BBC reporter, Bob Stimson, and my photographer friend from Associated Press, Max Desfor, in case of any trouble. I had cabled London some time earlier for more film as I was getting dangerously short and filming Gandhi at Birla House had used up the remainder of the footage I had. Ten thousand feet went to Karachi for onward transmission to Delhi but the customs in Karachi would not release it unless I went there personally – a case of 'backsheesh' required – not unusual. I was due to go to Ceylon at the end of the month for its independence day on 4 February, so I decided to go via Karachi to pick up the film. Consequently, with no film, I stopped going to the prayer meetings. The bomb explosion was worrying but as I had just over a week before going to Ceylon it seemed pointless going to Karachi to get the film, returning to Delhi and then leaving again. How wrong was that decision. The BBC reporter continued to attend the prayer meetings but Max Desfor had a special assignment with one of the maharajas and flew off on 29 January. I had arranged to go to Karachi on 1 February and on Friday 30 January I went to the cinema in the afternoon. Suddenly, about 6 p.m., the screen went blank, there was solemn music and the lights came on. The manager appeared on the small stage in front of the screen and announced, first in Hindi and then in English, that the show had ended as Gandhi had been shot at his prayer meeting and was dead. There was no reaction from the large audience; they were too stunned. They filed out quietly. It was eerie and very dramatic. But apart from the dreadful news as such I realised it was dreadful news for me. I had no film with a world story on my doorstep. I knew the BBC would have a world scoop but for Max Desfor and me there was nothing – we had missed out. I remember hurrying from the cinema in a panic. My immediate hope was that they would have a lying-in-state for a day, or several days, so I could get to Karachi and back with the film before the funeral.

I went to Birla House where there were already large crowds and was relieved to see Ved Parkash. He had managed to get some early shots. He, too, was short of film, as I had kept him supplied and he had been hoping to get some from me. I arranged to meet him later at the Imperial Hotel and tried to contact Karachi but it was too late in the evening. Then came the news on the radio that the funeral was to take place the following day from midday. More feelings of panic. My only hope then was that I could work out something with Parkash. And thank goodness for that resourceful man. When he arrived at the hotel he told me he knew a lot of film cameramen in the town and in the past had used some of them as assistants in filming stories. So we made a list of those most likely to have film, including his brother Mohan, and set out to see what we could get. I must confess I had little hope, but the situation was desperate and we could only trust that if any had film they would not want to use it themselves. One thing was fortunate. Those were the days before television's 16mm film so whatever film was around was likely to be 35mm. Parkash told me if anyone would not part with film he would blackmail them

Mahatma Gandhi on an open bier for his funeral, following his assassination. From the newsreel.

ITN Archive/Reuters

The body of Mahatma Gandhi. From the newsreel.

by telling there they would never get another job with him in the future. A true newsman! We spent almost the whole night locating those people. Parkash was as good as his word. When we found someone reluctant to release film, my good friend used his persuasive powers. By dawn we had collected a number of tins containing variable lengths of film. We sorted it out as best we could and I finished up with approximately 2,000 feet and Parkash had some 1,000 feet. We had no idea how reliable each piece was but it was remarkable that we had managed to find so much. Most of the people we contacted were very generous and handed over without any problems. But it was a daunting day ahead for both of us. In addition to the camera it meant carrying tins of different lengths and constantly having to reload the camera via the changing bag in the street and the crowds, and all the time wondering whether one was filming vital scenes with faulty stock. I can say without reservation it was the worst day in my whole career as a cameraman. But it transpired that all the film was usable and that was indeed a miracle.

I arranged with Parkash for him to film scenes at Birla House at the start of the funeral procession and whatever else he could in that area while I would make my way to the other end for the cremation. What saved the day was the time the procession took to get from Birla House to the banks of the Jumna river where the pyre awaited, a distance of about four and a half miles. With the vast crowds and stops it took the cortege five hours to make the journey. It gave me time to get pictures on the way – the shrouded Gandhi, head exposed, surrounded with flowers, the crowds and the general atmosphere – and to tin-up exposed film as I made gradual progress along the road. There had been no opportunity to arrange for an assistant or for transport. With all that gear it was a long, hot walk and if there had been less time I would not have been able to finish the story. When I finally arrived at the pyre it was to be confronted with a crowd of around half a million waiting for the climax. In the front were the VIPs: the Mountbattens, Nehru, ministers, ambassadors and military top brass. I took some pictures of all this but surveyed the scene with some disquiet. I needed some elevation to show such a setting. A high pair of steps would have helped. However, I seemed to be blessed with miracles. A local photographer whom I knew had somehow managed to fix a small platform on a single pole which he had embedded in the ground and which was about ten feet high. There was just room for two and I pleaded with him to let me join him. Understandably he was not keen but he agreed. I cannot remember how I got up there. Probably on someone's shoulders but up there I got, festooned with equipment. We were very close to the pyre and ideally placed to show it when it was alight. When the cortege arrived, drawn by members of the state services, Gandhi's body was placed on the pyre and the sandalwood logs set alight by his son. As the flames rose high the crowd went wild and broke through the police cordons, and the VIPs disappeared in the ensuing pandemonium. Police horses came in to restore order and continually brushed past our pole. It really was a wonder we did not fall off or get knocked off. However, due to the generosity of my photographer friend I managed to film the whole scene. I had kept my longest piece of film – it seemed to be about 200 feet – for that part of the proceedings and it was just enough for the arrival of Gandhi, the pyre alight and the chaos that followed. Parkash had done well at Birla House with good close-ups and the start of the procession. Thanks to him and his efforts during the night we got a good coverage when it seemed we were in an impossible situation. When the film was dispatched to London all we could hope was that the stock was OK. I never found out what the laboratories thought when they received all those short pieces of film. I thought it wise to say nothing about having run out of film. I was also very lucky not to have been on my way to Ceylon, for if Gandhi had been assassinated two days later I would have been unable to return to Delhi in time for the funeral. So ended the life of that frail individual at the age of seventy-nine, one who had tried so hard to end violence but died by violence. In the Hindu language of Sanskrit 'Mahatma' means 'Great Soul', a fitting epitaph for the man.

The next day I was on my way to Ceylon with little time to prepare for its independence on 4 February 1948. I left behind a sad city with flags at half-mast, places of entertainment shut, and most shops closed for the thirteen days of mourning that had been declared. I picked up my film in Karachi, satisfying the customs of my claim to the film by a suitable handover of rupees. Ceylon is just twenty miles south of the Tamil states of India and is roughly the size of Ireland. It is a Buddhist country in spite of being so close to Hindu India. As one approaches from the air one can see many of its tea plantations, tea being its main export. On arrival in Colombo l made for Mount Lavinia and the Galle Face Hotel next to the sea. I was pleased to see from my hotel bedroom that there were still vendors of pineapples and mangoes on the beach. Apart from that it was a different city from the wartime days. The harbour was as busy as ever but the warships had gone. No sailors, soldiers, airmen, Fanys or Wrens filled the restaurants and bars, or walked the streets, or waited for buses or boats. Now flags, bunting, ceremonial arches lined the processional routes and there were very large crowds to cope with again. I had the advantage, this time, of knowing the town, but I made no attempt to put up stands. I was on my own and needed to be mobile to cover as many aspects of the proceedings as possible and with the prospect of excitable crowds as in Delhi stands were not all that useful.

The programme in Ceylon was on a smaller scale than in India with no country to be divided and no communal troubles looming. They came some years later when the Tamil Indians tried to establish a permanent home for themselves. The initial ceremony at midnight took the form that was to signify the transfer of power at all future independence ceremonies – the lowering of the Union Jack, the raising of the national flag and the singing of the national anthem. Local cameramen had arranged for this to be lit. Throughout the night there was much jubilation until the next day, 4 February. Early that morning the inaugural ceremony, at which the governor of Ceylon, Sir Henry Moore, was sworn in as Governor-General, took place in a special structure in one of the large gardens in Colombo, as the parliament building was too small for the numbers they wished to accommodate. It was a covered hall with open sides and room for several thousand guests including schoolchildren. With the new Governor-General installed and the British henceforth represented by a high commissioner, a spectacular festival was staged and the rejoicing went on into the late evening.

Although there were a number of parties and displays of fireworks after the inaugural formalities there was a break in the proceedings until the opening of the first session of parliament on 10 February by the Duke of Gloucester, who arrived in Colombo with the Duchess on 8 February. They were greeted by Sir Henry Moore, a guard of honour, and a twenty-one-gun salute at the airport which was about twenty miles outside the city. Large crowds lined the processional route to Queen's House, the Governor-General's residence. The following evening there was a very large garden party in honour of the royals. The next day, the 10th, the Duke, in smart white uniform, opened the new parliament in the presence of representatives from more than twenty nations. After greetings and a gun salute the royal procession moved through the specially constructed open-sided hall to a dais on two levels. On the upper level was the throne of the Kandyan kings in gold and red, a gift from King George V in 1934. On the lower level were two thrones for the Duke and Duchess. After the proclamation of King George VI's commission authorising the Duke to open the first parliament of the new dominion, the Duke read a speech from the King and declared the parliament open. Very large crowds were in the park outside the Assembly hall to see the conclusion of the proceedings when the Singhalese prime minister, watched by the Duke and Duchess, unfurled the Lion Flag, standard of the Singhalese kings. There was some query as to which flag to hoist on Independence Day and it was decided that it should be the Lion Flag for its close association with the Kandyan court of past days, but a new national flag was to be designed as soon as possible. The next day it was up to Kandy where, at the Temple of the Tooth, the Duke raised the Lion Flag. This was followed by a perahera – a torchlight procession of Kandyan chiefs, dancers, elephants adorned in finery and ornaments and tom-tom beaters. There was a lot to picture and I was glad I had plenty of film.

Before I returned to India I was invited to dinner at the house of one of the white tea-planters with whom I had become acquainted when looking for some elevation on one of the processional routes. It was almost palatial and I was treated to one of the best curries I have ever had. I had had one or two when I was in Ceylon during the war, but nothing like that one. I returned to India on fire.

Mourning for Gandhi had ended when I arrived back in Delhi. The next few months were spent travelling all over India, sometimes with Lord Mountbatten, sometimes solo. There were goodbyes or thanks to maharajas, heads of states and officials. Sometimes there were festivals with their processions of elephants, horses, dancers and singers and religious statues of Hindu gods like Ganesh, the elephant-headed son of Shiva. There was a visit to Madras. There was Bombay, the home of the film industry where thousands of feet of film was exposed every year, for the Indians loved their films. Bombay with its elegant Parsi women, its slums, its Gateway to India arch, and where just outside its boundaries stretched miles and miles of paddy fields and where a little over a hundred miles away in the hills was Poona, the Simla of the south. There was Hyderabad where the very wealthy, miserly Nizam drove around in his old banger of a Rolls-Royce. There were farewells to tea-planters and the military. I regretted that on some of these journeys there was not always time to see the places other than cursorily. I would have liked to see more of the temples, the paintings of Hindu gods and the wildlife. No matter where one is, this is one of the frustrating things for a cameraman, for he has to concentrate on the story, leaving little time to enjoy the locality.

I did manage, however, to get up to Srinagar in Kashmir and see something of the place. I flew there in a single-engined plane between snow-covered mountains of the Himalayas, a rather unnerving flight but very beautiful. There was no trouble in Srinagar while I was there and the houseboats, lakes and flowers provided a welcome relief from the hot, steamy country 5,000 feet below. The city, situated on Dal Lake, was transversed with canals and the Jhelum river. It was a lovely place for a different kind of picture of India as one took a trip through the canals and lakes in a *shikara* (gondola). I was only there for a few days but it was certainly a nice break to be able to show a peaceful scene, although, of course, what I saw was a facade. I was just lucky, for Kashmir was by no means to remain a peaceful state after independence.

The time came for Lord Mountbatten to leave India and for an Indian Governor-General, Mr Rajagopalachari, to be sworn in. In the evening of 20 June 1948 the Indian Cabinet gave a state banquet at Government House followed by a reception for thousands of guests to give them an opportunity to say goodbye to the Mountbattens, who left early the next morning before the new Governor-General was sworn in. They drove down to the main gates in the state landau escorted by the colourful, turbanned Governor-General's bodyguard, watched by large crowds. Then it was by motor procession to Palam airport where, after Lord Louis inspected a guard of honour, the Mountbattens were seen off by Pandit Nehru, the new Governor-General and a number of diplomats and politicians. I had followed in the motor procession from Government House and took my last pictures as the plane disappeared into the distance to end my coverage of that historic assignment.

Then it was my turn to say farewell to the many friends I had made, to those at Associated Press and in particular to Ved Parkash. I told him to be sure to contact me if he came to London in the future. Some years later I was delighted to see his cheerful face and tubby figure when I took him to dinner in London's West End. When I called him several days later I was devastated to learn he collapsed and died in an Indian restaurant. It was a very sad end for a very nice, generous and likeable man. And the other participants in those dramatic days did not survive for very long. Jinnah died in September 1948, Patel in 1950, Nehru in 1964. And Mountbatten was assassinated in 1979. A sobering thought.

In the plane returning to England I thought back to the journey the other way when I was heading for India and to what had happened between those two flights. I would no longer hear 'Yes, Sahib' or call out, 'Bearer!' I would no longer see the straight-backed Parsi women in Bombay, clad in their beautiful saris. I thought of the excitement of Independence Day and the awful days that followed in the Punjab; of the squalor in Calcutta and the bodies in Delhi. In a way my look at India was superficial. One needed more than a few months to appreciate all its intricacies, its customs, its temples and to understand its peoples. In writing this account of my stay in India I should emphasise that my thoughts of the country were strictly as I saw it as a newsreel cameraman. I saw it in exceptional circumstances and I could not claim to know it in any way otherwise. It is a fascinating country and has much of the romance with which I surrounded it. I was so grateful to have seen history in the making, when, after 163 years of British rule and ninety years of the Raj, the country became two countries, each with a future that depended on its own initiatives. As my plane touched down at Heathrow I returned to my very first thoughts – India is, and always will be, 'news' – a good thought for a newsreel cameraman.

Chapter Eight
Changing Times

When I returned from India in the middle of the summer of 1948 it was three years since the war had ended, and although there were plenty of signs of the havoc the war had caused there were noticeable changes in general and a positive feeling that things were getting back to normal and life had a future. The speed-up in life over the next four years brought about a faster service of events to the reels. Faster cars, long-range aircraft with travel by air instead of by sea meant stories thought impossible to cover because of the distance and time involved in getting to and from a location were now in the diaries. A job which took a week in the country became a one-day affair or at the most a night away. There were no motorways during this period and these changes of course did not come about overnight, but nonetheless we were changing our ways of working all the time.

To complement these changes there were new, more sensitive film emulsions. With new film stocks we were able to film at times and in areas never considered before, especially at night. We were often testing new film stocks. I remember being called into my production manager's office and being given some rolls of a special film to test. It was very secret; we all tried to keep our experiments from the opposition, although this was defeated to some extent because the producers of the films were anxious to get coverage from whatever source they could. However, I took this particular film, I believe it was from Ilford, down to Southampton as I had a job to do aboard one of the big liners meeting some celebrity from America. After I had secured the story on current normal stock I wandered off into the main lounge of the ship. The decor was of the old-fashioned plushy type – heavy furnishing and drapes and subdued lighting, a sort of orangey effect which gave it a very comfortable look in the stately home style, very different from today's liners. So the room was not ideal for filming. But I was going to do a test and there was no point in making it in good light. I exposed a 100 foot roll of the new film and expected to see a blank negative or at best a few shadows. The result was outstanding. The picture looked as if it had been lit in a studio. True, the film was given special processing and although not quite ready for general use it was a very decisive step forward.

Another advantage the improved stocks gave us was in the use of telephoto lenses, which we were able to use in quite poor light whereas previously they had

The cameramen of the five newsreels at Epsom, early 1950s. Note the production managers wearing hats.

Diagram with identifications (page 139) by John Turner and Norman Fisher.

Name	Newsreel Company	Name	Newsreel Company
1. Martin Gray	Movietone	21. George Richardson	Movietone
2. John Rudkin	Pathe	22. Jock Gemmell	Pathe
3. Len Dudley	Paramount	23. Arthur Irwin	Gaumont-British
4. Eddy Edmonds	Gaumont-British	24. Bill Hooker	Gaumont-British
5. Bill Jordan	Pathe	25. John Corbett	Pathe
6. Adrian Consoli	Gaumont-British	26. Cedric Baynes	Pathe
7. Peter Cannon	Gaumont-British	27. Jimmy Gemmell	Paramount
8. Harold Morley	Gaumont-British	28. Ronnie Hubbard	Paramount
9. Ronnie Read	Paramount	29. John Collins	Movietone
10. ?	?	30. Nobby Clark	Paramount
11. Paul Wyand	Movietone	31. Stan Crockett	Paramount
12. John Turner	Gaumont-British	32. Arthur Farmer	Paramount
13. Derek Scott-Leslie	Movietone	33. Albert Wherry	Gaumont-British
14. Adolph Simon	Pathe	34. Tony Green	Gaumont-British
15. David Samuelson	Movietone	35. ?	Gaumont-British
16. Ken Hanshaw	Movietone	36. Jack Ramsden	Movietone
17. ?	Gaumont-British	37. Bert Bishop	Gaumont-British
18. ?	Pathe	38. Bill McConville	Pathe
19. Terry O'Brien	Movietone	39. Leslie Murray	Universal
20. Jack Harding	Paramount		

required good light for good definition. The lenses themselves were also improved with good quality components. With better black-and-white film there also came a breakthrough in colour film. There had been a few instances when we had used Technicolor for the big occasion. The results were superb but unless the cameras were in fixed positions they were not generally suitable for newsreel work. We needed a film that could be used in any camera, one film base, with quick processing, unlike Technicolor which required special cameras which could run three colour negatives at the same time with the consequent slower processing of the three negatives which had to be superimposed on each other. Technicolor did, in fact, achieve some remarkable results in later years when we required a special film the day after filming. Kodak came up with the answer for us with Eastmancolor, a film with one base which could by used in any camera. As in the days when sound took over from the silent era and old stories became new ones so it was with colour – old stories became new ones. Ilford, Agfa and others soon followed Kodak but in my opinion Eastmancolor was the best.

One other difference the faster films made was in cutting our lighting costs when filming in black and white. This helped tremendously on occasions when filming interiors where space was limited, and it usually was. It was amazing in those early days how accommodating organisers were in providing room for the cumbersome two-, five- or ten-kilowatt lights we used. The presence of VIPs or royalty added to the problems. It was compromise every time. So when we were able to use smaller lights and fewer electricians some of our problems were either solved or helped and our costs reduced. The latter was very important, for no matter how expensive a job was to light we did not receive any more money for the reel.

These were important changes which affected our working lives. For me this period from 1948-1951 was an extremely busy one with some quite challenging events, and it was the start of a complete change in my future newsreel career. On my return from overseas it took me some time to get used once more to the fact that it did not matter how you planned your day, your week or even your year, if you were in the news business you could be absolutely certain it was not going to work out as you had hoped. When we arrived at the office in the morning we usually had no idea what awaited us. It could be a tragedy, it could be Downing Street, it could be a foreign trip or it could be just a game of cards. Our wives had to be saints – and were. A nice dinner in the evening with friends often had to be partaken of without the host. We generally managed to keep our annual holidays but there were occasions when they had to be cancelled, too. On every other public holiday we were always working. This was the perennial lot of the newsreel cameraman.

While I had been away the new state of Israel came into being and the railways and electricity industries had been nationalised, to be joined by the gas industry in 1949. My favourite battleship, HMS *Valiant*, 72,700 tons of fighting steel, was scrapped, and my favourite cruiser, HMS *Euryalus*, suffered the same fate in 1949. Both ships had been platforms for me to get historic war films. Sad days.

Each year had its hardy annuals such as the Grand National, the Boat Race, Ascot, cricket and football. These formed a kind of skeleton for the newsreels on which we could add the special events and the unexpected. In this period there was much to add. The Olympic Games, the Festival of Britain, the Canadian tour of Princess Elizabeth and the Duke of Edinburgh, the birth of a future king and the birth of a new princess were some of the stories in which I was personally involved. Football was at its peak at weekends (few mid-week matches then) and enjoyed very large crowds. The cinemas, too, had large audiences, not surprising, as for *1s. 6d.* or less, people saw two films, shorts, newsreels and a stage show or the mighty Wurlitzer organ giving a recital of popular music.

So from the heat of India it was back to the traditional British summer – cold, heavy rain and very hot spells. At the end of July 1948 there was a heatwave with 93 °F being recorded and three days later on August Bank Holiday (at the beginning of the month then) it was cool and it rained. One of my first jobs in July was not a pleasant one. I had to go to the scene of a bad air crash near Northolt airport. An aircraft of RAF Transport Command and a Skymaster of the Scandinavian Airlines collided in poor visibility and both planes crashed to the ground in flames in woods close to Northolt. It happened in the afternoon and I was able to get to the scene soon after the disaster. There only remained the charred wreckage of the two aircraft and personal belongings scattered everywhere, as always in such tragedies. Although the fire brigade reached the scene quickly there was no hope of finding anyone alive in the inferno and thirty-nine people died. When they managed to lift what remained of the Skymaster the bodies were all huddled in a heap in the main section. The High Commissioner of Malaya was among the dead. Not a good beginning to the month.

One of the most important July stories we covered was the inauguration of the National Health Service, a sound story, which began with the slogan 'Security from the cradle to the grave'. In those first days before computers everyone was allocated an insurance sheet kept in ledgers at the insurance ministry near Newcastle. There were millions of these sheets which recorded the insurance history of each registered person throughout his life. It was an outstanding feat of organisation. July also saw the Shah of Persia pay a state visit, Lord Mountbatten made a Knight of the Garter, and the King and Queen were at Southampton visiting the liner *Queen Elizabeth*, nostalgic for the Queen, who had launched the ship just before the war. And this busy month ended with the opening of the Olympic Games at Wembley Stadium.

J. Arthur Rank had secured the filming rights for the Olympics for *Gaumont-British News*. It was forty years since the games were last in Britain and our newsreel was determined to make it a very special occasion. Everyone on the staff was involved and many freelance cameramen were hired. We were very well organised by our production manager, H.W. Bishop, a former cameraman, and were dressed in very smart blazers and trousers and looked like one of the competing teams. Apart from the newsreel coverage our director, Castleton-Knight, made a film in Technicolor, XIVTH OLYMPIAD – THE GLORY OF SPORT. The sun shone on the crowd of some 80,000 who filled Wembley to watch the ceremonial opening of the Fourteenth Olympiad by the King, who arrived with the Queen, Queen Mary and other members of the royal family.

The proceedings began with the King, in naval uniform, greeting the International Olympic Committee who, curiously, had lined up on the track wearing top hats and frock coats, the etiquette of an earlier era. Next came the march past of the athletes, 6,000 competitors from fifty-eight countries, massing in the centre of the ground after the march for the opening speeches and to await the arrival of the torch-bearer to light the Olympic flame. The King proclaimed the games open, the Olympic flag was raised as trumpeters of the Household Cavalry sounded a fanfare, and thousands of pigeons were released, circling the stadium before disappearing into the distance. The torch-bearer, a former Cambridge Blue, arrived to loud cheers and after running round the stadium lit the Olympic flame. Finally the Olympic oath was spoken in the centre of a semicircle of flag-bearers, after which the athletes left the arena and the games began with the runners racing anticlockwise round the track with the finish just beyond the royal box in the centre of the main stand. All this kept us very busy and the next two weeks were spent covering the events at twenty-one centres apart from Wembley. This involved travelling to Henley, Bisley, many football grounds, Torbay and the other sites. Little else was filmed during that fortnight. On 4 August, on her forty-eighth birthday, the Queen spent the afternoon with the King and the Duke of Edinburgh watching the games. The crowd, led by a band, greeted her by singing 'Happy Birthday to You'.

The weather had not been particularly good during the Olympics and in the middle of August there were very heavy rainfalls in north-east England and southern Scotland – a disastrous downpour which lasted only two days but resulted in cattle and sheep being swept away in floods and drowned, over twenty bridges being damaged or destroyed and many people made homeless. We were back to filming hard news stories.

Bombed sites were being cleared and new buildings began to appear. On the Thames south bank an area from Waterloo Bridge to Hungerford Bridge was in the initial stages of clearance. This was to be the site for an exhibition that would be part of the Festival of Britain in 1951. It included a concert hall and a national theatre. The Festival Hall, as the concert hall became known, and the Royal National Theatre are, of course, very much part of London's attractions today.

A welcome diversion was when the reel was asked by a cinema, often one of our own, to cover a particular local event for showing only in that area. The story was usually a carnival or a bathing-beauty contest, the object being to film as many local dignitaries and crowds as possible in order to attract the people into the cinema to see themselves on the screen. It was well advertised by the cinema that *Gaumont-British News* would be filming in the town. The cinema manager organised positions and obtained any necessary passes, and often we would be taken to the town hall to meet the mayor and council and frequently be entertained to a buffet lunch. Wet or fine it was a pleasant day away from any pressures. I usually filmed about 400 feet which would be edited, a commentary added and the story attached to the current issue of the general reel destined for that cinema.

Each season had its quota of hardy annuals and special events so that we were rarely without a job throughout the year. The weather, always unpredictable, seemed to give us a story any time. The longest day was well past and the days began to be noticeably shorter. With the approach of winter events in the open started earlier, but I do not recall any great difference or problems in filming stories outdoors. Perhaps sometimes we had to allow more exposure by opening the apertures on the lenses more widely, and the newer and faster film emulsions helped to compensate when the light was poor. There were many more indoor events, more exhibitions and trade shows in the cinemas, an expensive time with the extra cost of lighting.

Earls Court staged the International Motor Show, the first for ten years due to the war. To light each model we wished to film we had small units consisting of a two-kilowatt or five-kilowatt light with electricians to establish supply points and run cables, which had to be protected against the public falling over them. Each time we moved to a new stand the whole procedure of new supply points and running of cables had to be repeated. It was quite complicated especially with the large crowds which surrounded each car. Hand-lights were particularly useful for showing close-ups of engines and people climbing into or peering into cars. The new Morris Minor caused a lot of interest as did John Cobb's world-land-speed-record Railton. Most cars were going overseas – the industry had exported 40,000 since the war, a fine achievement as steel was in short supply. This resulted in buyers in the home market having to wait from twelve months to two and a half years for delivery. Disappointing when a Ford Anglia could be bought for around £300.

Hunt meetings made nice pictures in the countryside and were a pleasant way of showing the land in winter. We did not have to contend with the difficulties that hunting has to face nowadays. At the beginning of November President Truman was re-elected for a second term against all predictions, as the experts had said Mr Dewey would win. We received that story from our American associates.

In the middle of the month, on the 14th, Princess Elizabeth gave birth to Prince Charles at Buckingham Palace just after 9 p.m., and when Queen Mary arrived soon after the birth to join the King and Queen and the Duke of Edinburgh, she was cheered by large crowds massed around the palace and on the Queen Victoria Memorial. I was there with hand-lights and when a copy of the court circular announcing the birth was posted on the palace railings my electrician and I had the greatest difficulty avoiding being trampled underfoot by everyone wanting to read it. Queen Mary left at midnight and the crowds again cheered her enthusiastically, forcing her car to slow down and almost to stop. She seemed to enjoy it. It was well into the night before things quietened down.

The end of the month brought a pea-souper – dense, yellow, very dirty fog. It lasted for more than a week and caused chaos all over the country. London Airport and Croydon were closed with aircraft diverted to Hurn, near Bournemouth, and the large liners including the *Queen Elizabeth* were unable to leave Southampton. We could not venture far because the fog around London stretched for thirty miles round the city. It was extremely dangerous to drive and often almost impossible, for visibility at best was fifteen yards but mostly nil. It was eerie filming in those conditions. Conductors of buses and trolleybuses walked in front of their vehicles with flares until forced to stop when visibility became nil. Thus ended an eventful few months on my return to England.

In the new year, 1949, all the basic annual stories were pencilled in for coverage. They remained very popular with cinema audiences as did tragedies – the voyeurism in our make-up – and royal stories, which had a big following. But for me 1949 was a year in which aircraft played a major part. I was filming flights of machines that were the prototypes of many of those flying today. The English Electric A1, Britain's first jet bomber, powered by two Rolls-Royce turbojet engines, made its test flight in May and in the same month a test pilot tried out the first ejector seat from an aircraft. Saunders-Roe at Cowes, Isle of Wight, were building three Princess-class flying boats, each of 140 tons with an estimated speed of 400 m.p.h. and a range of 5,000 miles. There was the first flight of the de Havilland Comet, the first passenger aircraft designed solely for jet engines, and in September the Bristol Brabazon, a very large plane for the time with eight Rolls-Royce engines, made its maiden flight. During the year I was despatched to Culdrose in Cornwall, the headquarters of the Fleet Air Arm, to show the work of that branch of the navy. I stayed at Culdrose for some time and was flown out to aircraft carriers most days to show take-offs and landings and to make a number of flights myself, filming activities on the carriers from the air. Being catapulted off an aircraft carrier was a different experience from my first one of being launched in a Walrus from HMAS *Australia* during the war. Everything seemed so much bigger although the tensions were very similar before take-off. When I landed it was on the deck as opposed to the Walrus, which landed on the sea. An interesting plane I filmed was the de Havilland Vampire jet-propelled aircraft which had made its initial flight from the aircraft carrier, HMS *Ocean*, in December 1948. I made so many flights that the commander who flew me on most occasions made me an honorary member of Culdrose and gave me a beautiful little brooch which entitled me to visit there at any time. Unfortunately I left it on a jacket which I sent to be cleaned when I returned to London, and I never got it back.

Apart from the advances made with the new planes 1949 had a bad time in the air. At least 140 people were killed in crashes worldwide, a high figure for the times when passenger lists were small. On the subject of flying for pictures, in the early days we had to dress up in full flying kit to film from open cockpits. Paradoxically, flying in a closed cockpit and at increased speeds we had to dress in even more gear and had G-force to contend with. There were others more skilled than I at filming from the air but I agreed to have a go at flying in a Hunter with an aerobatic team. It was not the most pleasant of experiences. My camera got heavier and heavier as we dived and pulled out of formations. Apart from trying to cope with the uncomfortable and constant change of direction, which made me dizzy, I was boiling hot and the increases in the G-force made the camera so heavy and un-manageable that it was impossible to keep my eye to the viewfinder. That kind of flying required the camera to be screwed down. I tried three times to get something worthwhile but was not successful and at the end of each effort I was completely exhausted. I decided henceforth that Black Arrows, Red Arrows or whatever coloured Arrows would be filmed from the ground if I was involved.

Some important political stories made the reel. The North Atlantic Treaty was signed in Washington by twelve countries that did not include the Soviet Union, which believed that it was an aggressive rather than a defensive force. American associates supplied us with that film. Eire opted out of the British Commonwealth and became a republic at Easter, thirty-three years after the 1916 Easter Rising. There was much rejoicing, especially in Dublin where there was a great military parade. And after almost a year the Berlin blockade was lifted and the lights came on again in western Berlin. It ended the remarkable airlift of the British and American air forces who flew hundreds of Dakotas every day with thousands of tons of supplies to feed the city, thwarting Russia's attempt to take over the whole of Berlin. Our German associates supplied us with that story. Three significant historic events.

While all the above was taking place sweet rationing was lifted with long queues immediately forming at stalls and shops to satisfy the sweet tooth of the nation. Clothes rationing also ended. An interesting fact about what we wore was the disappearance of hats. Everyone wore a hat before the war but this year saw both men and women go bareheaded. Another relaxation was the end of soap rationing and perhaps the prospect of getting clean again prompted the opening of the first launderette in Bayswater, London. All stories to brighten the reel.

I had a nice little story at the London zoo. A baby elephant about six months old, born in Assam, was flown to London from the Calcutta zoo, which offered it to our zoo, as it had been abandoned and would have died in the jungle. I had not been to the zoo since my very first story as an assistant in 1936 when I went with one of Gaumont's cameramen to film the arrival of an okapi. I enjoyed my day with the animals, a change from people.

At the end of July HMS *Amethyst*, which had been held hostage on the Yangtze river by the Chinese since April, managed to escape down the river, an extremely skilful and daring operation, under fire at times and with very tricky channels to negotiate in the dark. At the end of October I was once again back with the navy. I flew out to Gibraltar on an official Admiralty rota facility to witness the arrival of the ship in the harbour and to return in her to Plymouth. Her commanding officer, Lieutenant-Commander Kerans, was very cooperative and I got some good pictures of the crew and the ship apart from the scenes in Gibraltar and the welcome as she steamed into Plymouth Sound. So ended another eventful year.

A new decade began with a general election in which Labour got back in with a majority of just five. When covering general elections the cameramen and editors had to be particularly careful to present an impartial story. It was not always easy when we might be faced with a charismatic individual who made a better picture or was more articulate than an equally important opposition candidate. It would have been so easy to show preference or to emphasise one's own political leanings.

Each year had its tragedies and 1950 was no exception. Early in the year a charter aircraft bringing back Welsh rugby fans from an international match between Wales and Ireland crashed in South Wales while preparing to land, breaking into three pieces as it hit the ground and killing eighty passengers and crew. I am glad I did not have to cover that one. We received film from a freelance cameraman. Later in the yea, in September, eighty miners died in an underground fire at Cresswell Colliery in Derbyshire. Scenes at such disasters were always dramatic and poignant with rescue teams going down into the mine, often returning to the surface empty-handed or with the body of a victim, to face the sad, distressed groups of relatives and friends waiting at the pit-head for news of the trapped men. This one happened very early in the morning, giving time to get to the colliery while rescue operations were in progress.

In May the Queen launched a splendid new *Ark Royal*, the fourth of that name. It revived memories of my first encounter with the enemy as a naval war correspondent when I filmed her predecessor straddled with bomb splashes during an air attack in the North Sea. Over 40,000 people at Cammell Laird's yard at Birkenhead made the launch a festive and happy occasion and cheered and waved as the ship slid into the water. She was a larger ship than the previous *Ark Royal* and was greeted with a twenty-one-gun welcome from the carrier HMS *Illustrious* stationed midstream, while a force of aircraft saluted her in a fly-past. It was always an anxious and exciting moment to see a large vessel glide gracefully into the sea.

Came the day for which all motorists had been hoping – the end of petrol rationing. This came just before Whitsun, resulting in a rush to the seaside with the strange sight of full car-parks. There were inevitably more breakdowns with the longer journeys as many motorists had got out of the habit of preparing for such excursions. It did not affect us as much as others as we had special allowances to enable us to get to our various locations, but nevertheless it was very pleasant to join in the general euphoria in tearing up our coupons and telling the pump attendant (no self-service then) to fill the tank.

We tried many times to film events which featured an orchestra or a stage show, such as at the Edinburgh Festival. We wanted to show what happened behind the scenes, the location, artistes off-stage, etc. We needed a few feet of an orchestra playing or a play in action to establish the basis of the story. We were always frustrated by the Musicians Union or Equity, which insisted we would have to pay full fees for the privilege. That meant a fee at the top rate for each member of an orchestra or for actors. The cost was prohibitive for the few feet we required. We tried to get some workable arrangement such as an agreed footage for an overall payment. We were never successful. Consequently, the players got nothing and the events lost free publicity.

In an earlier chapter I referred to cricket test matches and the long waits, which became quite boring when wickets would not fall. Although I usually had a roving assignment from ground level, there were occasions when I was on the rostrum from which the five reels worked with long lenses. When nothing much was happening we used to amuse ourselves by swinging our telephoto lenses on to the crowd on the other side of the ground, partly to get crowd reactions such as people asleep and partly to be peeping Toms. It was amazing what the long lens revealed on a warm summer's day. We refrained from filming such revelations.

On 15 August Princess Elizabeth gave birth to Princess Anne, this time obligingly in the morning. The baby was born at Clarence House, where the Princess and the Duke of Edinburgh then lived. Only the Duke and the Queen were in London, the rest of the royal family being on holiday at Balmoral and Sandringham. Dense crowds gathered outside Clarence House to read the official bulletin and in daylight we were able to film more easily than at Prince Charles's birth at night.

In 1943, to prevent numbers of photographers, cameramen, journalists and radio reporters following the King's various wartime activities and to keep his visits secret, it became necessary to impose a rota system. The newsreel cameraman assigned to accompany the King was Graham Thompson, a Scot employed by Movietone who was not working as a war correspondent. When he started it was not intended as a permanent appointment but after some months the King requested that he should be accredited indefinitely to Buckingham Palace. The newsreels agreed to this providing he was based in a different company every three months, thus avoiding Movietone having an exclusive royal cameraman. Thompson remained in this capacity until, mysteriously and almost without notice, he gave up his accreditation and announced in July 1950 that he was joining BBC Television. Soon after this I was called to the Newsreel Association offices and was stunned to be told that I was to be the next royal cameraman. It had yet to be decided whether the assignment was permanent and whether I would follow Thompson's routine of moving from company to company. Castleton-Knight, my boss, opposed the latter and it was agreed that for the time being I should stay with Gaumont, probably with the thought that the cameraman would be changed every few months. Apart from royal stories to which I had to give preference I was available for other stories for my own newsreel. I was given a special Buckingham Palace pass and met the King's press secretary, Commander Richard Colville, who briefed me on general procedures and the way I would work with the Palace. More of that later.

My first taste of a special facility came with the christening of Princess Anne in October when I was allowed very close to Princess Elizabeth and the baby. Also in October I was involved in a major royal story – the opening by the King of the restored chamber of the House of Commons, the original having been destroyed when London was bombed during the war. The main ceremony took place in the vast Westminster Hall and significantly for us was televised. It was the first time I had worked with television. We jointly established positions and lighting with the Ministry of Works, which was responsible for building the stands for the sound cameras and fixing overhead lights. I learned a great deal about how to handle such events from this job, which stood me in good stead later. This was a very splendid occasion with all the principals in ceremonial dress. From overseas twenty-nine speakers or the equivalent from Commonwealth parliaments accompanied the Speaker from the Mother of Parliaments in his procession into Westminster Hall. It was essentially a story for the sound cameras and on the day my job was to film the arrival of the King, the Queen, Queen Mary, Princess Elizabeth and other royals.

There was nothing special for me for the remainder of 1950 in my new capacity. George Bernard Shaw, always awkward but often featured in our reel, died aged ninety-four in November and we gave him a good send-off in an obituary which showed much of his life in pictures.

Nineteen fifty-one, the fourth year of this changing period, saw me establishing myself as royal cameraman although it was still not confirmed as a permanent job, and I continued to film other stories. I was given a boost in April when, at a meeting of the Newsreel Association, Commander Colville requested that I should cover the Commonwealth tour by the King and Queen in 1952. It seemed that I was getting established.

Ernest Bevin, former foreign secretary, died suddenly in April and space was given in the reel for film of the high points in his life. A high point in my life also came in April. As St Paul's Cathedral was chosen to stage the opening ceremony of the Festival of Britain it was decided to have the great cross above the dome cleaned for the occasion. I was given the job of showing this operation being carried out by steeplejacks from the top of St Paul's. I do not suffer from vertigo but was seriously tested this time and did not enjoy covering the story. The cross is 365 feet above ground level and can only be accessed by climbing above the dome. Accompanied by a steeplejack who carried my camera I began my journey upwards by ascending over 500 steps inside the cathedral, in itself an endurance test, and arrived at the Stone and Golden Galleries, just above the large dome. It was then necessary to go up vertical ladders to reach a smaller dome above which was the ball on which the cross was mounted. There was a strong breeze up there which seemed like a force nine gale to me, and by the time we got to the base of the smaller dome I was shivering with cold and nerves. My steeplejack was magnificent, giving me confidence to get to the next ladder which would take me above the curve of the smaller dome and from which I would be in a position to film the steeplejacks at work cleaning the cross. To get to that ladder we had to negotiate round the base of the curve of the dome, a ghastly experience edging round with nothing but space behind one. Finally in position on the ladder, with the steeplejack leaning on my legs to steady me, I managed to take my pictures. Back at the base of the small dome

I had to take a shot looking down to give an idea how high the cross was from the ground. Looking down from a height through a small viewfinder can play havoc with one's sense of balance. I found that when I had some feeling of protection, however slight, such as a low railing or low parapet, I was not troubled. If there was only wide open space in front I had to fight hard not to lean forward and fall off, a very unpleasant feeling coupled with a fear of dropping the camera. I asked my steeplejack to hang on to me while I took the shot. I was very relieved when I was inside the cathedral again. The steeplejack said I had done well. That was kind, for he must have been aware how nervous I had been. I certainly could not have done anything without his help. His job is definitely one I could not do even though generally I have a good head for heights. My thoughts of the cross as I left the cathedral were not entirely religious.

A month later on 4 May I was at St Paul's again, this time at ground level. After a service of dedication attended by most of the royal family, the Lord Mayor, politicians, diplomats and a congregation representative of people from many parts of the country and from overseas, the King opened the Festival of Britain from the steps of St Paul's in a speech which was broadcast. It was a spectacular scene with much of London's history portrayed in the tunics of the heralds with their coats of arms and in the uniforms of the Honourable Corps of Gentlemen-at-Arms with white plumes and glittering helmets, of the Yeomen of the Guard, the Yeomen Warders of the Tower, the trumpeters of the Household Cavalry, the honourable Artillery Company which included a company of pikemen and the Lord Mayor in his ceremonial robes holding high the pearl sword of the City. To the left of the King were most of the royal family and somewhere in the vicinity of all this, endeavouring to be unobtrusive, was me. Opposite the steps were the newsreel sound cameras and the BBC, depicting and recording the whole scene. It was a grand opening to an equally impressive festival. The King and Queen, Princess Elizabeth, the Duke of Edinburgh and Queen Mary had driven to the cathedral in a carriage procession along beflagged streets lined by cheering crowds. We had cameras at strategic points – on the Queen Victoria Memorial for the departure from Buckingham Palace, on a stand along The Mall, at Temple Bar for the traditional ceremony when the Lord Mayor offers the King the pearl sword and outside St Paul's.

In the evening the King with the Queen opened the Royal Festival Hall on the South Bank and attended the opening concert, a programme of British music. The following day he paid an official visit to the South Bank Exhibition and many of the royal family joined him as, with the Queen, he looked at the exhibits in the large Dome of Discovery and the various pavilions. There was much to film. The organisers of the Millennium Dome of the year 2000 and other millennium projects would have done well to follow the example of the organisers of the 1951 Festival of Britain and its exhibitions. As the King said in his opening speech at St Paul's: 'The Festival was planned as a visible sign of national achievement ... a symbol of

Britain's courage and vitality ... a record of our national character and its history ....
activities and displays of lasting value which will maintain the prestige of our arts
and industries, proof of our world-renowned skill in design and craftsmanship ... and
the vital part played in industry by scientific imagination and research'. Such
sentiments were borne out in the exhibitions, which offered a wonderful picture of
British achievement past, present and with a look to the future, emphasising quality
and not quantity. The festival was a nationwide event with many pageants and
exhibitions in cities and villages all over the country. Although some areas other
than London were covered by the newsreels, we concentrated on the capital. The
large Dome of Discovery housed many intriguing records of British contributions
to scientific discovery. Among the fascinating exhibits in the Transport Pavilion was
a display of railway locomotives and a carriage of a tube train in which one could
open and shut the doors, an amusement for the adults as well as the children. Other
exciting pavilions were the Sea and Ships, the Lion and Unicorn, and Homes and
Gardens. The whole exhibition site was impressively floodlit at night and of
particular interest was the Skylon, a vertical structure which when floodlit and
viewed from the opposite side of the river appeared to be suspended in the air
without any visible means of support. Many of the exhibits were filmed, with my
efforts directed at following the royals in their numerous festival interests.
Altogether a very enjoyable few days both in filming and in seeing what the festival
offered.

Four days after the festival opened the King and Queen of Denmark paid a state
visit. For me this involved being at Victoria Station for their arrival and at Windsor
when the King of Denmark was installed as a Knight of the Garter. I will give more
details of what was involved in these ceremonies as they affected me in the next
chapter on my royal appointment.

Sadly, later in May, the King became unwell and was forced to cancel some
engagements. It was announced in June that his lung was troublesome and he was
advised to take a complete rest. His engagements in July were cancelled and he
went on holiday early in August, intending to return to London in October. This
reduced the number of royal events I was to cover and for a time I was assigned to
more general coverage. In July I was at Earls Court Stadium when Randolph Turpin
surprised the boxing fraternity by beating the famous Sugar Ray Robinson to
become the middleweight champion of the world. The fight went the full fifteen
rounds with Turpin winning seven on points and with three even. It was not a
spectacular fight and going right to the end meant exposing quite a lot of film.
Boxing was a real test of endurance then, before the number of rounds was
permanently reduced from fifteen to twelve.

One day our managing director and editor, Castleton-Knight, popularly known as
C.K., showman extraordinaire, came into the camera room very excited. I do not
know the exact circumstances as to how he came to make the deal but he told us he

had acquired a wonderful new film which the newsreel was going to splash in a big way. He had 25,000 feet of it and it was going to be used at once. It was infrared film. This was a specialist film used in aerial photography to cut through haze and to use at night. It had medical and scientific use and there was unconfirmed speculation that it could penetrate walls and, let it be whispered, peer through clothing. The only use one could see for it in the newsreel was perhaps for the odd special effect. We did not think C.K. would use it seriously in the reel. Experiments maybe, but not for stories. However he decided we should cover a race meeting in the 'fabulous infrared film' as it was to be billed. We tried to talk him out of it but he was adamant; no doubt he had to justify the purchase of the film. He chose a meeting with a pretty course and one attended by well-dressed racegoers. We duly filmed it, preceded by a great deal of publicity. As the film was used in daylight with normal lighting conditions we used very deep red filters in order to get a result. And what we got was a most peculiar effect and not entirely unpleasant. In some ways it was like a negative. The grass had an eerie pale look, the trees were white, faces were white and the sky was black. It appeared in the reel as publicised, and C.K., with the instincts of the showman, got away with it. We got very few complaints and even received some congratulations on an interesting film. Lucky C.K. His stunts always seemed to work. It was certainly an attempt to be different and in that he succeeded. However it was the only time infrared was used and I do not know what happened to the balance of the stock.

In September 1951 I was told by Gaumont that I was to cover the royal tour of Canada by Princess Elizabeth and the Duke of Edinburgh due to start in October. The King returned to London earlier than expected from his holiday at Balmoral. He was seen by his doctors in mid-September on account of a deterioration in the condition of his lung; it soon became apparent that he would have to have a serious operation. The Princess and the Duke were due to leave for Canada on 25 September by sea in the *Empress of France* but because of the King's health this was cancelled, and subject to the operation being successful they arranged to fly to Montreal to begin the tour as planned.

The operation on the King for 'lung resection' as officially announced (removal of the lung in lay terms) was carried out on the morning of 23 September at Buckingham Palace and a bulletin was posted on the Palace railings in the afternoon for the benefit of the large crowds waiting for news. I was there for a while to record the comings and goings to and from the Palace and the activities of the crowd and took it in turns with other cameraman to keep watch during those first vital hours after the operation. There were anxious days to the end of the month, and then at the beginning of October the bulletins stated that the King's condition was improving. With this news the Canadian tour, which had been delayed a week, was now set to begin on 8 October with the royal couple due to leave London Airport for Montreal on the night of the 7th. When it was decided in September that I was to go to Canada we held a number of meetings to work out how the visit would be covered. Now that we had confirmation that the tour was to go ahead we met again to finalise those earlier preparations deferred by the uncertainties which arose because of the King's health.

My coverage was not on rota as the other reels had not expressed an interest. This gave Gaumont a marvellous exclusive and as it transpired this was the last big occasion the Princess undertook before she became Queen. As we did not have to consider the other newsreels we decided at our meetings that we would try to operate a very fast service to the Canadian and British cinemas geared to getting my material back to London without delay, processing, editing and printing overnight with a reel back to Canada within two days and in Britain the following day. In Canada it would be shown at the next main stopping place on the tour with more copies following for showing in all the principal cities and towns. Although my coverage was not required by the other reels it was officially on rota and it had been agreed by Buckingham Palace that I was to travel across Canada on the royal train which simplified the problem of how to get from place to place and made possible the plan worked out with our production manager, the cinema managers and others throughout Canada and myself. This involved the cinema managers being on the platform of every agreed scheduled stop of the royal train, my handing them the

Princess Elizabeth and the Duke of Edinburgh arriving in Canada. From the newsreel.

exposed film and their sending it by local plane to the main Canadian airport where an agent would transship it to a transatlantic flight to London. It was a very ambitious, elaborate, organised plan which even today would be hard to beat. It was certainly one of the most difficult and demanding assignments I had ever undertaken. I had to have the exposed negative tinned up, labelled and with dope sheets ready at the agreed stations, sometimes with only short stops. On arrival I had to look for the cinema manager, hopefully identifiable, who would be at an agreed spot such as by the locomotive or the fifth carriage, hand over the film and then keep up with the tour. This had to be accomplished while the Princess was introduced to local dignitaries on the platform, sometimes inspecting a guard of honour, and it relied on a quick hand-over so that I could get to the car in which I was to travel in the procession before it moved off. The arrangements as planned worked absolutely perfectly. The cinema managers were very efficient, often spotting me before I saw them and they had the local plane ready for onward shipment of the film. It could not have been easy for them to get permission to be on the platform but no one missed out. It was as well we had pre-planned the tour in September before the King's operation as this gave us time to make the complex arrangements with those involved across the whole of Canada. Not one plane was missed – it really was a marvellous effort. My part in it almost gave me ulcers as sometimes I was left with only minutes to get to my car when the Princess had only a few people to meet and there was no other ceremony at the station.

I joined the royal train in Montreal. It was very luxurious. There were ten coaches – two for the Princess and Duke, some for the royal household, sleeping quarters, a club car, a dining car in which I ate with members of the royal staff, a lounge and an observation platform at the rear of the train. Shortly before we left Montreal I learned that the King and Queen had abandoned the Commonwealth tour due to start early in 1952 and that the Princess and Duke were to take their place. This journey through Canada on the royal train thus gave me an excellent opportunity to get my face known before 1952.

We arrived at Wolfe's Cove in Quebec province where General Wolfe had landed in 1739 to conquer Canada, but this time it was the place where the Princess started to conquer Canada by her charm and personality and where she had originally planned to begin her tour had she come by sea before the King's operation. Quebec City gave her a great welcome with large crowds who had come from all over the province. Everywhere, too, were vast numbers of Canadian, American and French photographers, cameramen, journalists, and radio commentators – 250 of them. I was the only newsreel cameraman from Britain and I had to struggle hard to film in that jostling mass, with all endeavouring to be first with their pictures and stories at this initial appearance of the royal couple. A hundred and twenty-five of them followed the royal train in a back-up train and I felt very privileged to be

153

travelling with the royal couple and to have an official place in a car in the royal processions.

So began that wonderful journey across the six provinces of that great country. It was a long first day in Quebec meeting people, speeches of welcome and replies by the Princess, sometimes in French, processions through the city, a large military parade and a drive through the old town with its narrow streets and shaded houses – the truly French area of Quebec. Then up to a high point above the St Lawrence river with marvellous views and finally a state banquet with the Princess looking very attractive and stunning in evening dress, diamonds, tiara and wearing the Garter star and ribbon.

As the train drew into the beautiful city of Ottawa in Ontario the next morning it was looking its best on a sunny day with the trees decorated with colourful red and gold autumn leaves, forming an effective backdrop to another great welcome as the royal couple drove through the crowded streets to a huge park where 12,000 children waited to greet them. Not having any supporting cameramen I had to work out how to get shots of processions through the crowded streets wherever we stopped. It was an essential part of my coverage to show the marvellous reception the Princess was receiving from the people in every province. It meant leaving my place in the procession at some point where there was a halt, moving ahead to somewhere near to where there would be a further stop, filming the approach through the cheering crowds and rejoining the procession before it moved off again. It was as well I had a very detailed programme to assist me in deciding where to leave and rejoin the processions.

Every city and town had its welcoming officials, its presentations, its speeches, its drive through the streets, its official lunch or dinner or state banquet and visits to the special features of the area. Toronto, one of the largest cities, gave a sort of ticker-tape welcome, showering the royal car with torn-up paper from the tall office buildings in what was said to be the richest street in Canada. The morning programme included a journey by train to Trenton, Canada's largest air station, stopping several times along the line. At one station the Princess met two Indian chiefs in full war dress, one wearing white-tipped eagle feathers and carrying a pipe of peace – very good for pictures. At Trenton the Princess and Duke were greeted by a boys' band wearing gold suits and blue trousers. A large air demonstration was staged including a fly-past of Canadian jet fighters. Back in Toronto they made a thirty-mile drive through the city and its outskirts in an open car on a cool day, watched a parade of 30,000 children, looked in on an ice-hockey match and ended the day with an official dinner.

After that long, very tiring day the couple made the one-and-a-half-hours' journey from Toronto to Niagara Falls for a more relaxing break. It was hot and sunny as they spent some time on a spur of rock looking down at the thirty-seven million gallons of water that flowed every minute over the Horseshoe Falls, falling 170 feet with a deafening roar to the rocks below. Clad in waterproof clothing the royal couple then descended by lift to a platform on a rock at the foot of the falls to stand covered with spray from the booming cascade of water. They enjoyed that very pleasant time off after a most hectic first week of the tour.

There were stops at several stations for short ceremonies and a number of unscheduled halts to enable the Princess to wave to the crowds which lined the railway on the way to Windsor on the Detroit River. Many Americans crossed the river to see the travellers, and the city of Detroit welcomed them by floodlighting all its skyscrapers. After a visit to the very large Ford Motor factory in Windsor the tour left Ontario to cross into Manitoba for Winnipeg. It was a breathtaking sight to see the size of that wheat-growing province as we passed across the vast prairies, and I got some good pictures from the observation platform of the train. It was cold in Winnipeg with some early snow falling. Fortunately officials had had the foresight to get a transparent roof made to fit over the open royal car to protect the couple from the bitingly cold wind. In spite of the cold and the snow people had come into the city from farms and homes many miles away to the north of the province. From this great grain centre, one of the largest in the world, situated on the banks of the Red River, the train steamed across another border into the province of Saskatchewan. Light snow covered the countryside, which looked like a giant Christmas card as we entered Regina, the headquarters of the Royal Canadian Mounted Police. To date we had only seen the police on motor bikes or in cars but here they were true 'Mounties' on horses. The Princess and Duke visited the riding school to see a special performance of their musical ride, very spectacular as they rode round in their scarlet tunics and flat-brimmed hats with pennants flying. More good pictures. The Princess had already received many gifts both for herself and for her children; here she was presented with pairs of beautiful caribou slippers for herself, Charles and Anne, made by Indians from the North. The Duke was given a pair of caribou gauntlets.

It continued to snow and was very cold as we left Regina for Alberta and one of the highlights of this memorable tour – Calgary. First the royal couple were greeted by 9,000 Indians in an Indian village. Some of the chiefs who met the Princess had the intriguing names of Maurice Many-Fingers of the Blood tribe and Chief Yellowhorn and Ben Calf Robe from the Blackfoot. Arriving at the stampede corral Indians with feathered head-dresses and wearing blankets of many colours welcomed the visitors, and braves performed a war dance to the beat of tom-toms. Then came the rodeo – bronco-busting, calf-roping, steer-riding and the climax – a race between covered wagons, something exclusive to Calgary. All these activities gave me many feet of superb film.

We left Calgary to pass through the Rockies on the last leg of the journey westwards to Vancouver in British Columbia. It was almost dark and the snow made it difficult to film anything other than an impression of the mountains, and when we

Princess Elizabeth and the Duke of Edinburgh with the Americans in Washington following their Canadian tour in 1951. From the newsreel.

ITN Archive/Reuters

came to pass through the most spectacular views it was quite dark. The weather was bad and rain persisted all the time the Princess was in Vancouver and later in Victoria on Vancouver Island, but she carried out a full programme and the crowds were as dense as ever and appeared undeterred by the wet.

A well-deserved break – a three-day holiday on Vancouver Island – preceded the second phase of the tour through that huge country. During this period we learnt that Churchill was back as Prime Minister after the Tories won the general election, albeit with a small majority. No Downing Street for me this time, however. On the way to Edmonton in Alberta we again passed through the Rockies, this time in the early evening with the sun still shining, and the following day at dawn and I was able to get some grand shots. Some time earlier I had put in a request through the Royal Household to get some pictures of the Princess in the cab of one of the locomotives. Permission came on this part of the journey and the Princess drove the train with the Duke as fireman, giving me some very intimate pictures. I was using a French camera for this tour – a LeBay – instead of my usual Newman Sinclair. It was very quiet and ideal for close shots of the royals and just right in the cab of the locomotive. It was a very light camera with a two-lens turret enabling me to change from wide-angle to close-up with no delay. It held 100-foot magazines which I sometimes found tricky as I had to carry a number of them pre-loaded and was constantly unloading and reloading the camera. This also meant a lot of tinning-up when I had to get the film away. Incidentally, the engine the Princess was driving was one of twenty-three locomotives used to pull the royal train on its journey west and east.

In Edmonton, the most northerly city of the tour, there were visits to an oil refinery and a floodlit football match before heading eastwards, with many un-planned stops for the crowds who, as elsewhere, had travelled many miles from outlying areas to see the Princess. At Port Arthur, back in Ontario, the royal couple saw one of the world's largest grain elevators with a capacity for ten million bushels of wheat. Among the many interesting processes they watched was the grading process and a ship being loaded with wheat.

Montreal was the last city to be visited before flying to Washington for a three-day visit to the USA. The crowds here were the largest of the tour and it was a very different Montreal from the first day of the tour when the royal couple had flown in from London. This time there were fourteen engagements in one of their busiest days since their arrival in Canada. In Washington they were met by President Truman and his wife and daughter. The streets were not decorated, as this was not a state visit. But it was an extremely tiring one. As usual in America the press were very much in evidence, recording receptions at the Canadian and British embassies. There was a meeting with Congress and over 1,500 people to shake hands with, plus official dinner parties.

On their return to Canada the couple went to Prince Edward Island where they embarked in a Canadian cruiser which took them to Newfoundland. There they joined the *Empress of Scotland* to return to England by sea. The royal train finished its journey in Charlottetown on Prince Edward Island and I made my arrangements to return to England by air after that most challenging and successful tour, not only for the Princess but also for our newsreel. It showed what could be done with superb organization and good teamwork. We received plaudits from the Canadian press and the *Daily Mirror* stated that the newsreels of the tour had been one of the biggest attractions in British cinemas. It described how we had got the films back to London and returned to Canada in record time, often beating the Americans at getting pictures on the screen, and it suggested that so popular were the newsreels that they should be made up into a ninety-minute film for global distribution. Praise indeed. I could not understand why the opposition had shown no interest in such a tour. I could have understood if they had not wanted rota coverage and perhaps covered part of the visit independently. As it was they gave us a wonderful exclusive. When I got back to London, Gaumont, which was not given to bonuses, gave me a rise in salary. Unexpected but very nice.

The four years had seen dramatic events which still affect us today, such as the inauguration of the NHS. For the newsreels there many good stories like the Olympiads, which continue to be staged in the new millennium. We filmed critical times that changed the lives of the royal family and shaped the future direction of the monarchy with the operation on the King, which led to his early death. For me my newsreel career was completely changed by my appointment as royal cameraman. Perhaps of most significance for the cinema newsreels was the increasing influence of television. More sets were being sold with the increase in programmes helped by the acquisition by the BBC of the Gainsborough Studios in Lime Grove, Shepherd's Bush, in London. Gaumont-British had been forced to move to the Rank Studios at Denham with the loss of the Gainsborough laboratories and editing facilities in London. For a while television screened both Gaumont and Movietone reels and there was even talk that we could make the BBC reel but everything was stopped by the Film Industry Exhibitors Association, which threatened to cancel bookings if we supported television. A changing time indeed. Colour enabled us to remain the dominant outlet for news on the screen for around ten years after the war.

At the close of 1951 I was preparing for the next big royal event – the six-month Commonwealth tour due to start early in 1952.

Chapter Nine
Royal Rota

The new year – 1952 – began in traditional manner in London. As they massed round the statue of Eros, the crowds in Piccadilly Circus were lit up by the brightness of the signs that shone down from the buildings all around, and some were lit up in the pubs that were still open. There were the annual bathers in Trafalgar Square, and fireworks, dancing and balloons added to the gaiety. The hotels and restaurants celebrated with fully booked parties and the Chelsea Arts Ball filled the Albert Hall with its own riotous merrymaking. But for me 1952 began in the shops. There is undoubted pleasure in spending someone else's money and I had been doing just that in the early days in January. I was getting together the things I would need for the six months of the Commonwealth tour. I required additional clothes suitable for living in the close environment of the royal yacht *Gothic*, including some for hot climates, and many small accessories which I might not be able to replace on a journey on the move. The expense sheet was like a bank account from which one could draw what was required. The newsreels were not parsimonious in their attitude to expenses. Paramount was the most generous; Gaumont was reasonable. One item often tried on new people joining a reel when helping them write their first expense sheet was 'taxi over Hungerford Bridge' – a pedestrian bridge across the Thames. I doubt whether anyone actually did claim that one. For the forthcoming tour my expenses were to be shared by all the reels, which was just as well as I was about to live free for six months – one of the perks of tours abroad.

For a long royal tour travelling with the royal party one's heavy baggage had to be left at Buckingham Palace to be sent with the royal and household luggage to the starting point of the tour – in this case it went to the *Gothic*, due to leave for Mombasa in the middle of January. My new suitcase was alongside an old one, there was a spare camera and thousands of feet of film stock was packed in suitable containers, all delivered to the trade door of the Palace, and looking splendid with special labels reading 'Royal Tour'.

As the departure date approached Princess Elizabeth and the Duke of Edinburgh left on 31 January to fly to Nairobi to stay at Nyeri, close to Nairobi, in a hunting lodge given to them by the people of Kenya as a wedding present. They had a number of engagements to carry out in Nairobi before going to the lodge, where they intended to spend a few days prior to joining the *Gothic* on 7 February for the start of the tour. My passport, medical checks, money arrangements and everything that had to be done for a long stay away, both personal and for the company, were in order and with goodbyes said I set out to fly from Heathrow to Kenya with my colleagues who were also on the tour – two agency journalists, Louis Nickolls and Ronnie Gomer-Jones from the Press Association and Exchange Telegraph, who were permanently accredited to the Palace like me, although my permanent accreditation had still to be confirmed. We embarked in the *Gothic* in Mombasa on 5 February. Most of the royal household were also in the ship and we all settled down for a fabulous tour and to await the arrival of the Princess.

On the following morning, 6 February, one of the journalists received an early call from his London office with the shattering news that the King had died. The senior household member on the ship was immediately informed and he telephoned Nairobi to ask Michael Parker, the Duke's private secretary, to tell the Duke to pass the news to the Princess. She was resting in the Treetops Hotel, where she had been observing the wild animals during the night and would not yet be aware that her father was dead. In the *Gothic* and in Nairobi the royal staff had to make immediate arrangements for the Princess, now Queen, to return to London, and we were told that the tour was cancelled.

Everything now was in reverse. We had to arrange flights back to London, while our baggage in the *Gothic* would be returned to Buckingham Palace. Few words were spoken as we packed up, hardly able to take in the anticlimax that had struck so suddenly. It took a long time to overcome the trauma of having to return to England in such tragic circumstances. One can only imagine what it must have been like for the new Queen about to undertake such an important visit to the Commonwealth countries, and for all those countries who had to cancel the elaborate arrangements they had made to receive her. They had already had to reorganise much of the tour when the Princess took the place of the King who was to have been the visitor in the original plan. I suppose, looking back, it was fortunate that it happened when it did. We could have been halfway across the Indian Ocean and that would have caused immense problems for everyone to return to London.

From the heat of Mombasa, just south of the equator, it was back to the chill February days we had left behind, a trauma in itself as we changed from our light clothes to heavy suits and overcoats. In London the newsreels had been filming the return of the new Queen and the public proclamations of her accession to the throne at ceremonies at Temple Bar and in the City, and at the lying-in-state in Westminster Hall with very long queues stretching from Westminster Bridge along the Embankment to Lambeth Bridge.

The state funeral took place on 15 February with all the sombre pageantry that the death of a King engenders. The cortege, a mile long, left Westminster Hall with the gun carriage, pulled by naval ratings, carrying the coffin surmounted with the crown, the orb and the sceptre. Ahead were various dignitaries on foot and bands playing Chopin's funeral march. Behind the coffin was the carriage with the Queen, the Queen Mother and Princess Margaret followed by the royal dukes, including the Duke of Windsor, walking together. The solemn procession passed along Whitehall, The Mall, and into Hyde Park to Marble Arch and on to Paddington station. Here the coffin and principals were taken by train to Windsor and then in another procession to St George's Chapel for the funeral service and burial. Everyone on our staff was engaged on this mournful occasion. I had returned in time to join this coverage and as there were no special facilities for royal rota I filmed from one of the positions on the route to Paddington. It was not an assignment I had expected to be undertaking just a few days earlier and it took a while to readjust, and for the Queen no doubt more so, but her training stood her in good stead as she undertook all the meetings and duties she had to perform on becoming Queen Elizabeth II. In the way fortune operates I had drawn a different card. I was now royal cameraman to a queen instead of a king.

In July there was another passing: Eva Peron, who inspired Lloyd Webber's musical *Evita*, died in Argentina. And another sad farewell as the last tram which ran from Woolwich to New Cross ended its days also in July and was mourned by thousands of Londoners. But July for me was an important month. Commander Richard Colville informed the Newsreel Association that the Queen wished for a permanent royal rota cameraman to be accredited to Buckingham Palace and that I should be appointed to that office. Although the reels obviously could not ignore this request it caused some problems at first as, other than Gaumont, they were opposed to my remaining in my present employment. To overcome this and the difficulties that arose with my pension and the way I would operate on a permanent basis it was eventually decided to form a new company – a subsidiary of the Newsreel Association to be called British Newsreel Association Services Ltd. Its terms of reference were 'to provide a cameraman and the necessary service to film the activities of the Queen and other members of the Royal Family, Her Majesty having expressed the wish that one man known to her should be appointed by the Newsreel Association for that purpose. The company would also have the authority to extend these activities to filming outstanding national and other important events on behalf of the Newsreel Association.' It was really quite something to have a company formed just to employ me because the newsreels could not agree to having one company enjoying the prestige of a royal cameraman. So now, permanently accredited, my duties were to film only rota stories, but if major stories other than royal activities were required, a royal story would take precedence. When the special company was eventually formed arrangements were made for BBC Television to be supplied with my coverage. I then had the unique experience of taking pictures for television as well as for the cinema newsreels. To the best of my knowledge no one had ever done that before or has done subsequently, that is, filming specific assignments for both media. Television later supplied us with sections from the big occasions when they had the rights but were not covering specifically for us. It was also my responsibility, when necessary, to make the arrangements if a story required additional cameramen.

Each week it became my business to go to Buckingham Palace to see Colville to be briefed on forthcoming events. In most cases I was told in confidence before they were publicly announced so I could plan ahead. Generally, also in confidence, I could inform the newsreels of future stories so they could decide what they wanted covered. Sometimes there were occasions when I had to keep the news to myself for a while. I would go to the Palace just after the Changing of the Guard in the morning, drive through the gates and park near the Privy Purse door on the right of the Palace and would be conducted through the carpeted corridors to the Commander's office, which overlooked the gardens. Until I got used to this procedure I must admit I felt quite important as I approached the Palace and was ushered through the gates by the duty policemen, who got to know me. That wore off! However, of course, it *was* a privilege to be briefed in this way.

Perhaps I should explain something of the background the newsreels experienced in filming the royals before royal rota and the appointment of such as myself. In my early days in the 1930s the royal family was kept in cotton wool. In the course of normal work a cameraman found it extremely difficult to get close to a royal personage when filming a royal event, necessitating the use of telephoto lenses to get a reasonably intimate shot. Sometimes the Foreign Office wanted something filmed, perhaps a state visit that was particularly politically sensitive. Facilities were offered but nothing very special and certainly nothing 'behind the scenes'. The result was that there were constant attempts to get an off-guard picture. The reels then were a filming paparazzi. At a hunt meeting a cameraman did get the Prince of Wales falling off his horse at a jump. The Prince was furious at being filmed. All this of course led to bad feelings and tension. There was some relaxation and cooperation at charity functions such as a film show, but generally our coverage of the royal family was at large public functions like Trooping the Colour, the state opening of Parliament, the Derby and Royal Ascot – events in the public domain. Everyone filmed and photographed these but they did not include any facility out of the public eye. It was a strange period, for the royals were very popular and the public always turned out in large numbers whenever they appeared. Possibly they and their advisers thought there was no need to make any further gestures. The monarchy was surrounded in mystique; their private lives were private. There had to come a change and the war did it. As I said in the previous chapter a pool system was started whereby everyone's filmed material taken on active service was available to all. There had been occasions pre-war when space was limited and there was only room for one camera when the event was pooled and this became known as the rota system. Royal rota came into being during the war when it became necessary to appoint one man to accompany the King in order to

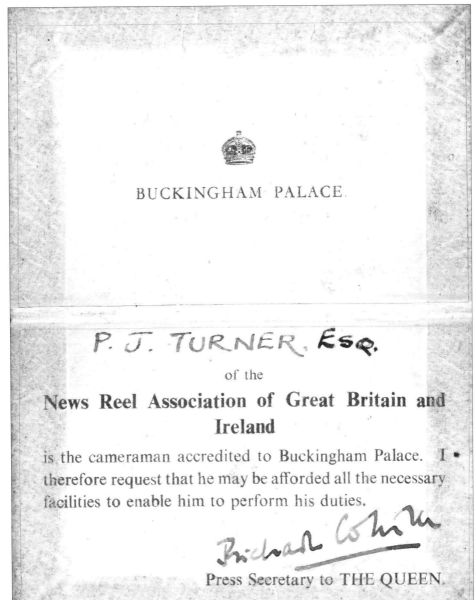

BUCKINGHAM PALACE.

P. J. TURNER, Esq.

of the

News Reel Association of Great Britain and Ireland

is the cameraman accredited to Buckingham Palace. I therefore request that he may be afforded all the necessary facilities to enable him to perform his duties.

Richard Colville

Press Secretary to THE QUEEN.

My pass to the front of the queue.

keep his movements secret, a temporary arrangement at first but which became permanent at the King's request. From then on we began to get more informal pictures of the royals. When I became the royal cameraman I was always allowed to work very close to them, but it was some while before I got the kind of pictures the newsreels wanted, namely off-duty shots. Of course that was only the beginning of the opening-up of royal lives we see today. Television documentaries and radio programmes and some newspapers have changed attitudes to the royals – very different from my time. My job would not carry the same prestige today as it did in the 1950s.

Royal rota was not an easy job. I was faced with a divided loyalty. In the ordinary course of events when royalty was not involved our duty was to record everything as intelligently as possible without any question of censoring what we took. Our job was to get the picture whether nice or nasty. That did not mean we had to be tough or cause distress but it was necessary to get what was happening, which often meant filming incidents which might be questionable. If one exercised restraint too rigidly the picture could be lifeless and dull. It was an editor's job to decide what went into a reel and to avoid the distasteful. When filming one had to rely on his good sense and generally this worked out satisfactorily. There *were* editors who were not too held back, and the cameraman usually got the flack in such cases. But when it came to royal rota it was a different situation. I had five editors to think about. I had somehow to play the game on both sides. It was a question of compromise and common sense but in some respects royal rota was a disadvantage to the newsreels for compromise often had to be weighted in the royals' favour. The newsreels would expect wonders; the Palace would expect restraint. I had always to remember that I was at an event to film a special part of it and I was trusted to observe Palace protocol and not to take advantage of my privileged position by taking something that could be embarrassing. I was there to get as intimate a picture as possible and that was acceptable, as Colville told me. Sometimes the royals could be very relaxed and generally I could film them, for they knew I would not intentionally take them in a compromising situation – difficult sometimes when one considered how one had been trained. However I was well aware that if I did take an off-guard shot it was likely to appear in one of the reels. There might be a very windy day which revealed a great deal of a royal lady's underwear. While I might take such a shot unwittingly I had to take care not to wait for it to happen as I might have done with someone less exalted. If such a shot was taken I had to hope the editors would not make it difficult for me. I must say the principals on both sides were always very understanding and I am glad to say I did not have too bad a time. I was personally treated with the greatest courtesy and support from both the Palace and the reels.

So back to 1952 and stories other than royal. Elizabeth Taylor married Michael Wilding, a wedding which drew large crowds who were no doubt glad to partake in a happy occasion. Newcastle beat Arsenal in the Cup Final. A de Havilland Comet made the first passenger flight to Johannesburg. The American ship *United States* won the Atlantic Blue Riband. There was trouble in Egypt and in Kenya the Mau Mau were causing mayhem, murdering white farmers in an effort to drive Europeans from Kenya. Sir Stafford Cripps, much involved in the negotiations leading to India's independence, died in Switzerland. All stories during the year which kept the newsreels and their associates busy in presenting world events as well as the domestic scene.

All the Queen's activities, being firsts, had an interest in a new reign, but, understandably, there were few major royal stories with the coronation due to take place in 1953, and the reels concentrated on other news for a while. The Queen changed places with the Queen Mother, moving from Clarence House to Buckingham Palace. However, the year had more than its fair share of disasters and tragedies. Some of these required a full turn out of staff. They were not on rota but as the new company would not be formed until 1953 and I was still at Gaumont I was given permission to be available for these stories providing always if a royal story was required it would take precedence. The year began with the sinking of the *Flying Enterprise*. Then came the King's death. Nine inches of rain fell on Exmoor in a day, flooding a very large area. It caused rivers to overflow, including the West Lyn whose swollen waters cascaded down on to the small resort of Lynmouth completely destroying it, and over thirty people lost their lives. Standing on the steep Countisbury Hill which descended into Lynmouth it was unbelievable to see what had happened. Hardly a house still stood, much of the town had been washed info the sea, and it was a problem to know where to begin to film such a scene.

At Farnborough Air Show, always a spectacular event, a de Havilland 110 fighter had just broken the sound barrier when it fell to pieces, killing the test pilot. One of the engines dropped on to the dense crowd killing twenty-six of them and injuring sixty-five. One cameraman had a narrow escape, as he was close to the area where the plane fell. I was in Scotland at the end of September to film John Cobb's attempt to break the water speed record on Loch Ness. I was alongside Jock Gemmell of Pathe on the south side of the loch opposite Drumnadrochit where Cobb had his headquarters. We were set up and waiting because Cobb was going to make his run as soon as conditions were right. I was suddenly recalled to London. The next day Cobb made his attempt and Jock got an exclusive scoop as the speedboat *Crusader* disintegrated right in front of his camera and Cobb was killed. Thus each newsreel has its luck – and its disappointments. There came a little light relief after this when Charlie Chaplin arrived in London after twenty-three years away and was mobbed wherever he went.

Then came the worst of the series of disasters in October with the terrible train crash at Harrow station. The sleeping-car express from Scotland, ninety minutes late, ran into the back of the Watford-to-Euston local train standing at the station platform, throwing wreckage across another line into which a second express from Euston with two engines ploughed at 60 m.p.h. One locomotive and the local train were buried beneath a ghastly mass of twisted metal thirty feet high, which demolished the Harrow footbridge across the line. We were used to tragedies, seeing the results of major road crashes, air crashes and train smashes, but this was one of the grimmest I ever had to cover. A hundred and twelve passengers were killed and over 200 injured. All the pathetic signs of a major disaster were there – handbags, brief cases, raincoats, clothing and tickets lying by the track – journeys finished abruptly. Who knows to whom they belonged, whether they were on their way to work, to happiness, to meet someone or whatever. On such occasions one realises how frail is the human body as I witnessed the sickening scene of pieces of victims placed in bins by the gallant rescuers and as stretcher after stretcher was put into ambulances, most with the shattered remains of some unfortunate traveller. There was the bewildered survivor, her face covered in blood, and the weeping man, his clothes torn to pieces. Those men and women who were involved in the rescue of victims and the removal of the dead were heroes indeed – railwaymen, firemen, voluntary civilians and the medical people. Everything had to be filmed, for such horrors were part of the job, and as always one tried not to get involved emotionally and one hoped that much of what one took would not get into the reel. Nevertheless I came away from Harrow with a heavy heart and very sad. I have never been able to understand the ghouls who stop to see these awful accidents. To have to witness them in the course of one's job was a degrading experience; to voluntarily stand and stare – beyond comprehension.

From that terrible event I was glad to get back to filming royalty. On 4 November the Queen opened Parliament. I was at the entrance to the Lords to get close-ups when the Queen, the Duke and other royals arrived to enter the House. At that time the state drive and my shots were as much as we got of the opening of Parliament. A few years later, with the aid of television, we were able to film the splendid pageantry inside. The year ended on a gloomy note; dense fogs and smog caused, it was reported, 4,000 deaths. I was not sorry to see the year depart but 1953 did not begin on a high note.

Abnormal tides coupled with strong gales created havoc at the end of January. Sea defences gave way in low-lying areas along the east coast causing disastrous floods. Canvey Island was almost completely under water drowning 100 people trapped in their houses and bungalows; hundreds of caravan dwellers and residents had their homes washed away near Woolwich in the Thames estuary. There were few coastal towns from Yorkshire down to Kent that were untouched and hundreds lost their lives. The Queen and Duke spent several hours visiting flooded areas in King's Lynn and other parts of Norfolk, as they were staying at Sandringham. I did not film them for there was no official car and it would have been impossible to keep up with them without one. I did cover some of the flooded areas in Essex and devastating it was. The services were mobilised to help rescue people and to fill sandbags throughout the night. Pictures from the air showed the true scale of the floods. There was not a green field to be seen all along the coast. It is unfortunately true that the worst disasters always provided the most dramatic pictures for the newsreels and we had plenty of these in the last months.

When not on domestic tours or overseas the royal routine was usually to spend the Christmas break at Windsor followed by a stay at Sandringham until February, when they would return to London for their public engagements during the spring and summer. August and September were spent at Balmoral after which they were back in London again for more engagements until the end of the year. So with the Queen at Sandringham I was able to meet some of the household and staff still in London in the early part of the year on less formal occasions than when on duty. Commander Colville's number two, Anne Hawkins, was always very helpful. I had met many of the senior members of the households when filming so an opportunity to meet some of them off the road was very pleasant. Martin Charteris, assistant private secretary to the Queen, and later to be knighted, was a very charming man and always very friendly. I very much liked Sir Martin Gilliatt, the Queen Mother's private secretary, and her press secretary, John Griffin, delightful hosts over a drink. Admiral Bonham-Carter in the Duke's household was another of my favourites. He sometimes referred to me as 'extra equerry' and marvelled at the weight of my camera. Commander Colville was later knighted to become Sir Richard Colville KCVO. Some people thought he was too autocratic and unhelpful. I did not find him to be like that and got on well with him. As I came to know him better we used to meet in the evening, precisely at six, to go to the Ritz cocktail bar, sometimes at his invitation, sometimes at mine. We both drank gin, his was always neat, mine was pink. I suppose the navy was responsible for that. In ships it was always the cheapest drink – not so at the Ritz. All these officials helped me in various ways to make a success of my appointment. There were two individuals who figured very much in my world when I was filming. They were the detectives of the Queen and Duke. Chief Superintendent Clark was the Queen's detective at first but Chief Superintendent Perkins took over from him and was there for most of the time I was royal cameraman. The Duke's detective was Superintendent Frank Kelley. They were very important, for if I was pushed aside or stopped from moving near to the royal by a policeman or official who did not know why I was there the detectives would come to my rescue and bring me forward to the position I sought. Perkins was sometimes a little pompous but never restrictive. Kelley was what one might call a buddy, and when staying away somewhere either in Britain or overseas we would often have a drink together in the evening when he was not on duty.

After the floods preparations were in hand for the coming coronation of the Queen in June. We were regularly filming anything that suggested a coronation was approaching – street decorations, designs for special robes. There were meetings to fix camera positions on the processional routes and in Westminster Abbey, alongside television on many of these. The abbey positions were rota and the most experienced cameramen from all the reels were assigned to that very important job.

I think Peter Cannon from Gaumont and Henry Hawkins from Paramount were two chosen. I could not have undertaken that rota position because I was not used to the cameras required to film such an occasion. But there were still dark days to come before the sun came out. Early in March Stalin died in Russia, which meant an obituary in the newsreel, but I do not recall our receiving any footage from Moscow. Then on 24 March Queen Mary died. Again, so soon after the funeral of King George VI we were once more filming a solemn procession, this time from Marlborough House to Westminster Hall for the lying-in-state.

The gun carriage was used again to carry the coffin of Queen Mary. There were no more processions after this as there were for the King. The coffin was taken privately to St George's Chapel in Windsor where the funeral and burial took place. I did not go to Windsor. I was at Marlborough House and Westminster Hall.

In spite of this setback the Queen managed to carry out a number of important engagements before June. That kept me busy. In April Winston Churchill was created a Knight of the Garter but because of the arrangements for the coronation the customary splendid procession through the castle precincts to the service in St George's Chapel did not take place. Also in April the Queen launched the new royal yacht *Britannia* from John Brown's shipyard on the Clyde. The Duke had laid the keel in 1952 and he was with the Queen for the launching. It was a very wet day but the many employees and families of the ship's builders invited to the ceremony seemed to enjoy the occasion, singing lustily as the band played 'Rule Britannia' as the ship went down the slipway. At the beginning of May the Queen and Duke were at the Cup Final. It was a memorable match in which the legendary Stanley Matthews starred, his team Blackpool beating Bolton by four goals to three, the winner scored in the last minute. A week later new colours were presented to the Grenadier Guards by the Queen at Buckingham Palace. It was quite a spectacular ceremony. The old colours were trooped for the last time and marched slowly off parade to a subdued 'Auld Lang Syne'. Four new colours were then consecrated. Also in May the Duke received his 'wings' and was able to fly solo. Rehearsals and the final preparations for the coronation filled the remainder of May. Our own preparations for filming were finalised and everyone was in their positions in the early hours of 2 June. I was at Buckingham Palace.

The weather did not fit the occasion. The skies were not bright with sun but clothed in the white and grey of cumulus clouds and as the day progressed the rains began to drench but not dampen the large crowds that lined the processional routes or were in the specially built stands on the way to and from Westminster Abbey. We had a special stand built on the Victoria Memorial to film the departure and return of the Queen at Buckingham Palace and for the appearances on the balcony. The stand was in two tiers and quite long, for it had to accommodate all the newsreels, television and the photographers from all the Fleet Street newspapers. Everyone had telephoto lenses, so it must have looked quite daunting from the Palace balcony.

The Queen in the state coach in 1953 on the coronation processional route. From the newsreel.

ITN Archive/Reuters

This stand was built for every major state occasion but was made larger for the coronation to make room for increased television and radio, there in force. This and all the stands on the routes were built by the Ministry of Works, the positions agreed at our earlier meetings. The costs were shared by all the users. For our cameramen on the processional routes the rain made filming difficult. Covers over the cameras became sodden and they were continually wiping lenses and viewfinders praying that the rains would ease when the procession reached them. Judging from the end result they managed to overcome these difficulties.

In 1937 at King George VI's coronation we had received complaints that each camera had only filmed the same sections of the processions, i.e. the coach with the King and the immediate parts of the pageantry in front of and behind the coach. This time everyone certainly had to film a similar section with the queen in the gold coach as a protection against camera trouble at other positions. Apart from that each cameraman was given a specific part of the procession to film with the proviso to film anything unexpected. One such highlight was the Tongan Queen Salote, a dignified figure who sat in an open carriage in the rain waving to the crowds, who responded to her unselfish gesture with enthusiastic cheers. They loved her.

In addition to the newsreel coverage, Castleton-Knight, ever resourceful, made a film of the coronation in Technicolor entitled A QUEEN IS CROWNED and had it in the cinemas in just a few days. It was a remarkable achievement with wonderful cooperation from Technicolor and it beat all opposition efforts both in superb colour and overall coverage. The cinemas and newsreel theatres were well patronised to see C.K.'s film and the newsreel coverage which included many of the festive scenes which carried on well into the night. When the Queen was back in the Palace the crowds made their way through the West End to see the decorations, which were magnificent. In the evening there were fireworks over the Thames and all important buildings were floodlit. Although it was unnaturally cold for a June day and the rain continued to fall at intervals all day and into the night, it did not deter a vast throng from massing outside the Palace, along the Mall and in St James's Park to hear the Queen's broadcast which was relayed through speakers at strategic points, and later to cheer the Queen and her family when they appeared several times on the floodlit balcony. It was indeed a joyous day even for a number of bedraggled, very damp technicians who arrived very late at night at Denham laboratories with their evening's efforts. The daytime coverage was already processed and in the cutting rooms with the editor. Insofar as television was concerned we had the advantage of colour whereas all their coverage was in black and white, but the coronation was a major advance for them as they were able to show the complete ceremony in the Abbey as it happened.

Just four days later the Queen was at the Derby. This was styled the Coronation Derby and thousands of racegoers turned out to cheer the royal party when they arrived to drive down the course to the grandstand. The Queen had a horse in the race and everyone wanted it to win. But it was Sir Victor Sassoon's horse, Pinza, ridden by Gordon Richards, which was the winner, with the Queen's horse, Auriole, coming in second. Although this was disappointing for the crowd and the Queen it was nevertheless a popular win on account of Gordon Richards. Only a few days earlier he had been knighted, and although he had won almost every other classic race this was his first Derby win. A memorable week for him and he got a great reception as he rode into the winner's enclosure.

Over the next two months, following this one day of relaxation, the Queen, supported by her husband, embarked on a daunting series of engagements related to her coronation. They began with drives in London to give the ordinary citizens of the city a chance to see them from their own doorsteps, and very popular they proved to he. The boroughs were divided into four areas, north, east, south and west, with the drives, in an open limousine, taking place over four afternoons, each lasting just over two hours. Islington, Knightsbridge, Hammersmith, Peckham,

Greenwich, Hackney, Stepford and Bermondsey were among the places visited. There were stops at town halls to greet the mayors, town clerks and council members of each borough. Every street and home was gaily decorated with bunting, photographs, flowers and flags. There were nurses outside their hospitals with patients wheeled out in their beds, there were schoolchildren by their schools, workmen in overalls, and in some places there were bands which played the national anthem as the car passed by. It was an imaginative undertaking for it brought every type of Londoner from the well-to-do to the poorest in the East End into close contact with the monarchy and they showed their appreciation by the very large, cheering turn-out.

On 15 June it was down to Portsmouth for the review of the fleet at Spithead. The Queen and Duke were in HMS *Surprise*, normally used by the C-in-C Mediterranean, and converted for this exercise into a royal yacht. Rain had been forecast but it held off and the review was held in sunshine. Each reel had men strategically placed, some in ships, some on the shore. I was in a ship following the *Surprise* filming on rota. There were no press aboard the royal yacht as the Queen had spent the night before the review in the ship and was joined the following morning by the Queen Mother, Princess Margaret and other family members. Over 200 ships of all kinds were assembled at Spithead. Dressed overall, with flags streaming from masts in the high winds, they were a marvellous sight. Pride of place was given to the battleship HMS *Vanguard* where in the evening the Queen was entertained to dinner in the company of many admirals and captains from the British, foreign and Commonwealth ships. There were eight aircraft carriers, plus cruisers, destroyers, frigates, minesweepers, submarines, merchant ships, overseas ships and the many smaller vessels that made up the navy. Sailors, lined up on each ship, cheered and bands played the national anthem as the *Surprise* steamed past. All round the edges of the fleet were small yachts, big yachts and ferries, their crews and passengers joining in the cheering as the royal yacht came into view. It took nearly two hours to complete the review which ended with a fly-past of 300 Fleet Air Arm planes headed by helicopters. In the evening the fleet was illuminated, each ship outlined against the darkness of the sky and with a big firework display adding to the spectacle. This was Royal Ascot week, a must for the Queen, and she and the Duke left Portsmouth the morning following the review for Windsor to meet her guests at the castle. Shortly after arriving she left for the races with them driving in open carriages along the course to the royal enclosure. In the evening the Queen went on the river to Eton College to watch a procession of boats and their coronation firework display. My colleagues and I had returned to London after the review with our negatives and arrived very late being caught in the streams of cars leaving Portsmouth for London but we managed to get to Ascot for the racing and more pictures of the royals.

After Ascot I travelled to Scotland to prepare for the Queen's coronation visit to Edinburgh and Glasgow starting on 24 June, another major occasion. The Queen and Duke arrived by train at Waverley station. Greeted by the Lord Provost and other officials, the Queen was presented with the keys of the city, which she returned to the Lord Provost for safekeeping (this was part of my coverage). There was then a state drive to Holyrood House, the official royal residence in Scotland. Eight members of the Royal Scots Greys on horseback in scarlet dress and bearskins led the procession. Then came the Household Cavalry with coaches with heralds in full regalia preceding the royal coach. Everywhere, as in all these coronation engagements, there were large cheering crowds. Later in the day there were visits to various functions in the city. The next day there was another state drive, from Holyrood to St Giles' Cathedral, for a service of thanksgiving and dedication. This time the royal coach was preceded by two carriages carrying the Honours of Scotland – the Crown, the Sword and the Sceptre. Royal archers of the Queen's Bodyguard for Scotland escorted both the royal coach and the Honours. I was at St Giles' for close-ups and other cameras covered the state drives. A visit to Glasgow followed where the crowds were almost uncontrollable in their enthusiasm. Whenever the Queen was in Scotland at that time huge crowds always greeted her, as they regarded her as their Scottish queen. As their car approached George Square opposite the City Chambers outside which a guard of honour was drawn up, the crowd broke through barriers and surrounded the car, and the Queen was only just able to manoeuvre round the guard for her inspection. Difficult to film. But she enjoyed it all, waving later to the masses from a window in the chambers and smiling in appreciation of the affection shown to her. Another successful day as in Edinburgh in this round of coronation events.

Early in July we filmed a very large parade of over 60,000 ex-servicemen and servicewomen sailors, soldiers, RAF and the nursing services, held in Hyde Park. The Queen and Duke drove round the assembled ranks, among them a group of Old Contemptibles from the First World War. After addressing the parade the Queen took the salute, with bands playing as each section marched past. It was an event which aroused emotions, pride, poignancy and nostalgia and was well deserving of the royal accolade.

Another service event followed with the review of the Royal Air Force at Odiham in Hampshire. It was a great display of our air power. On the ground were 300 aircraft and all the equipment and types of vehicles used by the RAF. All were inspected by the Queen following a march past by units from RAF commands from all over the country. I was there for close-ups. Then came a fantastic fly-past of more than 600 aircraft of all types – helicopters, flying boats, jet and piston planes, bombers – flying at different speeds but managing to pass overhead in a continuous line. It took half an hour for all to fly by. That was in the middle of July. After this the royal family went to Scotland, to Balmoral, for a well-deserved holiday and to prepare for the postponed, long Commonwealth tour due to take place from November 1953 to May 1954. I had been advised some time earlier before it was made public that the tour was to take place and that I would be going, so I also took a holiday and made preparations for six months overseas.

British Newsreels Association Services, my new company, was finally formed and I had to say goodbye to Gaumont-British. It was sad to be leaving a company that had treated me well for sixteen years. They were a very friendly bunch of cameramen, sound men and news staff and I got on well with Castleton-Knight. There was no jealousy whenever I was given a prestigious assignment or when I became royal cameraman. Everyone was generous when one did well and understanding if things went wrong. We got on well with each other's wives and friends and whenever there was cause for celebration everyone joined in. My new office was in the Newsreel Association building in Soho Square. At first it was rather lonely with no mates around anymore. I shared an office with a pleasant girl with titled parents, the secretary to the Newsreel Association's company secretary. I was desk-bound for quite a lot of my time, arranging future royal visits, going to each reel in turn for extra cameramen, but occasionally slipping away for a lunch with someone I needed to persuade to give us some special facility. The servicing of my equipment and the supply of film and accessories was taken care of by each company in turn on a rota basis. One thing I did miss was car parking facilities. Gaumont rented a large section of the second floor in a nearby garage to house the trucks and our private cars. In the congested streets of Soho, even in those early days, this was a great boon. A motor mechanic was also employed to keep the cars serviced and that was helpful too. Other reels had parking arrangements but space was tight with no room for an extra car. Fortunately with the royal job I usually knew where I was going each day and did not always need a car to hand. When I did I became adept at finding parking places.

The year passed quickly and the day came when I packed my bags for the start of the six-month tour of the Commonwealth, which began for me in the Caribbean in Jamaica. I stood on the balcony of my room in the luxurious Montego Bay Hotel on a reasonably cool morning to look across a lovely wide sandy bay to the deep blue sea of the Caribbean and was pleasantly warmed by the tropical sun as it rose to begin its special day over Jamaica. It was November. Nearly two years earlier I had prepared for this Commonwealth tour and was in Kenya when it was aborted by the death of the King. Now it was on the royal agenda again. The four of us permanently accredited to the Palace, the two agency reporters, Godfrey Talbot of the BBC and myself, had not gone to Bermuda where the Queen spent just one day after leaving London on 23 November. We left England on a cold winter's day for sunny Jamaica and were in Montego to await the Queen's arrival on the island. She was due to carry out some engagements before embarking in the *Gothic*, berthed at the capital Kingston, to begin the long journey across the seas to New Zealand

The *Gothic*.

and Australia, the two major countries of her Commonwealth tour. Fortified with one of the hotel's splendid rum punches and almost in holiday mood I went to the airport to film the Stratocruiser landing and the Queen and Duke welcomed by the island's officials. After inspecting a guard of honour with the Jamaican military band at full blast she met envoys and delegates from the other West Indian islands – Grenada, St Lucia, St Vincent, Barbados, Antigua, Montserrat and the British Virgin Islands. It was a very colourful Caribbean scene.

While the Queen was making her way along the north coast I went ahead on part of the route she was to take on her way to Kingston and passed canefields soon to be harvested to be turned into sugar, an important product in Jamaica's economy. I passed, too, an area of rich bauxite lands, some of the largest deposits in the Commonwealth. On arrival in the capital I fixed on points where I would film the Queen's engagements in the city and then joined the *Gothic*. As before, all our heavy baggage had been delivered to Buckingham Palace and mine was now safely deposited in my cabin. As I unpacked this time I offered a short prayer that the tour would go ahead successfully. Although places had been added to the itinerary most of the things I had acquired in 1952 were fortunately still suitable for this tour.

The *Gothic* was a one-funnelled ship which normally made sailings carrying passengers and cargo from the UK to Australia and New Zealand and had a speed of just under twenty knots. Now converted into a royal yacht the royal apartments were situated in the after part of the ship on the boat and promenade decks. The original dining room on the saloon deck was divided into two, with the royal dining room on the starboard side, and a dining room for the royal staff, the ship's officers and us four press on the port side. The normal passenger lounge had been divided in a similar way. Everyone had a separate cabin. The royal party included Lady Pamela Mountbatten and Lady Egerton, ladies-in-waiting to the Queen; Sir Michael Adeane, the Queen's private secretary; Lieutenant-Commander Michael Parker, the Duke's private secretary; Colonel Martin Charteris, assistant private secretary to the Queen; Commander Colville, press secretary; and Surgeon-Commander Steele-Perkins, the medical officer. There were equerries, secretarial staff and Bobo Macdonald, the Queen's personal maid, who was always with the Queen wherever she was and was a law unto herself. And of course there were the two private detectives, on this tour Messrs Clark and Kelley. So I was in good company and settled in with those who had joined the *Gothic* ahead of the Queen. After the engagements in Kingston and with the Queen, the Duke and the remainder of the royal party aboard, we left Jamaica in the evening of 27 November to cross the Caribbean for Panama accompanied by the escort cruiser HMS *Sheffield*.

I had not realised how close Panama was to South America. The Panama Canal was absorbingly interesting. I had read the history of the canal, how it was built, begun by the French in 1881, and of the corruption and delays and of the many deaths from yellow fever until it was opened in 1914. It really was a wonderful experience quite apart from providing some worthwhile pictures. We stopped at Christobal, the Atlantic terminal, with the Royal Marine band on board playing as we docked. I filmed the activities around the *Gothic* as the president of the Republic, Colonel Remon, and British and American officials came aboard to pay their respects to the Queen. As the royal couple left the ship the Queen inspected a guard of honour formed from America's three armed services. It was extremely hot and humid as it was the wet season, but the rains kept off and the sun shone down mercilessly on the Queen as she drove with the president into the nearby town of Colon in an open car. In streets lined with many old wooden houses a huge, excited cheering crowd almost stopped the car as they climbed over the barriers and pushed and shoved to try to get close to the royal couple. At the town hall where the Queen met the mayor there was another great welcome with the police having the utmost difficulty holding back the surging mass of people. The American authorities and the Panamanians had really done their best to make the visit a happy and splendid occasion and the populace fully responded; every street, house and shop was gaily decorated and most of the crowd carried flags or something to wave.

After this reception a very damp cameraman decided to stay with the ship because I wanted to show the *Gothic* passing through the canal and because

Panama was a foreign country and not strictly part of the Commonwealth tour. First we came to the three Gatun locks which raised the liner eighty-five feet above sea level on the Atlantic side. Then we came to the Pedro Miguel locks where we descended to the very large Miraflores lock, fifty-four feet above sea level, 1,000 feet long and 116 feet wide. The Queen and Duke had driven there from Colon to see how the lock worked and to operate some controls and then came aboard the *Gothic* in the afternoon for a church service as it was a Sunday. The service was conducted by an American bishop. Then they were off again in the early evening to Panama City for further receptions and wild crowds. Meanwhile the *Gothic* descended through more locks to pass into Balboa, the Pacific terminal of the canal. There is no doubt that the canal is an impressive engineering feat, fifty-one miles long with an average time of eight hours to traverse it. Generally it allowed two-way traffic but sometimes there were hold-ups in one narrow five-mile stretch between the Gatun and Pedro locks. For a third time the Queen and Duke returned to the *Gothic*, on this occasion to change into evening dress to attend a state banquet at the presidential palace in Panama City followed by a large reception given by the government. In the oppressive heat it must have been a very tiring day for the royal couple but they seemed very cheerful as they went ashore for the evening's functions. At daylight on 1 December with everyone back in the ship we passed through the Gulf of Panama and into the Pacific Ocean to begin the 6,000-mile, seventeen-day journey to Fiji.

I suppose the opportunity to go round the world in a ship is a pipedream many have but never achieve. To make such a voyage in the company of the Queen must be even more fanciful but this was just what was happening to me – a journey of a lifetime as the cruise adverts might describe it – and all expenses paid: 30,000 miles of travel from the Caribbean islands, through the Panama Canal, Fiji, Tonga, to New Zealand and Australia; then the Cocos Islands and Ceylon. I remember sitting in the sun on the deck of the *Gothic* and it seemed almost unbelievable that this was actually taking place. My thoughts turned to the evening to come, however. Each of my colleagues and I had been invited to dine with the Queen and it was now my turn. Although I was used to meeting people in all walks of life this was something very different.

I was seated next to the Queen on her right, with the Duke and Colville opposite and the rest of the household round the table. The royals are so skilled at dealing with guests on these occasions and the Queen soon put me at ease, asking how I was getting on and speaking of general topics. I confess to not being a good conversationalist but it seemed to go reasonably well. I remember I remarked on a gadget she used to support her handbag at the table and she told me 'Philip' had given it to her as a present. I cannot recall what we ate or who was sitting on the other side of me! The men wore dinner jackets and the ladies evening wear but generally it was quite informal with across-the-table banter. There were plenty of pre-dinner drinks and wine at the meal and I managed to avoid sliding under the highly polished table. An occasion I had not expected but certainly one on which to reminisce.

The journey across the Pacific was very relaxed and pleasant. We crossed the equator soon after leaving Panama but there was no special ceremony. It was nice to meet Lady Pamela Mountbatten again after the hectic times in India. I was able to get some pictures of the Queen and Duke and some of the sporting activities of the household and staff but generally there was little to film and my camera stayed in my cabin most of the time. There was one fairly dramatic event. One of the ship's crew developed acute appendicitis and an emergency operation was performed by the Queen's doctor, Surgeon-Commander Steele-Perkins. His assistant, the anaesthetist, was in the escort ship, HMS *Sheffield*, and had to be transferred to the *Gothic* by bosun's chair. That made a picture and I noticed the Queen was busy with her camera. When the bosun's chair was returned to the *Sheffield* I wished I could have gone across to get some shots of the *Gothic* at sea, returning later to the *Gothic* when the assistant doctor went back to the *Sheffield*. However I did not have the nerve to ask permission under the emergency conditions of the operation. With hindsight of course I should have asked – how I hate hindsight! A chance of a good picture missed. The transfer between the two ships brought back memories of my efforts during the war in the Mediterranean. The member of the crew had a story to dine out on having been operated on by the Queen's medico. As I leaned on the rails of the *Gothic* watching the sea passing by I remember thinking that these tours took a large chunk out of one's normal life. A year in India, six weeks in Canada, six months on this tour and a number of other shorter times away were very hard on those left behind who were not seeing new places or participating in world events. Admittedly one had to work and it was not always glamour, but I have to say, a journalistic job is a selfish job.

The days of relaxation were over as we approached Fiji, and months of hard work lay ahead for everyone. One tends to think of Fiji as a single island but in fact the area of Fiji is very extensive, comprising some 320 islands, some large, some tiny, many volcanic. Entering the spacious harbour of the capital Suva on Viti Levu, we were escorted to our mooring by Fijian war canoes, very proud with their large sails made of bamboo matting. Many of the Fijians had come 200 miles or more from the outlying islands and with their woolly, tight-curled hair and the lower half clad in the broad leaves of the banana plant they presented a truly tropical greeting. The harbour was alive with many other small sailing boats and larger vessels, all gaily beflagged and full to overflowing with welcoming islanders. After formal greetings by the governor aboard the *Gothic* a party of chiefs offered the Queen a whale's tooth, one of many she was to receive, a ritual of welcome inviting the recipient to come ashore. Alighting from the royal barge the Queen was presented with a bouquet of exquisite flowers by a tiny Fijian girl who then sat on the ground and clapped her hands, greatly amusing the Queen. It made a lovely picture. Again we were in the wet season, making it very hot and humid, but it did not rain as the royal couple carried out their many engagements – processions, speeches, a visit to a sports ground, which they drove round perched on the hood of their open car to the delight of the crowd. There was a visit to sugar plantations which supplied the huge refining mills, some of the largest in that part of the world. The main welcoming ceremonies took place at Albert Park, where a splendid feast had been prepared. The Queen and Duke, seated on a dais, were offered cups of kava which they gamely drank, giving much pleasure to the watching crowds for it is a powerful alcoholic traditional drink given to welcome visitors. Later on the journeys round the island there was an opportunity to see the beautiful scenery and lovely sandy bays which were part of the attraction of Viti Levu. Suva has a mountainous backdrop and the hills were illuminated at night when the Queen gave a dinner party in the *Gothic*. A happy if rather hot curtain-raiser to the Commonwealth tour.

Tonga is the main island of a group of 150 islands closer together in a smaller area than the Fijian ones and are aptly named the Friendly Islands. I flew there in a back-up plane preceding the Queen, who also went by air in a flying boat in order to have more time in Tonga. On arrival at Nuku'alofa the tall, stately figure of Queen Salote greeted the Queen and Duke as they came ashore. There was some rain as

The Queens Elizabeth and Salote and the Duke about to tuck in to a Tongan feast during the Commonwealth tour 1953–54. From the newsreel.

ITN Archive/Reuters

they drove into the town for the official welcome. There followed a typical Tongan feast, which, as in Fiji, was provided for all important visitors, but this was very special with 2,000 sucking pigs cooked and chickens, lobsters, fruit and coconut milk in vast quantities were laid in rows on banana leaves. After some filming I was able to join in and partake of the goodies. We sat on the ground and ate with our fingers, eating whatever we fancied. The two queens were at a top table in a special pavilion, but it was taboo to film the royals eating. Although utensils were provided for visitors, I believe the royal party joined the guests, and also ate with their fingers. There was dancing, singing and bands during the meal, making it all very jolly. Later the ships' companies of the *Gothic* and escorts were treated similarly. The ancient royal tortoise of Queen Salote was filmed by the Queen in the grounds of the royal palace, a wooden building with an iron roof. The tortoise is ranked as a chief with a Tongan title. I do not know who took precedence when he met the Queen. The next day, a Sunday, began with a church service, then visits to ancient monuments and to a display of hula dances, and that was all there was time for in the short visit. The Tongans were a warm, simple country people who gave their visitors a truly genuine show of affection. Queen Salote in her homeland was the perfect hostess to the Queen at whose coronation she had herself been the guest and had endeared herself to the British people when, in the royal procession, she sat in an open carriage in the rain waving to the crowd.

Embarked again in the *Gothic*, which had arrived from Fiji, we steamed for New Zealand. Up to this point I had been on my own in covering for the newsreels. On a long tour such as this and with the coming visits to the two major countries, it was obvious I could not film everything and I had to try to decide what to leave out. Initial entries into capital cities and important towns had to be filmed. Anticipated highlights and areas of political significance were on the agenda. Otherwise I considered it meant being present at as many functions as was practical and to film anything unexpected or which made a good picture. There were going to be cameramen at most places covering the general story, and except when I was the only one able to get to a location my brief as royal cameraman was to concentrate on close-ups of the royal party. We arrived at Auckland on 23 December 1953.

After Fiji and Tonga, Auckland was pleasantly cool. Anyone who thought a royal tour was a rest cure or a holiday for a cameraman would have been quickly disillusioned on seeing the number of events in the programme. There were similar engagements in every city and town visited. Civic welcomes, guards of honour, childrens' rallies and wreath-laying had to have some coverage but it was necessary on such occasions to look for incidents which made them different from the norm and so avoid repetition. I filmed the decorated streets and shops in Auckland, for it was Christmas and in addition to the flags and bunting always evident on a royal visit there were coloured lights, Christmas trees and gifts in the shops – almost like

London's West End in December with the weather adding to the illusion – it was very wet.

Sir William Norris, the Governor-General, and his wife organised a Father Christmas to arrive at his residence on Christmas Day. The Queen and Duke were staying there over the holiday period and when the red-coated gentleman arrived, the Queen was there with her camera to record the distribution of gifts and I was there to record that scene. Later in the evening the Queen made her Christmas Day broadcast to the Commonwealth from Government House.

With Christmas over the tour of the North Island began with journeys by air, train and car. The Maori influence was of especial interest to the royal visitors, first at Waitangi, 300 miles north of Auckland, where there were good pictures of tribal rituals and displays of singing and dancing to be had. As the Queen left her car a mat of kiwi feathers was laid out for her to step on, an honour normally reserved for Maori chiefs. I was not alone in filming such events and concentrated on close-ups as was my brief and was helped by the royal detectives to remain close to the royal party for longer periods than other cameramen. Generally, as happened on long tours, except where by virtue of travelling with the royals I was enabled to be the only cameraman at an event, my coverage was by no means exclusive.

The next important gathering of Maoris was at the popular resort of Rotorua, situated in a volcanic area by a lake surrounded by hills. On the way we had spent a noisy night in the country-style Commercial Hotel. The crowds outside were

The Queen and the Duke at the opening of Parliament in Wellington, New Zealand. From the newsreel.

ITN Archive/Reuters

constantly calling for the Queen until she came out on a balcony to wave to them. In Rotorua I filmed the royal couple watching the continual thermal activity in the area – the geysers, the bubbling pools of mud and the lakes of hot, very hot water. These were exciting pictures with Maoris in attendance, faces painted with their special designs and dressed in flax skirts. The chieftains wore cloaks of kiwi feathers and all later performed the haka and old rites and dances, with rolling eyes and tongues out and much yelling and leaping into the air. That was very different film from processions and official welcomes and I was very pleased to film those events with the Queen and Duke either in the foreground or background, for although I was involved in close-ups whenever the picture was of special interest I also endeavoured to show the scene that went with the close shots. Everywhere there were huge crowds, in the villages or towns through which we passed or stopped.

There was a week in Wellington where the highlight was the opening of parliament, closely following the London ceremony. The Queen, dressed in her coronation gown and wearing a diamond tiara, looked very much the monarch. It was an important occasion which emphasised the close bonds between the Commonwealth countries which that tour was designed to strengthen. In touring through the North Island the Queen and Duke saw beautiful country, volcanic mountains, Maoris, growing industrial schemes and everywhere were greeted by large crowds, not only as a spectacle but with real affection.

On the South Island there was a similar reception. First to the sunshine state of Nelson where I filmed the royals in the large orchards which produced apples and pears, much exported to Britain. Christchurch, the capital of the next province, Canterbury, was a large city with long straight roads, its houses mostly wooden dwellings with the iron roofs common in towns in those parts. We travelled there by royal train across the Southern Alps, a journey made for film others could not get. There were a number of drives in an open car through Christchurch and a lot of press and cameraman to picture them. I took closer shots of the car to fit into the more general shots of the others. There was a visit to one of the many dairy farms which produced marvellous butter and cheese, also largely exported to the UK at that time.

After a stop in Dunedin, founded by Scots in 1848, where I filmed the kilted residents meeting the Queen, we continued southwards, passing beautiful cattle feeding in the shadow of snow-covered peaks until we came to the port of Bluff where the *Gothic* was waiting. Five weeks and 3,000 miles of travel had passed very quickly. Maoris in skirts and cloaks of kiwi feathers performed the haka on the quayside and bade us farewell with their song 'Now is the Hour' and boats in the harbour full of cheering people had their sirens going at full blast to say goodbye to the Queen and Duke waving from the *Gothic* as we left to cross the Tasman Sea for Australia.

Australia, divided into seven states, six of which the Queen visited, was the most arduous of the countries in the extensive journey around the Commonwealth. Each state is autonomous with its own parliament, its own governor and Prime Minister. In each capital there were processional drives and civic ceremonies and, in contrast to my close shots, I endeavoured to get a sample of each to show the huge crowds and receptions the royal couple experienced everywhere. Later, in the outlying areas I showed in general shots the vastness of the country and the farms with their masses of sheep and cattle. Of course, as in New Zealand, there were cameramen in every main city and town who covered the tour in general terms throughout, but I took my general shots where there were no other cameras or where I could feature the Queen and Duke prominently in them. Otherwise I continued with close shots to emphasise the interest and enjoyment of the Queen and her husband in the things they were shown. The journeys through the states were a massive undertaking with such a large area planned for the Queen to visit. Over thirty flights were scheduled. On some we four press were in the royal plane, on some in a back-up plane going ahead with baggage and staff and, occasionally, we had to make our own way in civil aircraft assisted by the organisers of the tour. There were royal trains in which we travelled, cars in processions and sometimes we were back on the *Gothic*.

We had a fairly rough passage across the Tasman Sea to New South Wales and its capital Sydney. As we entered the large and beautiful harbour the scene was made for filming. There were hundreds of ships, yachts and boats of all kinds, all flying flags or pennants in the strong breeze, all gaily decorated and all crowded with cheering people. For me it meant pictures others could not get, with the Queen and Duke waving often in the foreground of my general shots. Certainly a tremendous welcome as the *Gothic* came to her anchorage. I managed to get ashore before the royal barge arrived at the quay where Sir William Slim, the Governor-General and Mr Menzies, the Prime Minister of the federal government, were waiting to welcome the Queen and Duke. The long processional drive into the city through boisterous crowds to a civic reception by the Lord Mayor completed an exceptional and spectacular arrival both for the royal visitors and for the newsreels.

Among the many engagements in and around Sydney was a visit to the famous Bondi beach where I filmed the Queen watching the lifeguards demonstrating their

The Queen and the Duke of Edinburgh see lifeguard demonstrations on Bondi Beach, Sydney during their Commonwealth tour of Australia in 1953-54. From the newsreel.

rescue work. It was hot and the beach was crowded, many running by the royal car as it endeavoured to circle the sands. Those were good, mostly informal, pictures although not easy to film in the pushing and shoving of the mob of people. Being on that beach took me back to a brief stop in Sydney during the war when I had quite a fright when swimming off the shore. I got caught in the treacherous undercurrents and was unable to move in any direction. Just when I thought I would have to signal for the life-savers to rescue me the currents changed direction and I was able to struggle free.

We travelled north from Sydney by air, rail and road to the coal-mining area and centre of heavy industry at Newcastle. There were good relaxed pictures when the royal couple showed great interest in the furnaces, flaming coke and molten metal in a large iron-and-steel works. Further north at Lismore the crowds were especially wild on the way to the hotel where the royal party, including our four press, were to spend the night. At hotels the Queen, Duke and household occupied the top floor and lesser mortals – the secretaries, staff and press – were accommodated on a lower floor. All those night stops were tiring for my companions and me for we all had dispatches of one sort or another to prepare. For me film had to be packed up, dope sheets written and if possible sent by air back to a main city for onward dispatch to London, with phone calls and cables informing destinations of relevant details. Occasionally, if the Australians required a particular event or area, the film was processed in Sydney and a duplicate made from the negative before it was sent on to London. They really wanted colour but my instructions were to keep to black and white except where colour would be useful for future films. That posed problems, for so much was colourful and as I had no idea what future films were contemplated I generally took the easy way out and stuck to black and white. When I was the only cameraman at an event with the subject demanding colour there was no difficulty in deciding which stock to use. I would have liked to film the whole tour in colour but it would have been very costly with five newsreels and associates involved in processing and making prints for each apart from time factors in getting the stories into the reels. After dealing with dispatches we had to have our baggage ready for collection at a given time the next morning wherever we were staying and be ready to travel as instructed each day. I must say the organization by the tour authorities and royal household was very impressive.

Coming south again the Queen said goodbye to New South Wales at Wagga Wagga, a small farming town, and proceeded to Canberra, the capital and seat of the federal government of Australia. As in New Zealand, only on a larger scale, the two royals had seen industry and manufacturing, dairy farms and mountains and arid desert, thousands of wool-producing sheep, herd upon herd of cattle, wheatfields, canefields and glorious scenery – a scenario that was repeated in essence in each of the states visited.

In Canberra the principal engagement was another opening of parliament with the Queen again in her marvellous coronation dress, the blue sash and star of the Garter, and wearing a diamond tiara. Some lighting had been installed for part of the ceremony but this time I left the coverage to the local cameramen and our associates and filmed the royal arrivals and crowd reaction outside Parliament House. Later I filmed a mixture of other events in Canberra which were mainly semi-official and centred around Government House.

The *Gothic* took us to Tasmania and I had an opportunity to get more film stock from the store I kept in the ship. In Hobart, the capital, there was yet another opening of parliament with the Queen this time in a white gown and the Garter sash. It was a small chamber for the ceremony and no extra lighting so I just shot general scenes outside, leaving the engagement to be told in commentary. We flew to the north of the island over sizeable lakes which supplied the efficient hydroelectric system, providing cheap electricity to the islanders. It made good general views. We drove on a pleasant journey between white sandy bays and mountains and hills, past orchards and potato fields on the north coast to the port of Burnie where the royal couple saw commercial paper being produced and, as always, production in factories made interesting pictures. Tasmania had a prosperous paper industry and supplied mainland Australia with a large proportion of its newsprint. The Queen and

The opening of Australia's parliament. From the newsreel.

Duke spent the night at Connorville, a big privately run sheep farm. I stayed nearby in Launceston from where, after a short visit the following morning, it was into the air to fly to Victoria, the third state in the royal programme, and to land at Melbourne, the capital. There was a stay of two weeks in Victoria with much of the time spent in Melbourne. In the famous cricket ground there was a review of ex-servicemen and women with the royal couple standing in a Landrover as it circled the stadium to very loud cheering by friends and relatives situated in the stands. There were nice relaxed shots as the two visitors chatted with the servicemen and women. Later in the same venue there was a spectacular rally of 17,000 children dressed in red, white and blue. After an inspection they gave a wonderful display of gymnastics and dancing. Again there were relaxing pictures with the Queen and the children.

There was a fifth opening of parliament before joining the royal train for a two-day tour of the northern parts of the state. Everywhere at the stations we passed through or stopped at there were massed crowds and cheering children overwhelming the Queen with the joyous receptions and genuine affection shown by the Australian people in those remote outlying regions. It was pleasant filming both in general and in close-up. The first night was spent in the train in Ned Kelly country on the plains he used to roam to rob the stagecoaches passing through.

This story with the general views of the wide plains offered the reels good commentary material. On the next day's programme I again filmed general views as the basis for good commentary, for we were at towns which in Victoria's early formative years were at the centre of a gold rush. In those days they were just shanty towns but they became the forerunners of the growth which made Victoria the second largest in population although the smallest of Australia's mainland states.

After a second night in the train and a return to Melbourne there came a change in climate to tropical heat following a flight of 900 miles to Brisbane, the capital of Queensland. The crowds seemed more relaxed than in the south. The city was friendly, lively and merry with everyone gaily dressed for hot days and nights and my pictures pleasantly contrasted with the more soberly dressed people further south. Most of the homes, as elsewhere in Australia and New Zealand, were of wooden construction with iron roofs but there in the tropics were built up from the ground to avoid white ants. At night buildings, bridges and streets were floodlit or brightly lit with coloured bulbs, giving enough light to get an exposure.

Because of the vast area to be visited in Queensland, the second largest state on the continent, most of the journeys were made by air. At a town bordering the rich wheatfields, I had an opportunity to film Aborigines who had trekked many miles from the north. With their tall, lithe bodies, carrying spears shoulder-high, faces painted red and yellow, with head-dresses of grass and feathers and wearing brightly coloured loincloths, they were quite intimidating as they performed a display of tribal dancing. Good colour film. The town was also famous for its racehorses, of great interest to the Queen.

A further 700 miles north by air took us to Townsville on the east coast. Serious flooding in the west caused by monsoon rains prevented sheep farmers, families and friends from reaching the town, reducing the size of the welcoming crowds. Lying some way out from Townsville, whose waters were too shallow for her to come alongside, was the *Gothic*. The ship was waiting to take the Queen and Duke to see the coral wonders below the surface of the Great Barrier Reef, which formed part of the 1,000-mile Queensland coastline. On the way to the royal ship in an Australian destroyer the royal couple visited one of the escort ships, HMAS *Australia*, a cruiser that was one of my wartime ships. They posed for a picture with the entire ship's company – a different crew from my days in the ship. A nostalgic moment nonetheless. Sadly, thirty years old, the *Australia* was to be broken up after her escort duties. The *Gothic* anchored in the waters of the barrier reef and the Queen was able to see the fabulous coral and colourful tropical fish from a glass-bottomed boat.

As I mentioned, on the way to Tasmania I was able to get more film from my stock in the ship. On long tours it was always difficult to carry sufficient film. If I took my complete supply my baggage would have been too heavy. So each time I returned to the ship on the journey round Australia I was able to get more film. It worked well, for I knew in advance from my overall programme when we would be in the ship and I could work out how much to carry in between visits, sometimes only just making it.

On the long flight to South Australia, the fifth and penultimate state, we stopped at Broken Hill in the outback, the first time the two royals had actually been in bush country, for their journeys by air had only taken them over those remote areas. Broken Hill had grown from its days when rich uranium ore was discovered into a region of large lead and zinc mines. It was also the base for the flying doctor service connected by wireless to many mining camps and farms, some of them 500 miles from the base. The Queen broadcast over the network to those in their lonely desert homes and looked at the flying doctors' aircraft, which made something different to film.

After Queensland it was decidedly cool in Adelaide, the capital of South Australia, but the drive into the city was undertaken in an open car passing through welcoming crowds into a town with wide avenues, many churches and high buildings. Five days of engagements included the last of the parliaments to be opened, dances by almost-naked Aborigines, and a visit to Wyalla, where Australia's biggest ships were built. The Duke flew to Woomera on his own to see some of the atomic research programme. South Australia had low rainfall but imaginative irrigation schemes enabled it to establish sizeable sheep and cattle farms and vineyards which produced most of Australia's wines – all part of the royal tour. I kept mainly to close-ups in this state to supplement the coverage of others. The Queen and Duke left Adelaide by air for Perth in Western Australia, the last and largest of the states in the programme and where the tour of Australia was to end.

I was unable to film anything in Western Australia and travelled to Fremantle in the *Gothic* with most of the household. A serious outbreak of polio in the state meant everyone in the ship apart from those absolutely necessary to be with the Queen were not allowed ashore. The royal headquarters were changed from Government House in Perth to the *Gothic*. Everything eaten ashore was taken from the *Gothic* and most of the programme was either cancelled or modified. There was no shaking of hands or large assemblies of people. It was very disappointing for everyone but they arranged for as many people as possible to see the royal pair as they drove through the town, although this time not to a civic reception.

So, on 1 April, almost two months after we arrived in Sydney harbour followed by well-nigh non-stop travelling, we left Fremantle to steam out into the Indian Ocean. Aircraft flew overhead in salute, guns fired salutes from shore batteries and Australian warships took up positions to escort the *Gothic* from their shores. Apart from the salutes it was a quiet departure. Only Prime Minister Menzies and his wife, the governor of Western Australia, and the officials who had organised the tour were at the quayside to wave goodbye to the royal ship, a sad anticlimax to a very successful tour. All I could film was the royals waving as we cast off from the shore and the warships taking up their positions around our ship. One disappointment for me was that I had not seen a kangaroo or a koala bear. The Queen broadcast from the ship to thank everyone for the wonderful time and the deep affection she and her husband had experienced in every part of the country.

It was nostalgia again as Australia faded into the distance. The last time I had been in those waters I was in HMAS *Australia* during the war steaming the 3,000 miles to Ceylon as we were now doing in the *Gothic*. That same warship was almost alongside us as escort ship. This time we stopped halfway across at the Cocos-Keeling Islands. The Queen was only ashore for ninety minutes, so apart from an arrival and some general shots I did not attempt any further coverage. As we continued on our journey the Australian escort was replaced by cruisers from Ceylon. Close shots of ships at sea make good pictures and help to provide a link from one country to another. The Indian Ocean was as enchanting as ever – the flying fish, the balmy breeze, the Southern Cross bright like a regal jewel among the thousands of stars that beautified the heavens, and the phosphorescence sparkling in the wake of the royal ship.

It seemed like a step back in time as on 10 April we turned into the port of Colombo, my fourth visit. This time in addition to the little boats and dhows hurrying around the harbour or attached to buoys whilst their owners dozed in the sun, there were gaily decorated crowded boats cheering the *Gothic* to her berth. I was on familiar ground. Colombo had a similar look to the last time I was in the city for the independence ceremony in 1948. The streets were decorated with great arches, some symbolic with lions, elephants and peacocks woven into them. The Union Jack flew alongside the new flag of independence and bunting and photographs of the Queen were now added to the gay scene. It was very hot and oppressive as the royal procession proceeded to the town hall. The crowds were not demonstrative in the way we saw in Australia and New Zealand, clapping hands being their usual way of greeting, but they were there in vast numbers, thousands having come in from outlying parts of the island. Their loyalty and expressions were just as genuine as in the other Commonwealth countries. The women looked very attractive in their long saris and the men complemented them, dressed in white. Such scenes made good introductory pictures to this closing part of the Commonwealth tour. The royal car was open and it must have agonisingly hot for the Queen and Duke as they made slow progress along the processional route past those crowds who had stood in that burning sun waiting to see them. I was steaming in a closed car although filming from an open window. The weather played a dirty trick, however. A ball given by the governor in the grounds of Queen's House in the evening was ruined by a torrential tropical rainstorm just after the Queen came out and dancing had begun. It also cut short my efforts to show something different, as the garden was floodlit and the newsreels rarely had an opportunity to see such a social scene in the open.

The Queen opened parliament for the last time on her Commonwealth tour and for the third time she was in her coronation gown in spite of the heat. After official engagements in and around Colombo and visits to various shrines and historical ruins, some of which I filmed, the royal couple left the heat and humidity to go by train to the hills and coolness of Nuwara Eliya. They attended a reception given by the Planters' Association of Ceylon celebrating its centenary. I did not film it, but later when they visited a tea estate I showed them watching various processes in the production of tea, Ceylon's major export. There was a walk round the Royal Botanic Gardens with its wonderful collection of tropical flora, unforgettable beauty and good colour film. The climax in Ceylon came with a drive down the hills into Kandy.

Normally the town had a population of around 50,000 but it swelled to more than a million with those who had come in from outlying areas to see their Queen and watch the spectacular procession – the raja perahara, arranged specially for the visitors. The Queen met Kandyan chiefs before the perahara and shook hands with more than fifty of them. They had arrayed themselves in fantastic robes with priceless jewels – emeralds, rubies, sapphires and gold fastened to their dress or hung from their necks. I managed to get some individual pictures of them but unfortunately their meeting with the Queen took place in an unlighted room. The Queen and Duke entered the Temple of the Tooth, where they were shown the sacred relic which is carried in the annual religious perahara in August but was not in the one the royals saw. I could not film inside the temple for there was insufficient light and no permission.

The perahara began at dusk. The surrounding scenes were a suitable backdrop to the splendid pageantry. Kandy has many temples and all were floodlit. All the trees were adorned with tiny coloured sparkling lights. I filmed much of the assembly before it got dark. There were well over a hundred elephants, and hundreds of musicians and dancers performed a short sequence of their act before moving off. The procession was lit by flaming torches carried on long poles and began with the beating of drums as it moved past a specially built royal pavilion. All the elephants were illuminated and decorated. The temple elephant was completely covered with richly embroidered red velvet and looked magnificent as it lumbered along, preceded by men who laid a white cloth before it to walk on. Traditional dances, martial music and gesticulating acrobats with men on stilts made a very memorable spectacle. I could not film the true magnificence of that wonderful procession, but there was sufficient light at early dusk with the light of the torches and the illuminated elephants to get a fair impression of the perahara. It was strange being in Kandy again, for close by were the gardens in which Lord Mountbatten had established the headquarters of South East Asia Command to which I had been assigned when the war in Europe ended. Ceylon had many memories for me.

A final engagement in Colombo was a review of the Ceylon military forces, which took place in heavy rain. It was 21 April, the Queen's birthday, and she was greeted by the crowd singing 'Happy Birthday'. It was my final coverage and the end of the Commonwealth tour for my colleagues and me. We were not covering the short stay in Aden where the Queen would say farewell to the *Gothic* and it was impractical to get to Uganda and the Mediterranean where the Queen would join the new *Britannia* to complete her tour. I watched the *Gothic* disappear into the hazy distance and realised that some years before I had stood in the same place watching HMAS *Australia* go out of my life – two ships in which I had sailed on memorable journeys, both unforgettable and unrepeatable, encompassing most of the world. The six months I was away this time seemed to pass quickly. My cameras and equipment stood the test of travelling 30,000 miles in all sorts of conditions with very little trouble and the thousands of feet of film I exposed had been safely delivered without loss, but I had no idea how much of it was used in the newsreels. One of the things I liked about those tours was the opportunities to meet the cameramen and technicians of the different countries and to see their ways of working. Generally we were very much alike; sometimes perhaps there were those who were more aggressive than we in England. Since those days long ago times have changed and attitudes have changed but the Commonwealth tour was a fantastic episode in my life; there has never been anything like it since, and I imagine, too, for the monarchy, who must have fond memories of a time when royalty was at its peak.

With the Commonwealth tour at an end it was back to Soho Square and Wardour Street. In spite of the prestige attached to 'royal cameraman' and all the tours and jobs I have done throughout my career it was grand to return to Soho. I am a Londoner and that was the heart of London. I was always glad to see its seedy streets again, its many restaurants – Italian, French, Chinese – its cosmopolitan continental shops, its pubs of every type catering for every type of person from writers, painters, drunks, petty crooks and not-so-petty crooks, homosexuals and lesbians, tarts young and old resting from the doorways they normally occupied, onion sellers and ordinary chaps like newsreel technicians. That was Soho, a bohemian city within a city. My favourite pub was The George in Wardour Street, conveniently close to Film House and run by two elderly ladies. Each newsreel had its own special drinking haunt. A different place today but I always get a buzz when there, for it is still Soho. Buildings and restaurants have changed and the film companies have disappeared from Wardour Street. However, Wardour Street, Dean Street, Greek Street, Berwick Street, Poland Street, Old Compton Street and Soho Square are all still there, no wider than they were in the 1930s. Film House in Wardour Street still stands but Nascreno House in Soho Square, where the Newsreel Association lived and where my royal rota office was, has been rebuilt. It is not so nice as the old building with its comfortable, spacious offices. It now houses my bank on the ground floor, moved from Wardour Street. At least that gives me an excuse to go to Soho and perhaps look for old haunts.

The world was becoming a different place as the war receded, and the 1950s reflected changes which the newsreel companies recorded in their reels. Although conditions were generally quite austere we saw rock and roll, Teddy boys, Premium Bonds, and Mary Quant's shop with its new dress styles for the young. Less welcome were parking tickets and even less welcome for us was television, which began to take the place of the newsreels in providing the news.

There were plenty of royal events which followed a pattern year by year. They were mostly domestic stories in all parts of the country, visits to hospitals, flower shows, factories, charity shows, exhibitions, races, agricultural shows and visits by foreign heads of state. There were short visits overseas – often with political or trade overtones. Added to these were the state occasions and the spectaculars – the opening of Parliament, Trooping the Colour and the Garter ceremony. Finally there were the once-only stories like weddings, deaths, long tours overseas, birthdays, launches of ships, disasters and births. The newsreels obviously did not want every royal occasion filmed, for there would be over a hundred in a year and neither is it possible for me to recall every story I covered as the royal cameraman, so I have chosen events in this period which show some of the problems of royal rota coverage or engagements where there was some special interest either in general or for me personally.

Just before the Queen returned from the Commonwealth tour on 15 May 1954 Roger Bannister had run the mile in under four minutes. How important that seemed then. Louis Lumière, French pioneer of the cine-camera and early cinema news including the beginnings of colour photography, died in April. A hundred thousand people crowded into Wembley Stadium to listen to evangelist Billy Graham. With the Queen back there was the Derby and Royal Ascot; an eclipse of the sun occurred at the end of June and all food rationing ended then. The newsreels had plenty of stories apart from royal stories.

While the Queen was on holiday in Scotland in August and September I had a call from Richard Colville to tell me that it had been arranged for me to go to Balmoral to film the very young Prince Charles and his sister Princess Anne. This was a story that did not require prior agreement from the reels, for I knew they would bend over backwards to get such pictures. I travelled to Scotland feeling a little nervous. I was not unduly worried about the technical side of filming though, as always on important stories, there was the awful thought, suppose the film in the camera jammed, or the speed control got accidentally moved, or the lens turret had not locked in tight after turning and everything was out of focus. These things should not happen if everything had been properly checked but they could – and sometimes did. My worry was not being sure whether I would be asked how I wanted to film the children and if so what I would say or whether the Queen would decide. When I arrived at that great granite building, the castle, with its high tower and set in 25,000 acres, I was shown into a room and told the Queen would he along shortly with the children. I noticed a large rug had been spread out on the grass in front of the castle. It was dry and a pleasant day and it seemed the Queen had decided the location. I wondered what would have happened had it been wet. I had no lights, and anyway lighting a large area would mean electricians even though lighting equipment had become more portable. There were the unions to consider. I was spared that dilemma, however, and the Queen brought the children out with some toys and sat with them on the rug and I filmed away as they played together. I filmed them many times since that day but never were they so uninhibited.

Nineteen fifty-one was notable for a mass slaughter. The rabbit population was decimated with the introduction of myxomatosis, saving the country some £50 millions' worth of crops each year, which the rabbits consumed without the permission of the farming fraternity. My colleagues were out in the fields for that one. And there was more destruction when Churchill saw the painting of himself by Graham Sutherland. He hated it so much that it was destroyed sometime later. It had been a present from Parliament for his eightieth birthday! In October Haile Selassie of Ethiopia came on a state visit. Most heads of state were met at the port of entry, usually Dover, by a senior royal and travelled by train to London's Victoria Station and then proceeded to Buckingham Palace in a carriage procession. On the station platform were the Queen, other members of the royal family, political heads, the ambassador of the visiting country, the Lord Mayor and others connected with the visit, all assembled to welcome the honoured guest. Television by 1954 was covering these visits and we jointly arranged the lighting, mainly from overhead. The only press on the platform were my three colleagues and myself accredited to the Palace, and a still photographer. When a head of state arrived at an airport I usually had an additional cameraman for the general scene. On every royal occasion whenever I required an extra body such as an electrician to be close to me I had to obtain a special one-day pass from the Palace press office. The procession to Buckingham Palace, normally via Whitehall and The Mall rather than the shorter route, was also filmed on rota by whichever company I was dealing with at the time.

At the end of October the Queen and Duke made whistle-stop tours in Lancashire, the West Riding of Yorkshire, Northumberland and Durham in the space of five days. The royal procession would speed through the countryside from town to town, stop at a town hall for a brief civic reception and on we would go. Sometimes there would be additional stops to visit a hospital or a factory or something special relevant to the area through which we were passing. The procession consisted of a number of cars. In the first were the Queen and Duke, in the next two were members of the household such as the private secretaries, ladies-in-waiting, equerries and the Lord Lieutenant of the county. The fourth had the organisers of the tour and the fifth was for my three colleagues and me, with lesser officials and the police behind. Sometimes we were in the fourth car and the organisers in the fifth.

I had a disturbing time on one of these days. We were on the way to the next town when I was taken short in the worst possible way. When I first became a newsreel cameraman I realised there would be long periods when I would not be able to leave a scene and I had trained myself to be nice and tidy by the time I left home. On this occasion there was a very early start and things had not gone to plan. It was a desperate situation, with other cars behind ours and the police bringing up the rear. People lined the route at intervals and there was no possibility of stopping the car. All I could hope was that we would not stop to look at something on the way to the next town, that I could hold out until we reached the town hall, that I could find a loo and could rejoin our car before we moved on; there would not be much time. When we stopped I was away; I had to fight my way past the Queen and officials and with the aid of one of the detectives very fortunately managed to find a toilet open. That was extremely lucky, for normally everything was locked for security reasons. Otherwise I would have had to let the tour proceed without me. I just managed to get back to the car before we moved off; needless to say there was no coverage at that stop. It was very embarrassing and I was very relieved – in both senses of the word – and I thought my colleagues were equally so as I got back into the car! It was the only time over many years of covering stories that I was in such difficulty, thank goodness. I remember one of our cameramen, Eddie Edmonds, a lovely older cockney fellow of whom I was very fond, a man who could get into any occasion without permission or a pass, who was cursed with a weak bladder. He was always in desperate trouble, frequently disappearing behind buildings. He was once in a plane filming from an open cockpit when he had to 'go'. All he could think of was to use his hat – we wore hats at that time. He held it over the side of the plane to empty it and that was the last he saw of it as it was whipped away in the slipstream. Fortunately the contents went with it.

Nineteen fifty-five was a turning point for the newsreels. Although controlled by parent companies, the finances of each reel had been left in the hands of the editors-in-chief who were basically showmen, knew the technical side and were well able to control the cost of temperamental technicians. Since the war, behind the scenes there had been a gradual replacement in the managements of the controlling companies by accountants – a very different breed. This became more evident in the mid-fifties. Although the Newsreel Association made some restrictions the cinema reels were still paying sizeable sums for rights for stories as the only way to film important events. Television was becoming more widespread, however, with many more households having a television set and it was not long before television began to get the rights for the big occasions, paying sums against which we could not compete, especially with the accountants looking over our shoulders. Except for major events, the high cost of printing forced us to put only parts of our reels in colour, for we did not receive an increase in income for the service. Colour was important for we were aware the BBC was experimenting all the time and it gave a demonstration of the progress it was making at Alexandra Palace at the end of the year. Colour enabled us to remain competitive with television for a while and it helped too that they did not always give as full a coverage to stories on their news programmes as we did especially on royal items, when they would show a car pulling up somewhere, the Queen or royal personage alighting and that would be overshadowed by a reporter looming large in the frame telling the story in words and not in pictures.

At the end of 1955 Independent Television came into being and its news was a further challenge to us. With two television channels and the obvious fact that they would eventually have colour it was apparent that the influence of our newsreels was on the wane. The result was that some of our best cameramen, sound men and cutting-room staff began to move over to television, lured by higher salaries, better expenses and a more secure future, a combination that was irresistible. It meant, too, that with the increase in television Buckingham Palace agreed to its request for an accredited cameraman with the same facilities as myself. This ended my material being supplied to the BBC and henceforth we were five in the processional car. It was yet another blow for us as we could not compete with their speed of exhibition; they had to make only one print against our 250 and it was only our better quality, colour and fuller coverage that enabled us to survive for a year or two more. It had become noticeable, too, that the Palace was beginning to pay more attention to television than to us. Personally I thought the palace was rather too quick when considering coverage of royal stories. I could understand it for the big occasions when they were live but for quite a long time their television footage of events both royal and otherwise was certainly quite limited. My own relationship with the Palace was not affected, but the trend was there and each reel was fighting for survival by the end of 1955.

During the year there were some notable events. Princess Margaret announced that she would not be marrying Peter Townsend; Donald Campbell broke the water-speed record in his boat *Bluebird* at Ullswater and Stirling Moss won the British Grand Prix. Films were made in wide-screen Cinemascope and in 3-D, a pioneering device whereby cinemagoers were given red-and-green spectacles to look at the screen – it did not last very long. Some cinemas were adapted to show Cinema-scope, which was very impressive when on the very wide screen a plane or a car came zooming out towards you. At the Royal Academy exhibition in August a new portrait of the Queen painted by the renowned Annigoni received wide acclaim. We ended the year on a political note with the Tories winning the general election and Hugh Gaitskill becoming the Labour leader.

Like everyone I began 1956 worried about the future. I was in a curious position, for although I was employed by all the reels I did not belong to any. If all the reels

The Queen inspects a guard of honour during the tour of Nigeria in 1956. From the newsreel.

closed there would be no more royal rota and I could be out of a job. If one or two remained I assumed, as I was employed by them all, one of them would have to take me on. When British Newsreel Association Services was formed this possibility had not been foreseen and perhaps it had not foreseen that the newsreels might not survive the television era. I did think of trying to get into television but soundings suggested I stay with the cinema newsreels as my experience could be a challenge or embarrassment to management teams. I did not want to start all over again so I was not sorry at this advice as I was still busy on royal rota and there were still five reels operating. So I put such thoughts aside and on 27 January 1956 I was off to Nigeria for a three-week tour with the Queen and Duke. We left behind a very cold start to February – the coldest since 1895.

It was a long journey to Nigeria's capital, Lagos – 3,000 miles by air – and travelling independently I arrived two days before the Queen was due. The city was gaily decorated in red, blue and white and was crowded to capacity, thousands of Africans having come into Lagos from remote areas. The streets were narrow and when the procession proceeded from the airport to a civic reception after the Queen's arrival, they drove very close to the cheering crowds. That made an interesting picture as usually they were in the middle of the road well away from the people. After two days of official engagements the Queen received a loyal address in the Federal

House of Representatives, a modern building and Nigeria's parliament. There was no opening of parliament, for Nigeria had not at that time joined the Commonwealth, but the ceremony was very much like one. It had been well lit by the local film people, making it very hot, but the pictures were good, for there were many representatives from the north, east and west regions in their national dress of turbans and robes.

Distances are great in that large country and the real highlight of the tour was in Kaduna, capital of the northern region. The royal party, including me, went by air to the racecourse, an area larger than the capital, Lagos. Here was staged one of the most spectacular durbars ever seen, a tribute to the Queen by the emirs and chiefs of the northern region. Standing in their car the royal couple drove round the ground, passing a large enclosure of cheering spectators before reaching a specially built royal pavilion in front of which was a guard of honour formed by the Nigerian regiment. After the inspection the regiment marched past, a prelude to the fantastic march past of the provincial contingents, each province led by its emir and chiefs on horseback. Each section had its own speciality; these were so diverse it meant filming almost all of them coupled with shots of the obvious enjoyment of the Queen and Duke. There was music of every kind – trumpets, wind instruments, drums of all sizes with drummers on camels. There were masked dancers, pagan dancers, yelling spear-men, women singers, acrobats and men on stilts. There was so much to film I seemed to be changing film magazines every few minutes. The climax came with a wonderful display of horsemanship, a breath-taking event. Riders in groups charged at full gallop towards the royal party and pulled up dead only a few yards in front of the royal pavilion. It was terrifying to watch and film for it looked as if they could not possibly stop before charging into the royal party. Altogether over 6,000 participants and 2,000 horses took part in the show. I had never seen such a spectacular event anywhere else in all my filming days and in pictures that durbar alone was worth the visit to Nigeria. We left that developing country with its fascinating customs and wildlife of tigers, crocodiles, elephants, giraffes, monkeys, camels and more after a short stop at Kano from where the Queen took to the skies to return to England. Nigeria, a federation of states jointly administered by the British and Nigerians, later joined the Commonwealth. The Queen's three-week visit was perhaps influential in that regard.

In June there was more pageantry after the Russian leader Khruschev met the Queen during a visit to Britain, but he was not at Windsor Castle where I had gone for the annual ceremony of installing new knights to the Order of the Garter. The investiture took place in private in the Throne Room in the castle. Assisted by the supporters or sponsors of the knights to be installed, the Queen buckles the blue-and-gold Garter on the left leg of each candidate, attaches the ribbon and the star and drapes a velvet mantle and gold collar over the shoulders. The three to be installed on this occasion were Sir Anthony Eden, Earl Attlee and Lord Iveagh. These proceedings take place in the late morning.

The afternoon saw the service of installation in St George's Chapel. It was preceded by a slow, spectacular procession from the castle on a route lined by foot guards and dismounted Household Cavalry carrying swords. It passed the Round Tower and descended down through the castle wards to the Chapel, where I was stationed at the foot of the stone steps leading up to the entrance. I arranged an elevated position halfway down for a cameraman to film the general scene. Bands played as the Military Knights of Windsor led the procession, followed by the heralds and Yeomen of the Guard, all in full ceremonial dress. The knights in their blue velvet mantles walked in pairs behind the new knights to be installed, who in turn walked behind the ladies of the order – the Queen and Queen Mother – wearing the long mantle and Tudor velvet hats plumed with ostrich feathers. They all passed within a few yards of me as they reached the bottom of the slope and turned to mount the steps to the chapel. The installation is private. A pageant which evokes the origin of the noble order, limited to twenty-four Companions in addition to the royal family. It was founded in 1348 by Edward III to honour the Garter patron, St George. Its motto is the oft-quoted 'Honi soil qui mal y pense'.

We went to Coventry, where the Queen laid the foundation stone of a new cathedral to replace the 600-year-old former one which was flattened in one of the worst air raids of the war. Severe troubles in Egypt over the nationalisation of the Suez Canal held the world stage. British and French troops devastated Port Said resulting in Colonel Nasser, Egypt's president, making the canal impassable by sinking many ships in it.

Still in 1956, there were two outstanding events in sport. At the Grand National the Queen Mother's horse, Devon Loch, suddenly collapsed within sight of the winning post when leading the field – very dramatic and very disappointing for the Queen Mother – and for the punters. There was excitement on the cricket field. We won the Ashes! In the fourth test at the end of July at Old Trafford our cricket test team slaughtered the Australians. One man did it. Jim Laker created a world record by taking nineteen wickets in one test match. He bowled the Aussies out with nine wickets for thirty-seven runs in the first innings and ten for ninety-three in the second. I was not there unfortunately, but it was a field day for the cameramen who were. There was no looking at the crowd with long lenses for that match; there was almost no time to change the film, the wickets fell so fast.

The Queen was at the Braemar Highland Games, a show almost on her doorstep and I was in Scotland for that. Later, in October after her holiday, the Queen opened the first British commercial nuclear power station at Calder Hall on the shores of the Lake District. It has had its problems since then. Then there was a royal command charity film performance to see THE BATTLE OF THE RIVER PLATE. Outside the cinema, as was usual on such occasions, we floodlit the street to show the celebrities arriving (that could not be done nowadays). As always on those occasions very large crowds waited to see the arrivals, no matter what the weather. Inside in the line-up of those to be presented to the Queen was Marilyn Monroe. My early experiences in publicity at many such performances were very useful in placing lighting and knowing the procedures. Before the year ended there were visits to factories to see the fascinating way chocolate was made and orange juice bottled. Outside one of these I was astonished to hear a voice – 'You've dropped your filter' – it was the Queen. The year ended with Grace Kelly marrying Prince Rainier of Monaco, an assignment I would have liked to film, but it was the wrong royal.

At the end of that very busy year I was informed by the Newsreel Association that Commander Colville had written to the chairman a letter of appreciation of my work and loyalty to both the royals and the reels. Although it did not produce any more money it was a happy thought to carry into 1957, for the general situation for us had not improved. Most of the independent cinemas had given up taking a newsreel, causing the heavy hands of the accountants to be felt more intensely. But we battled on. Royal stories continued to be required and it looked to be another busy year. Royal events included state visits to Portugal, France and Denmark in the first half of the year, and later the Queen was the first reigning monarch to visit the White House when she met President Eisenhower. In January Anthony Eden resigned on the grounds of ill health, no doubt not helped by the Suez crisis, and Harold Macmillan became Prime Minister. Prince Charles started at a prep school in Knightsbridge and the paparazzi were out in force to witness his arrival. I missed the visits to Portugal and France as I had to have an operation which kept me out of circulation for several weeks. I had a surprise visit from Commander Colville in Westminster Hospital to wish me well and to convey good wishes from the Queen. It was pleasing to know I had not been forgotten. I was back in May in time to go to Denmark for that state visit. On short overseas tours I usually went in advance by air to reconnoitre and plan my coverage and to pre-film any useful shots, so I flew to Copenhagen ahead of the royal yacht *Britannia* in which the Queen and Duke travelled to the country.

It was an impressive arrival. King Frederick and Queen Ingrid went on board to greet the Queen and all came ashore together in the royal barge. There was an inspection of a guard of honour (I wonder how many guards of honour the Queen has inspected). This one was made up of soldiers of the Danish Royal Life Guards in red and blue dress and busbies. There was then a procession to the Amalienborg Palace, the two carriages carrying the royal party leading the way and escorted by the Royal Lifeguards also in dress uniform of red-and-blue and mounted with drawn swords. Soon after their arrival the King, the two queens and the Duke came on to the balcony of the palace to wave to the large crowd assembled below in a square which was formed by the four palaces which made up Amalienborg. In pictures it was a good start to the visit and the warmth of the Danes' greeting and the decorated streets and shops gave a feeling of genuine affection towards the visitors. I certainly liked the Danes, who were extremely friendly and helpful. Among the royal couple's engagements was a visit to the Royal Copenhagen porcelain factory to see the production of some of its beautiful objects and to the Carlsberg breweries to see brewing processes. A sample of their product was very nice. A function on every state visit is the state banquet. In Denmark it was partly televised to include the welcoming speeches and the Queen's reply. This was a first as far as I can recall and it emphasised the growing power of television, as did the televising of the Queen's Christmas broadcast at the end of the year. Altogether this visit was a very pleasant few days which I much enjoyed.

While the Queen was in America in October I went with the Duke of Edinburgh to the inauguration of the giant radar telescope at Jodrell Bank, near Manchester. We went in a lift to reach the bowl of the reflector. It was a weird feeling as we walked round its very large surface, the diameter of which is 250 feet. I could almost imagine we would take off, drawn to the stars and never be seen again. Unusual footage for the newsreels. At the end of the year there was a very bad train crash in thick fog at Lewisham; ninety passengers were killed and 250 injured. With this gloomy end there were forebodings of closures to come in the newsreels.

With two-thirds of the nation having television sets and a decline in the fortunes of the British film industry, 1958 was the beginning of the end for the cinema newsreels. Paramount was the first to close. Then Castleton-Knight, my former boss at Gaumont, was prematurely retired by John Davis, the Rank chief executive, and the following year *Gaumont-British News* and *Universal News* became a colour magazine called *Look at Life*. It was a melancholy time for me to see the end of the company in which I grew up and to lose the support of C.K. My own future had to be decided with only Pathe and Movietone remaining as newsreels. The Newsreel Association was wound up, meaning the closure of its offices in Soho Square. Pathe and Movietone still required royal coverage so for a while my company, British Newsreel Association Services, was kept on and I retained my accreditation to Buckingham Palace. With the closure of Soho Square I was moved to Pathe's offices in Film House, Wardour Street. This was full circle for me. I had been in Film House in publicity on the fifth floor and on the lower ground floor – or basement – with Gaumont, and now I was on the fourth floor with Pathe. I had not the heart to look in the basement to remind me of earlier happy times.

Despite the demise of their fellow reels and the menace of television, Pathe and Movietone continued to issue their reels without appearing to be curtailing the extent of their coverage. Stories on royal rota were generally concentrated on the more important events and I was busy on some short overseas tours as well as domestic ones. In March 1958 the Queen and Duke went on a three-day visit to Holland in the *Britannia*, starting in Amsterdam. As usual I flew ahead to film such things as decorations, shop windows with pictures of the royal couple, anything that added to the visit. I had to be careful in my choice of subject because the weather plays tricks. It may be sunny when pre-filming and raining when the royals arrive. As it happened, that time it was cold and wet on my arrival and for the visit. That did not stop large crowds lining the streets to see the processions, however. I filmed the *Britannia* arriving at her berth. I loved filming ships. They were impersonal and predictable, there was no waiting for them to turn round or smile or whatever. They always made good pictures. I filmed Princess Beatrix going out to the royal yacht to welcome the visitors and Queen Juliana greeting them when they came ashore in the royal barge. Prince Bernhard had a bad cold and was not at the quay but managed to attend later engagements. While there was an inspection of a guard of honour and the introduction of other VIPs I went ahead along the route to the Dam Palace to film the procession arriving there and was shepherded into a press enclosure with the Dutch press and some photographers from Britain. Fortunately it was a good position to show the arrival and the two queens and the two princes waving from the palace balcony to the huge crowd waiting in the large square in front. That was followed by wreath-laying at the national memorial in that same square. There were good close-ups when the Queen and Duke met men from the resistance forces from World War II.

At the centre of Dutch horticulture at Aalsmeer, a short distance south of Amsterdam, the Queen and Queen Juliana went to a Dutch auction of flowers. It made interesting film for the auction was mechanised, the buyers pressing buttons to indicate their bids, which were registered on a revolving pointer. Both queens had a go. Queen Juliana got a pot of orchids for around £10 but the British Queen, also bidding for orchids, paid nearly £50 for hers. From there I went ahead to The Hague where fisherwomen in traditional dress of black skirts, shawls and white lace caps surrounded the royal car, causing it to stop. They were very effusive in their greetings. Other engagements included a visit to a diamond works and to see a wonderful collection of early Dutch paintings. It remained cold with intermittent rain during the three days but as always in those years there were very large crowds everywhere.

A month later I was in a very hot and humid Trinidad for the inauguration of the West Indian Federation by Princess Margaret, deputising for the Queen. I arrived in Port-of-Spain three days ahead of the Princess to arrange positions for her arrival and the inauguration ceremony. It was an important occasion for the Caribbean islands, a coming together under the Federation of the British West Indies ten islands including Barbados, Grenada, Jamaica, Montserrat, St Lucia, Trinidad and Tobago. I filmed the arrival of the Princess and part of her drive to Government House, situated at the foot of densely wooded hills overlooking Port-of-Spain. The people in the city were determined that the Princess's visit was going to be a holiday. It was very gay with steel bands and dancing crowds and smiling faces along the processional routes. There was a state drive to open the first parliament of the new federation with the new federal flag of an orange sun on a background of blue Caribbean sea much in evidence. The local press and film people had installed overhead lighting for the ceremony, which, added to the extreme heat outside, was quite an ordeal for everyone. The heat was so intense in Trinidad that I ordered a lighter suit than I had brought with me and it was made in twenty-four hours. Even in that I was very uncomfortable. The Princess, dressed in a white gown with the sash of the Royal Victorian Order, entered in procession and occupied the speaker's chair. After speeches she formerly inaugurated the federation and opened its first parliament. I went outside after those proceedings to film the Princess, the governor and officials on the balcony of the council chamber waving to the crowds in the square below. The people in their gay attire made good pictures as they cheered the party on the balcony. In the evening the Princess met the West Indian and overseas press and shook hands with us all. I completed my coverage filming a splendid firework display. After several days of engagements in and around Port-of-Spain the Princess left for visits to Tobago, British Guiana and British Honduras. My brief was coverage in Trinidad so I did not cover those visits but returned to London.

Back in England the Queen opened Gatwick Airport in June. How that has developed since those days when there was just one long pier which ran alongside the single runway for arrivals and departures! Also in that year work began on building the Forth Road Bridge in Scotland, destined to be the longest road suspension bridge in Europe. Two important events for future communications in the air and on the roads.

The last year in that dramatic decade for the newsreels, 1959, was fairly quiet for us. The Queen went to America again for a joint ceremony with President Eisenhower to open the St Lawrence Seaway. I did not cover that. Later in the year Eisenhower came to Britain on a state visit. A large crowd gave him an enthusiastic welcome when he arrived at the American Embassy in Grosvenor Square. He was invited to Balmoral Castle to stay with the Queen, reviewing troops while there and sharing the visit with Harold Macmillan. There were several royal domestic stories during the year which I covered – a look at Kew Gardens, visits to Winchester and Portsmouth, exhibitions, and of course Trooping the Colour and Royal Ascot. A visit to Ghana at the end of the year was postponed when it transpired the Queen was pregnant.

We passed from one decade to another – to the 1960s. Just as the 1950s had changed my newsreel life to royal rota so next decade changed it again and in a way I had not expected.

Chapter Eleven
South America

The royals were in their castles; the turkeys were on their way to the nation's tables; holly, ivy and mistletoe hung from picture frames and lamps, and tinsel brightened rooms. Tiny angels sat atop trees decorated with baubles. The high streets of cities and towns were alight with twinkling bulbs and gaudy emblems were strung across their pathways. It was Christmas once again and it was 1959 and I sat wondering what the future held when the new year and the new decade began in a few days' time.

At the beginning of 1960 Harold Macmillan made his 'Wind of Change' speech in South Africa. 'Good old Mac,' I thought, for that seemed to fit in with my life as I had little idea which way the wind was blowing at the start of that new decade. After ten years on my own I was again in a camera room with cameramen I had been with many times on stories, whom I knew quite well superficially but who had not been part of my life other than on the road. It was like meeting someone in a pub but not knowing what they were like at home. They were a very different team from those I had worked with in my Gaumont days. Not unpleasant but different. British Newsreel Services and royal rota were still viable as company and employee but for the first two years of the sixties I could not see where my future lay.

Being in Pathe's offices I was more or less answerable to Tommy Cummins, Pathe's editor-in-chief, and had very little direct contact with Movietone. My relationship with Cummins was very different from that with C.K. I sensed he did not like my close connection with Buckingham Palace, believing that he should be the one to make the contacts. He was frequently on the phone to the Palace and it seemed to me he was intent on eventually taking over arrangements for royal coverage. I would find when additional cameramen were required he would send one of his cameramen to arrange the position, part of my job. I did not fight him on this for I was sure with only two newsreels and television getting stronger and more influential every month that royal rota was not going to last much longer and before long 'royal cameraman' would be just a memory.

On the royal front 1960 began with the birth of Prince Andrew, which meant a stint outside the Palace in the cool days of February. Soon after I was again at the Palace in great secrecy to film engagement pictures of Princess Margaret and Tony Armstrong-Jones (later Lord Snowdon). I took them on to the veranda at the back of the Palace overlooking the gardens. As Armstrong-Jones was himself a

Author's collection

My passport photograph at the time of the South American tour.

photographer the pictures were simple to arrange and the poses reasonably informal. In April General de Gaulle, having become president of France, came to Britain on a state visit. The last time I had seen him was during the war in the ill-fated battleship HMS *Barham* when, at Dakar, he tried to get the French fleet to capitulate, an attempt equally ill-fated. I was at Victoria Station for his arrival and it was decided Pathe and Movietone would make their own coverage for the state drive to Buckingham Palace and any of his non-royal subsequent engagements which they required. It became evident that apart from my own filming, except when space was a factor, rota coverage with only two reels was generally not required. Each company preferred to have its own original negative instead of a duplicate, and for the non-rota company it saved time, particularly important when there was an event the day before a reel was due to be issued. That was sensible.

Princess Margaret got married at Westminster Abbey in May. We had some coverage in the Abbey as did the BBC and ITV. Our two reels made their own arrangements for the processions; I was at Clarence House for the departure of the bride with the Duke of Edinburgh who acted as father to the Princess, and at Buckingham Palace in the forecourt for the return of all the royals and the bride and bridegroom. The appearance on the balcony was covered by both reels from the Queen Victoria Memorial. There were very large crowds lining the processional routes and at the Palace demonstrating the popularity of the royal family at that time.

During my time as royal cameraman very nice letters had been sent to the Newsreel Association by some members of the households and by the press secretaries of the Queen and Queen Mother as to my handling of my job, which was very pleasing. However I was surprised when I received a letter from the Chancery of the Order of Knighthood informing me that the Queen was going to appoint me a member of the Royal Victorian Order, an honour peculiar to and only bestowed by the monarch. In July I attended an investiture to receive that special 'gong'. It was a pleasant recognition of ten years of sometimes difficult work and an exceptional award for a cameraman. As far as I am aware no other cameraman has since become a member of that order and nowadays there are so many self-appointed royal photographers and royal correspondents, it would be interesting to know if any would be eligible. I was extremely pleased to receive a letter of congratulations from Castleton-Knight and to know that, although he was retired, he continued to keep in touch with newsreel events. The trade paper *The Cinema* gave me a mention but referred to me as being with Movietone. I rather enjoyed that. Cummins and Pathe were certainly not forthcoming.

The year continued with annual events – Trooping the Colour, Royal Ascot, royal command variety and film charity shows, the only rota coverage being mine inside the precincts of the Palace and interiors of events such as theatres at the charity shows.

In 1961 there were three overseas visits by the Queen to Italy, Ghana and India, the latter of which I would like to have covered to see how the country had developed since I was there in 1947. We did not send cameramen from London for any of these visits; with only two reels it was deemed too expensive. Each reel relied on associates to supply it with the stories. I was among the flowers at the Chelsea Flower Show, which the Queen and Duke attended in May. Afterwards I journeyed north to film the engagement of a charming and tall lady, Katherine Worsley, to the Duke of Kent at Hovingham Hall near York, the home of the bride-to-be's father, Sir William Worsley. I then went to York Minster to make arrangements for their wedding in June. It was a very special occasion for it was the first royal wedding in the minster for 633 years. Although the pageantry was similar to that at royal weddings in Westminster Abbey, in York there were noticeably fewer uniforms among the guests, most men being in morning dress and toppers, and the ladies wore informal short dresses. This gave a feeling of a family wedding and the crowds lining the streets seemed especially friendly. It seemed strange to see the Queen and other royals arrive in the city by train and drive to the church from the station instead of leaving from Buckingham Palace. I had cameras on the bride's processional route from Hovingham to the minster and inside alongside television, this time all positions on rota to save on costs. I was in the precincts of the church to film the bride, our royal family and many foreign royals arriving and departing. Very heavy rain drenched the crowd, the cameramen and myself for an hour before the wedding; when it left off and the sun came out just in time for the ceremony. Something different for a royal occasion and for the newsreels.

Since we had stopped filming royal overseas tours I was surprised to be told that I was to cover the Tanganyika independence ceremony at the end of 1961 and a tour of South America at the beginning of 1962, both to be undertaken by the Duke of Edinburgh. Tanganyika became independent on 9 December 1961. The Queen and Duke had been on a tour of West African countries due to end at the beginning of December. It was decided the Duke should remain in Africa to attend the independence celebrations while the Queen returned to England. I flew to Dar-es-Salaam, the capital, and arrived the day before the Duke. It was hot with a tropical heat of about 80 °F, but although there had been reasonably heavy rainfalls during the year it was not humid and was quite pleasant. Before the Duke's arrival I filmed a ceremony when a large independence monument was unveiled by Julius Nyerere, the future prime minister, and at which Jomo Kenyatta of neighbouring Kenya and of Mau-Mau fame was present. I filmed the Duke's arrival by air in the afternoon of 8 December, greetings by Nyerere and Sir Richard Turnbull, the Governor-General designate, and the beginning of the drive into the town through streets lined with schoolchildren. Otherwise there were not large crowds. While the Duke was at a state banquet in the evening I went to the stadium where the independence ceremony was to be staged at midnight and which seated 70,000 people. There was a tattoo preceding the ceremony and I filmed a little of that as the stadium centre was well floodlit. The midnight proceedings followed a general pattern which had become standard when a country became independent. The Union Jack, flying from a flagstaff, was floodlit in the centre of the stadium. As the clock struck twelve all the lights went out. After a minute or so of total darkness the lights came on again to reveal the Union Jack had been hauled down and

Tanganyika's new flag of black, gold and green was being hoisted up the flagstaff to cheers and applause from the crowd. The following morning in the same stadium there was another ceremony at which the Duke gave Nyerere the formal constitutional instruments of independence and Sir Richard Turnbull was sworn in as Governor-General. There followed a number of receptions at which gifts were presented to the new Commonwealth country from delegates of foreign countries invited to the ceremonies. There was a state ball and a garden party and where there was enough light I filmed a composite of those events. The three-day visit of the Duke ended with the state opening of the first parliament in the new Tanganyika. The Duke presided on behalf of the Queen. It followed the formalities of such occasions but was less colourful than an opening by the Queen. I managed to get some footage where the local press had installed some lighting. After this the Duke flew off, piloting a Heron of the Queen's Flight, it was thought to see wild animals in Serengeti National Park, and I flew back to England.

The year ended quietly with Christmas and new year passing without any special celebrations in the office. At Gaumont we usually got a bonus of a week's salary at Christmas and there was always a big card school when poker and pontoon were played with quite high stakes. It was not unknown for some to go home with bulging pockets and others with empty ones. We did not have an office party but there was usually a get-together in our local, The George, in Wardour Street – and sometimes a venture into one of the opposition drinking dens.

In the middle of January 1962 I received a letter from Richard Colville to say that the Duke of Edinburgh's household were inviting me to Buckingham Palace for drinks to meet them before the South American tour. In all the tours I had been on over the years this was the first time I had received a formal invitation to meet all the household. On previous occasions I had sometimes met the odd member with whom I was on friendly terms for an informal drink. Since on this tour we were going to be travelling together in a fairly small aircraft it was an imaginative gesture to get to know who everyone was before we started. On the press side, apart from myself there was Peter Tearall, a still photographer from the Central Office of Information (COI); Bruce Russell, a Reuters correspondent; and a BBC reporter, George Hills, so the party at the palace was an opportunity to meet them, too. My fellow accredited colleagues at the Palace were not on this tour as their primary duties were to follow the Queen's activities.

After this party Commander Colville advised me that he had asked the ambassadors in each South American country to arrange accommodation for myself and colleagues wherever we were due to spend the night so that we would be under one roof. That was a great help, as with so many places involved and last-minute changes of plans it would have been extremely difficult for my office to find suitably located hotels and to book them in advance and almost impossible otherwise to find somewhere on arrival at each night stop. There would have been the added complication of heavy baggage and equipment which had to be moved with the household luggage from the aircraft at each overnight stop. We had to make our own financial arrangements, and dollar traveller's cheques were the answer to that, with the assurance from the Palace that if in difficulty the Duke's treasurer, Admiral Bonham-Carter, would help out.

So on 6 February 1962 my heavy baggage, consisting of two suitcases of clothes, one camera and seven pieces of equipment and film stock, was left at Buckingham Palace that morning to be taken to the plane with the household luggage during the day. On that tour I used an Arriflex camera, battery-driven with 400-foot magazines, less heavy than my Newman Sinclair and with better lenses. A second camera was the 100-foot LeBlay I had used on the Canadian tour and which I kept with me together with a small personal case which acted as a spares bag with pre-loaded film magazines and some night things. In this way I was ready to film as soon as we arrived. I was at London Airport in the evening to join the royal plane – a Britannia 312 – to fly via Dakar to Georgetown in British Guiana to begin the two-month tour of Latin America. Apart from the crew there were sixteen of us travelling – the Duke, the household, secretaries, Superintendent Frank Kelley, who was the Duke's police officer, and we four press.

To write of South America could be a book in itself. It has always seemed a romantic continent with places such as Rio de Janiero, the Amazon, the Andes, Venezuela, Chile, Brazil and the Argentine. Each country is vastly different. One encounters high mountains, huge deserts, ancient cities, modern cities, even futuristic cities, and jungles, rivers and lakes of incredible size with differing climates throughout. As this book is of my newsreel life I have to describe what I filmed more than what I saw, and that of course related to the Duke of Edinburgh's schedule and to specific requests we undertook to film for the COI. There was a great deal of British interest and trade in every country. Britain had been foremost in helping to establish the independence of the various countries, aided by trade links between Britain and what were Spanish colonies at the beginning of the 1890s. It was this trade aspect that took up much of the Duke's time, visiting factories and associated organisations. Throughout the tour I took more arrivals, official receptions, meetings of British and Commonwealth residents at garden parties, than I would have normally taken for the newsreels, much of it to accommodate the COI requests. The COI had its own representatives in some cities either at an embassy or in a separate office and they would sometimes update me on a requirement. Occasionally when I was able to advise them in advance that I was going to arrive somewhere after the Duke they would arrange for a local cameraman to cover the arrival.

The tour was very different from those I had been on when the Queen was present. There were no openings of parliaments; there were formal drives into and around cities but not state drives in the accepted sense. There were the usual official welcomes, guards of honour and laying of wreaths but with a great deal of informality. Being generally on the same plane as the Duke presented some problems on arrival at the various airfields as I could not leave the plane before him. When possible the household were very helpful in letting me and the photographer precede them. With large press contingents at every stop, however, royal rota mostly meant joining the scrum and fighting for a position when one eventually landed. Superintendent Kelley did his best to help but he was usually fully occupied with the local police trying to keep the crowds from getting too close to the Duke; they always seemed to be able to break through the police barriers. With planes, particularly in South America when we were travelling in small aircraft, there is usually a support plane carrying baggage and some staff, and if it was scheduled to arrive before the royal plane I was sometimes aboard it. No matter what the transport it was always a problem keeping ahead when travelling with the royal party. In ships it was easier when alongside for there was nearly always a second gangway; if anchored offshore the royals would leave in the royal barge and sometimes I was able to get aboard with the household and remain below out of sight. Trains and cars were less of a problem except that one was some way from the royal coach or car and that meant a rush to catch up.

So began a tour which must have been one of the most singular assignments any solo cameraman had ever been given. We arrived on the morning of 7 February at Atkinson airport, British Guiana, about twenty-five miles outside the capital, Georgetown. As we flew over the city I filmed from the cockpit of the Britannia to get pictures of the city and the touchdown. It was a very wet welcome. Later the Duke went to the legislature to receive a loyal address. There was insufficient light to film inside but outside I found an interesting placard exhibited in the crowd on which were anti-Jagan slogans on one side and 'Welcome Philip' on the other (Jagan was the Prime Minister). The next day we flew in two helicopters to Port Mourant where we were greeted by a steel band playing the national anthem. The Duke visited a school; toured a display of agricultural exhibits; met Ameridians, representatives of the original race in Guiana; and saw some Creole-bred horses. It was then to New Amsterdam, which gave me a chance to take shots of the other helicopter from the air, such shots being a useful means of linking the various places visited. After a marchpast of schoolchildren we went to see a demarera sugar estate at Enmore by the Demarera river, after which we returned to Georgetown. Early on the final day in Guiana I took pictures around Georgetown and in the late morning we were again in the helicopters to fly sixty miles up the Demarera river to Mackenzie to see the very large, rich bauxite mines. How very different this was from the discovery of bauxite in England twenty-five years before – my first solo newsreel job. I saw some extensive bauxite mines in Jamaica during the Commonwealth tour in 1953, but those in Mackenzie were even larger, more widespread and made excellent film; a change from official receptions. At

Mackenzie it was goodbye to the helicopters and to British Guiana as we emplaned for the first time in the royal Dart Herald to fly to Caracas the capital of Venezuela.

Venezuela is tropical and seven times the size of England. Flying across the Orinocco river, which flows 1,000 miles across the country into the Atlantic and is deep enough up to 100 miles from its mouth to allow ships the size of the *Queen Elizabeth* to navigate its waters, we passed over some of the country's measureless plains. In the distance we could see the mountains of the northern Andes, some of which rose 10,000 feet, overlooking Caracas. As we approached the capital, a modern city spread over a large area, I was again able to get shots from the plane. Its mountain background made Caracas a particularly breathtaking picture. Later, whenever we approached a town or city I filmed from the air, sometimes successfully, sometimes not. I got the idea that the tour was going to be one where general views were going to be very important in establishing both the size and the contrasts of all those different countries whether taken from the air or the ground.

Taking arrival pictures in Venezuela was a battle indeed. The reception party came aboard the Herald to greet the Duke, which gave me a chance to leave the plane before him. I was confronted with representatives from twenty-five daily newspapers, seventy radio stations, five television outlets and over 300 magazines, Venezuela's press, all based in and around Caracas. There was another fight with the crowd and all those local press at an important wreath-laying ceremony at the Carabobo Monument, which commemorated the battle at Carabobo where Venezuealan and British volunteers fought together against the Spanish, won the battle and liberated the country. The leader of the Venezuelans was Simon Bolivar and the Duke visited Bolivar's birthplace, which had become a museum and national shrine. Among the processes shown to the Duke at the Reckitts & Colman's factory were mustard seeds being crushed and mustard being bottled, which made interesting shots. This was our port of call before taking to the air for Maracaibo, 300 miles from Caracas, the principal town at the centre of the oil-producing region. Venezuela's economy was mainly vested in oil and the greater part of its production came from under Lake Maracaibo. There was not much to film here as we did not see any oil production. After talks with trade unionists the Duke left for a weekend at the Vestey's ranch and we four press and the governor and his party flew back to Caracas. This gave me an opportunity to film scenes in the capital, including the marvellous road system of flyovers and network of ultra-modern roads. I also obtained permission to get some air-to-air shots of a Dart Herald. I only had half an hour and it was not a great success. I could not get both Heralds in the air, as one was with the Duke, so I had to film from a Dove aircraft. I could not get close shots for in spite of the Herald throttling right back and flying on one engine, the Dove was too slow to keep up with it. I tried to get them to fly over mountainous country but with the limited time available that was not possible. The Herald's crew said there might be another chance later, but it was not to be.

British Pathe

The Duke of Edinburgh meeting the people on his South American tour. From the newsreel.

Although not what I really wanted there were some useful pictures, and I was grateful for what must have been quite an expensive operation. There were more engagements in Caracas when the Duke returned before we left for Bogota in Columbia.

This country was very much a stickler for protocol. Everything was said nicely and politely for the people were pleasant but protocol was certainly on the agenda everywhere. It made it difficult sometimes to get into the processions and into good positions at some engagements. Royal rota was not in their vocabulary and I had to enlist the help of Kelley and one of the household to enlighten their officials that I was one of the royal party. We were there for three days. Approaching Bogata we flew over high mountainous areas and volcanoes, the fabulous Andes, which ran south some 4,000 miles to Chile. We arrived in heavy rain. As he left the plane the Duke said, 'Now it's my turn to get wet,' and he did. He had to meet the reception committee and inspect a guard of honour and then drive into Bogata in an open car, where, on arriving in the city, there was a wreath-laying ceremony at the Bolivar statue. The Duke was soaked. Meanwhile a band played, soldiers stood to attention, all equally drenched; protocol had been observed. A bizarre section of film taken by an equally sodden cameraman. Later I took an exchange of decorations at the presidential palace in drier conditions, but in poor light. At De la Rue's factory the

Duke saw stamps being printed and some of the machinery was restricted for close-ups. A Glaxo factory and an Austin assembly plant followed, all wanted by the COI as well as the newsreels; most operations at factories are very interesting. We flew to the walled city of Cartagena on the northern Caribbean coast of Colombia where there were pictures of an old fort, a drive past manned ships of the Colombian navy, and a visit to the navy school. On the way to Cartagena I was able to get shots of Prince Philip in his shirtsleeves at the controls of the Herald, writing a letter in his compartment, studying a route map with Admiral Bonham-Carter and looking out of a window. I got a special plug in Venezuela to use in the plane on the advice of one of the Herald's engineers and with his assistance rigged up lighting with photo-floods. The Duke was very cooperative and waited patiently when the lights had to be moved. I was also able to film the flight crew and the aircraft controls, all of which helped to link the move from country to country.

Before leaving Colombia I had to send off my film. This was necessary before leaving each territory. Wherever one was, at home or somewhere else in the world one of our most important jobs was to get the exposed film to the laboratories, if possible in time to catch the next reel. On a tour such as in South America it had to have priority even if it meant missing an engagement. On arriving at a new place I had to locate the post office, the cable office and the air dispatch centre. Cables had to include the waybill number, the expected time of arrival, length of film and important relevant facts that might be useful to know in advance, for example, if there were any sound tapes with the film. Packing film, dope sheets, tapes which I sometimes acquired from local radio stations, and programmes, each tin labelled to correspond with the dope sheet was a nightmare and time-consuming especially if I had to leave it to the last minute to include a particularly important item, with limited time before the Duke's plane left for the next country. When I was in a place for a long time, as on the Indian tour, I used a shipping agent to take a lot of the documentation off my hands and to dispatch the film, but on the move all the time in South America (and on other tours) that was not possible.

Ecuador took its name from the equator, which crosses the country almost through the centre of Quito, the capital, 9,000 feet up, where we landed at midday on 12 February. The Hotel Quito, where everyone including the Duke was staying, lay snugly between hills and snow-covered mountains rising to 16,000 feet, with rolling clouds crossing a clear blue sky adding extra beauty. This too was the lovely setting of the capital itself. The first day, which was generally quiet for filming, gave me an opportunity for some very attractive pictures. Cavalry escorted the drive from the airport to the presidential palace where, in reasonable light for the camera, there was a cordial exchange of decorations, the Duke investing the president as a Commander of the Order of St Michael and St George. In the evening while the Duke was at a small dinner party we four press visited a casino in the centre of Quito, played with one-armed bandits and had a go on the tables – for small stakes.

211

Later, with HRH safely in his rooms, Superintendent Kelley gave a midnight party to which I was invited; it was as well he had no further duties that night! Quito had some wonderful churches, and visits to some of these with the Duke, walking through tranquil cloisters with Franciscan friars, provided the basis of my film in that country. There were big crowds wherever the Duke went, giving the impression of a large population, whereas there were only four million people in the whole of Ecuador. Among the Duke's other engagements were meetings with diplomats and British and Commonwealth residents, which were not specially interesting for the newsreels, but I covered these as they were of interest to the COI. A spring in one of the cameras broke in Quito, but with the help of one of the Herald's engineers who had suitable tools I was able to make a replacement. He also recharged my Arriflex batteries overnight when opportunities arose, always a problem when travelling with battery-driven cameras, and on this tour it was marvellous to have such availabilty most of the time.

Peru – Inca country – provided some spectacular film. The buildings and the ambience in Lima, the capital city, were worth many feet of film. The tall, modern buildings such as the senate and the ministries of education and finance contrasted with the lovely Spanish-style houses and Lima cathedral. There was a street of flowers, there were vendors selling their wares from bicycle-like contraptions; there were rich and poor areas, the latter with many beggars which reminded me of India. Devastation by an earthquake, which fortunately had left some of the more beautiful houses and areas undamaged, resulted in splendid new road systems being built. I took general views both from the air and the ground with a wonderful backdrop of high mountains. The many marvellous churches and the mixture of old and modern made a different picture from what we were to see later in the mountains.

Soon after we arrived there was an exchange of decorations and presents at the presidential palace with the Duke personally robing President Prada with the mantle of the Grand Cross of the British Empire. It was an unusual picture to get especially as the atmosphere was very informal with everyone relaxed and smiling. This was followed by a press reception, one of several on the tour ensuring maximum publicity. There was a visit to the Central Railway shops in which the Duke, a train enthusiast, was greatly interested. On display was a British-built locomotive, thirty years old and still in use: Peru has the highest railway in the world, climbing to more than 15,000 feet. Peter Tearall, the COI photographer, was at most of the interior locations and I was sometimes guided by him as to COI interest. At the Engineering University the Duke cut a tape at the Heat Engine Laboratory to inaugurate a new section containing British equipment. And again, everywhere we went there were large crowds.

We left Lima in a civil aircraft for Cuzco, once the capital of the Inca empire, and situated in a valley of mountains 11,500 feet above sea level. On the way I took some splendid views of the Andes. The people of Cuzco were mostly American Indian but many had Spanish lineage. Every country in South America had beautiful churches and monasteries and Cuzco was no exception with a solid silver altar in its cathedral. We went by rail, a three-and-a-half hour journey rising between the mountains, to see the ancient hidden ruins of Macchu Pichu, which were only discovered in 1911. After shots of the Prince in the railcar I went on ahead filming scenery which showed torrents of water cascading into the rivers below. Peru has fifty-two rivers of which ten are major ones. At the approach to the foot of Macchu Pichu I took the Duke's railcar arriving. From here we went by bus to the top of the mountain where lay those vast ruins built in terraces. They made excellent pictures. We were there for nearly three hours, giving me plenty of time to choose my shots. That did not happen very often. Some of the ruins I filmed showed examples of the Incas' building skills. They used large granite stones, which they put together perfectly without mortar and which have survived *in situ*, despite earthquakes and earth tremors, over a considerable period. I was able to get some shots of the bus on the mountain roads on the return journey. Back in Cuzco the Duke drove round looking at places of interest with crowds surrounding his car every time it stopped or slowed down.

We left Cuzco, again in a civil plane, for a short flight to Juliaca and continued on by royal train to Puno, a town situated on the Peruvian side of the giant Lake Titicaca. In the market square there was a traditional folk dance, the women clad in long white skirts and bowler hats and dancing to music from wind instruments, which women also played. Peru had given me film different from the normal formal engagements which were inevitable in each country visited. There was much of interest in every city and territory but this was not a sightseeing tour so in Peru I was glad to be able to show something akin to one, which showed the contrasts and splendours of the whole continent.

We said goodbye to Peru from Puno in a different form of transport. We embarked in a British steamer for Bolivia to spend the night crossing Lake Titicaca, 350 fathoms deep, 150 miles long, sixty miles wide and 12,000 feet high in the mountains, the largest navigable lake in the world. More splendid pictures. After shots on the lake and passing local boats made of reed we arrived at Guaqui on the Bolivian side of the lake, where there was another royal train to take us to La Paz, over 12,000 feet above sea level and built on forty hills, with twenty bridges. This was another capital city which demanded filming. Grey-green eucalyptus trees, narrow cobbled streets, bowler-hatted women in colourful national dress selling their goods in the markets and huge snow-covered mountains all round. Pictures galore. As the Duke walked through the streets he was showered with confetti and flowers causing me to be constantly wiping the camera lenses. At those heights, in the rarified thin air, carrying my camera gear and moving quickly made me very tired and exhausted and everyone in our party had to slow up.

The Duke of Edinburgh arriving in La Paz (Bolivia), standing in his car as he did on every public drive. From the newsreel.

British Pathe

After the formal engagements we went by Landrover to nearby villages, passing llamas on the roads. In the village of Milluni at the Fabulosa mine, a source of mineral ores, the miners and their womenfolk, many with babies on their backs, gave the Duke a great welcome. After the inspection of the mine there was a marchpast by the miners' children dressed in spotless white pinafores, followed by the bowler-hatted women who took off their hats as they passed the Duke. Climbing to 17,000 feet along snow-covered roads, HRH went to the world's highest laboratory to see cosmic ray equipment. The going was really hard at that height. Finally in Bolivia there was a traditional dance by the Orura devil dancers, a very weird dance in weird costumes performed in the La Paz stadium and watched by large crowds in addition to the royal party. Before saying goodbye to Bolivia I packed up more extremely interesting film.

It was a seven-and-a-half-hours' flight to Santiago in Chile and we four press flew there in a civil aircraft, necessary as the Heralds had to carry all the heavy baggage in one plane and all the royal party in the other. On shorter flights we split up between the two planes. More film stock I had ordered from London, which I estimated would be sufficient for the remainder of the tour, was waiting in Santiago. I did not film much in Chile. It was more European than the places we had already seen. We saw damage caused by an earthquake in 1960 which made the whole area of Valdivia, south of Santiago, sink three feet with resultant severe flooding from the river. We visited a textile factory and went to the races. While the Duke took a day off after seeing Valdivia we four press returned to Santiago. On top of Mount Saint Christopher, overlooking the city, was a very tall statue of the Virgin Mary, which made an interesting general view with the lady in the foreground. As I did in each country I took establishing shots of the capital, which was very pretty set among the hills. There was also an opportunity to take further shots of the interior layout of the Herald other than those I had filmed earlier with the Duke in his compartment and at the controls. On those occasions when I was trying to get pictures from the air and the Duke was not flying the aircraft, when possible the pilot would position the plane to get the best view. This was very helpful for the COI photographer and myself in particular, and all the crew were always obliging if we needed assistance so I was very pleased to have an opportunity in the evening to host a party for them with my colleagues.

Paraguay was next. Excited crowds cheered Prince Philip as he left the airport for the capital, Asuncion. On the way from Chile we had experienced some very severe tropical rainstorms at 20,000 feet. Now, as we neared the centre of the city, there was a tremendous tropical rainstorm and it became so dark that I could not film. The chief interest in this country was its very extensive cattle ranches and we journeyed by car to see one on which there was a large herd which the gauchos (cowboys) were rounding up; one explained to the Duke the merits of a saddle in which he was interested. Later an exhibition of British goods provided an opening for British industry and from there we went to see a meat-packing factory. Paraguay's music was very individual, somewhat sad but very pleasant to listen to, and there were opportunities at some of the functions to hear a little of it.

Montevideo in Uruguay, where the battle of the River Plate and the scuttling of the *Graf Spee* took place in World War II, was the ninth capital on our tour. Uruguay is the smallest country in South America and one of the friendliest, its people very smart and very clean. It had beautiful beaches with breathtaking scenery bordering the coast with the weather fairly hot during the day and pleasantly cool at night. At a wreath-laying ceremony at the statue of General Artigas the crowd broke loose and the Duke and his party disappeared into the melee and eventually so did I. Like its near-neighbour, Paraguay, Uruguay had very large farms and we flew 100 miles north of Montevideo to see an estancia. I went ahead of the royal party to get shots of the Duke's plane from the ground as it landed on the grass runway. The gauchos watched the landing from their horses and after the plane was down they rode round the Herald to have a look at that strange bird. The skills of the gauchos were demonstrated as the Duke watched them breaking in horses, after which he rode off in an old Rolls-Royce to look at a herd of about a thousand Hereford cattle. Before leaving Uruguay the Duke met the players at the start of an international match between Uruguay and Argentina at the Montevideo football stadium. Everyone in that part of the continent was fanatical about football.

From the smallest country and comparative tranquility to the fourth largest in the world – Brazil – and the hurly-burly of sophisticated Latin America. We flew to Brasilia, the new capital of Brazil since 1960, and arrived on 15 March. Brasilia is 3,600 feet above sea level and about 600 miles inland from the Atlantic coast. The architecture was astounding in its futuristic modernity, almost impossible to describe. It provided a field day for something different in general views. The Alvorado Palace where the Duke stayed certainly did not look like the kind of palace that we were used to seeing. It had large glass windows and tapering columns along its front. The congressional office buildings were twenty-eight-story twin towers set very close together. The Chamber of Deputies was bowl-shaped rather like a cup and saucer. There were multi-level cloverleaf roads and wonderful vistas to be seen from the area of the parliament buildings. Some places were still being built including the cathedral and national theatre. There had been a lot of rain and the building was progressing in thick mud. The Duke spent several hours walking round to see all those wonders. Brazil, the only Portuguese-speaking country on the continent, certainly was way ahead of its Spanish colleagues in modern architecture. Whether I was overcome by seeing so much originality or whatever, whilst filming I fell off a wall on which I was standing for elevation. Apart from embarrassment and cutting my knee and trousers I escaped anything more serious.

From the extremely modern to the modern Sao Paulo, a busy city with many high buildings. There were two interesting factories to see and film. At Dunlop to watch the making of tyres and at Lever Brothers to see soap and detergents made. For my general shots of the city I concentrated on its skyscraper aspect and also endeavoured to emphasise a Portuguese angle by filming some of the older buildings and churches to contrast with the Spanish influence elsewhere. Before watching a football match in Sao Paulo's Pacaembu Stadium the Duke met the players, including the famous Pelé. To judge by the enthusiasm of the crowd watching the match our crowds are quiet. After four days of mostly official engagements in that expanding and thriving city, we flew into Rio de Janeiro. There were a number of official receptions, wreath-laying and similar, but apart from filming some of these wanted by the COI there was not a lot to film in Rio for the newsreels except to show its very attractive leisure side. I showed the long, curving Copacabana beach and Sugar Mountain in the centre of the bay where the people and tourists came to relax and some of the many jewellery shops fronting the sea, selling gems at bargain prices. And I had to take the towering figure of Christ the Reedemer which topped the 2,300-foot Corrovada Peak overlooking the bay and beaches. The three days spent in Rio were very pleasant before we left for Buenos Aires in Argentina.

It was 22 March when we reached Argentina, the last country in our South American schedule. There were very large and excited crowds at every engagement in the very large city of Buenos Aires, often breaking through police cordons and engulfing the Duke and his party. It was a wonder he was not thrown off balance in his open car, as usually in his drives through the cities throughout the tour he was standing to wave to the crowds. Almost miraculously we had gone all the way round in that often volatile continent without a coup, a head of state being deposed or an earthquake. However, in Argentina there was political unrest and when the Duke visited the Siam di Tella car factory there was a strike, part of a general one attempting to remove the president, and there were no workers on the assembly lines. But to the delight of everyone they all turned up in their Sunday best to give the Duke a great welcome, completely surrounding him wherever he went in the plant and making it difficult to get pictures of him looking at a completed car. Apart from this the troubles in the country did not affect the remainder of the Duke's programme. A huge power station was being constructed by British companies, destined to supply 600,000 kilowatts of electricity. From the outside it had a futuristic look; from the inside the Duke saw some of the mass of equipment required for the project. The general pictures in the capital, of wide spaces and imposing government and private buildings, were worthy of the second largest state in South America. Among the shops was an exact replica of Harrod's in London. I had some difficulty in obtaining some of those shots, as there were armed guards everywhere because of the poltical situation.

As a child I was sickened by what I saw at an abattoir which I came upon by chance in my wanderings alone in a back street somewhere in the Midlands. It may be different now, but the callous slaughter – and no one will convince me that what I witnessed then was other than callous – the cries of pigs and the terrified eyes of cattle remain with me even now. When we came to the Frigorifico Anglo meat factory, one of the Vestey interests, I was alarmed I was going to have to see similar scenes on a much larger scale. I was spared, however, as no slaughtering took place whilst the Duke was there. Dressed in a white coat he looked over the *corrales* where cattle and sheep were assembled to await their end. We saw them disembarked from road transport into pens, driven into baths by herdsmen, and after being cleansed, moved to the foot of a slope where they were marshalled to take their final walk up to the slaughterhouse. I again saw that frightened look in the eyes of the animals, for they were well aware of what lay ahead. From here we went inside for interesting shots of the various stages of meat production. In the chill room many carcasses were hanging, waiting to be cut up for corned beef. Bagged meat was stacked ready to be loaded into refrigerated ships; at that time over 1,000 tons of chilled beef was exported weekly from the Argentine to Britain from that one plant. The visit made good newsreel film but I was not sorry to leave. After that the Duke went to a British hospital, an old men's home and the Mission to Seamen, and he laid a foundation stone for a new Bank of London and South America, events which concluded my coverage in Buenos Aires before we left for Cordoba, a town about three hours' flight from the coast.

There were a lot of press and sound units from radio stations thrusting microphones unceremoniously close to the Duke's face whenever he stopped in Cordoba and I thought he coped rather well, perhaps rather better than he might have in England. On arrival I had a slight mishap when a cable from the camera battery broke requiring a hurried repair, especially as there were a number of engagements specially requested by the COI – meeting government officials, receiving the key of the city and talking to the British community. There was one more factory to see, where engines were being produced, before Prince Philip took off in his Herald to spend a few private days at an *estancia* owned by Bovril. I took a final shot of him at the controls of the Herald from the ground and the plane taking off and disappearing into the distance. That concluded my coverage and the Duke's official programme in South America. Before returning to England we were to go to British Honduras to complete the tour, and we four press were flown back to Buenos Aires in the other Herald and from there flew by civil airline via Miami to Kingston, Jamaica, to await HRH for that final visit. There was an alteration in the programme and we joined the royal plane at Kingston to fly to the Caribbean island of Grand Cayman before going to Honduras. On the island I filmed pictures of rope-making by the women, a look at 'Hell', a fantastic rock formation of eroded limestone, and some general shots of the beautiful tropical beaches.

We flew to Belize in British Honduras for a day's visit. In October 1961 Hurricane Hattie struck the town destroying most of it and making thousands homeless. The Duke saw some of the damaged areas with much still to be cleared up. Nearby was a temporary town, Hattieville, taking its name from the hurricane. The inhabitants are British, mostly black, and were intensely loyal, delighted to see the Duke. In some ways it was rather a sad end to the tour to see all those people without proper homes although they were very cheerful in greeting the Duke as he drove round in an open car, standing up to be seen and to wave to everyone. We returned to Grand Cayman in the evening. The following day was free until in the late afternoon of 5 April we flew back to Kingston and immediately transferred to the Britannia aircraft to return via Bermuda to London. Before we got on the plane I took some final shots of the Duke saying goodbye to the crews of the two Heralds and giving them signed photographs. We took off at 7.50 p.m. and arrived at Heathrow at 4.30 p.m. on 6 April, exactly two months since leaving London.

It had been a remarkable tour. There were some hair-raising drives along mountain roads, as we press were generally in the last car and had to travel the fastest to keep up with the royal party. Sometimes the food was hard on the digestive organs. In the tropics it was often a fight against the bugs; at night they vented their frustration at not being able to get to us by hurling themselves at the hotel windows. There were many different beds, mostly very comfortable. What did surprise me were the very large crowds everywhere to see an overseas celebrity. That might be expected in English-speaking countries, but in South America where the language and the populations were mainly Spanish or Portuguese it underlined the good relations between those countries and Britain, no doubt stemming from the early days when we helped them gain their independence. Such a turnout justified the royal visit and must have resulted in increased trade.

There were many cameramen in each country, often with assistants, while I was always acting as a sole operator, which I preferred, but it was quite a strain humping the equipment around in the mountains, keeping up with the royal party, packing and unpacking and dispatching the negatives. I made fourteen shipments back to London, shot 23,700 feet of film, travelled 36,000 miles in twelve countries. It says much for the general organisation behind me that on this and on all the tours I have been on rarely has anything gone badly wrong. Although a working tour, in between the filming there had been opportunities to experience the contrasts in each place visited. The mountains, the plains, the wonderful scenery, the industry, the very old and the very modern – all were very impressive. The personality of the Duke of Edinburgh, acting on his own without the Queen, held together the changes from one country to another and was a consistent factor throughout. Possibly, apart from India, this was the most interesting and enjoyable tour I had been on, even more so than the six-month journey round the world.

Of the people on the tour, Admiral Bonham-Carter was a kindly, very helpful member of the household. The Duke was always courteous and aware that pictures had to be taken whether he liked it or not. Of my three colleagues I liked Bruce Russell of Reuters best. He was always interesting and a character. We got on very well together, sometimes having to share rooms, but strangely in spite of working so closely together I never met or saw any of them again after returning to England. I suppose that tour was a fitting climax to my career as a newsreel cameraman for I was to hang up my travelling boots on returning to Pathe, where I learned it was my last job and that I was to join Pathe's inside staff. British Newsreel Association Services was to close and royal rota ended.

My job at Pathe was to be an assistant in the publicity and production department with my immediate boss the news editor and production manager – a woman – Grace Field. I learned this with some misgivings. I had not been consulted as to whether I wanted the job or what it entailed. It transpired that from a fairly creative occupation as a newsreel cameraman, I was to sort newspaper cuttings and do odd things no one else wanted to do. I felt it was back to the days when I had just started work. However, I thought it wise to accept the situation as it at least gave me a base with the opportunity to look around for something better without the desperation of being jobless, something I had never been since I started work. I was in an office with a middle-aged fellow who searched through newspapers for stories and the news editor's secretary, a bumptious girl I did not like although I thought she was brighter than Miss Field. She was instrumental in bringing the Beatles to the notice of Pathe before they took off and the reel got an exclusive session with them at just the right time. Grace Field was quite a pleasant woman, almost apologetic sometimes, but never made use of my experience on the production side. Whether this was a directive from Cummins I never knew. He did not like me. Having a full compliment of cameramen I think he resented having to take me on his staff and find a position for me. In doing so he certainly did nothing to give me any status. He was a complex character. Sometimes he could be quite charming but I had the impression he was suffering from an inferiority complex and that underneath his gruff manner he was essentially a nice man. However I did not trust him and our relationship was never close. When he turned on the charm he usually wanted to know something to do with Buckingham Palace. On that I must admit I was not forthcoming. I was keeping my contacts and friends to myself. Grace Field could have used me to advantage, for she was not very knowledgeable technically and whenever a story had to be contacted to make prior arrangements she sent one of the cameramen to deputise for her. I did not suggest otherwise, for it was a practice that had been going on over many years and I think it suited Cummins for he was very pro-cameramen – his cameramen – and sometimes would go out with them. He had been a cameraman himself. It was not a happy time. I was at an age when it was not easy to find another job where my experience would be beneficial, but I kept my ear to the ground for a move.

Then the fates stepped in. Tommy Cummins retired early, although he was by no means at retirement age. I think his decision was prompted by the fact that his wife was ill. This rather endorsed my earlier thoughts that basically he was a nice man. However his going was a godsend for me. His successor was Terry Ashwood, a former cameraman, one of the few I had never met, and a protegee of Howard Thomas, managing director of ABC Television. Ashwood had also become a director of the company by the time he came to the newsreel. We clicked at once. Life immediately had a different look. He thought Grace Field was not the right person for her position and it was not long before she was moved sideways and then out. She was not young and was given early retirement. Her secretary was not a favourite of Terry Ashwood either, and it was not long before she left. I was promoted to production manager and after Grace Field left became news editor as well. I was now able to appreciate fully what it was like to be behind the desk. The story researcher was efficient and I obtained a glamorous secretary who was very much on the ball. How I had scoffed in my early days as a cameraman when I was given a newspaper cutting to cover a story. Now instead of receiving them, I was handing them out! At first I gave out the more interesting events with reluctance, for I would probably have had such stories myself had I still been a cameraman. It took a while to become the executive and to realise that the team of cameramen was under my command and that I was no longer one of them. I did think they were an imaginative lot when I saw their expenses; I had obviously been missing a lot. They accepted the loss of Cummins and Miss Field with good grace and appreciated that the close life that they had had with those two was no longer quite the same with Ashwood and me. It must have been very traumatic for them to be faced with new management after so many years under the old. We were all facing change, however, and generally we got on well without any great difficulties. With give and take on both sides of the desk we continued and remained a good team.

I endeavoured to show no favouritism, but Pat Whitaker and Ken Goddard were the ones I liked best. They always accepted assignments without queries and inevitably often got the best ones. The portly, outspoken, likeable Ken Gordon was occasionally troublesome and Ced Baynes, the chief cameraman, took some time to be really cooperative, but with all of them the stories were always well-covered and that was what mattered. On major stories it was usual for the production manager to make the early arrangements. When meeting directors or other interested parties it was necessary to have the authority to agree or disagree with proposals which affected our coverage of a story. If it was a complex event one would be there on the day to coordinate everything. So I was often out to fix camera positions, lighting and sound feeds, often in conjunction with television. With the latter, regarding lighting, our problem was to try to avoid making the event look like a film studio. The television engineers were first-class and I worked very well with them. We normally were able to work out a compromise to suit both television and cinema.

With colour we required more light but a flatter light than did television in black and white. Too much light destroyed their contrast. With the aid of the laboratories and the skills of all concerned with lighting we somehow managed to obtain results that satisfied both parties. It was an interesting period with changes in film stocks and television working towards colour and we were not then cursed with the do-it-yourself brigade and the amateur. I would sometimes take a cameraman with me if he was to have a difficult job or position and I thought he would benefit by seeing the problems in advance. Often the cameramen would make useful suggestions, which I found helpful and would usually accept.

Sitting at my desk looking through the story possibles, I found it strange to be looking mainly for non-royal stories when for ten years I had only looked at royal events. It was of course more interesting to be involved with what was happening in the world, as had been the case before I became royal cameraman. My stories came from sources which must seem old-fashioned today. There were no mobile phones, no Internet, no computers, no e-mail or any of the advanced communication systems that editors enjoy (or perhaps do not enjoy) nowadays. We received many hand-outs from government departments, from the Central Office of Information (COI), from business, from entrepreneurs, from newspapers and news agencies and on the tape machine which all news offices had then and which poured out, in our case, news from Reuters, which was received from worldwide connections. All in all it was quite an efficient way of obtaining news. I worked some way ahead for the normal run of stories and compiled a list of possibles for the immediate Monday and Thursday issues, which I would discuss with Terry Ashwood. We would provisionally decide how each reel would be made up and which stories to drop if something unexpected turned up as it so often did. It was a busy life and I worked closely with Ashwood. I was often present when he had meetings or took someone to lunch. I had meetings too with the cutting-room staff and I was co-opted on to the management committee of the parent company, Associated-British Pathe. Although I was no longer accredited I kept my association with Buckingham Palace and had the entrée to the press office with Colville and those who followed him. One such was Bill Heseltine, later Sir William, who was a pleasant Australian who became a good friend and eventually became private secretary to the Queen. It was a life that had all the usual things a business manager had to do plus always being conscious of television taking the meat out of a story. But it was a life I eventually began to enjoy, looking at stories in the newsreel, not at what I had filmed, but with a critical eye on someone else's efforts. When it was wet and cold I was glad I was not the one out there probably trying to make time at night driving back in freezing conditions or in fog.

When there were five newsreels the COI would give commissions to each reel to film special stories for its overseas outlets, sometimes political, sometimes trade, and frequently it would take a story covered for our newsreels. The COI distributed to 120 outlets, made six newsreels for seventy countries in various languages; it was a useful source of extra income. With the closure of Paramount, Gaumont and Universal, Pathe and Movietone got more of those commissions and I was constantly in touch with its representatives and filming departments. The COI's requests sometimes caused me problems in providing a cameraman when we had a busy week.

During my years with Pathe there were many historic events which we either covered or received from our associates in other countries. I have picked out a few of these to show how we covered or obtained them or if there was an interesting story attached to them.

One of the first big events I became associated with was Operation Hope-Not – the coded reference for complicated advance arrangements for the funeral of Sir Winston Churchill when he eventually died. Tommy Cummins was personally involved in the undertaking for three years before I took over, not delegating it to his production manager, perhaps understandably as Grace Field did not have sufficient technical knowledge for such an important event. It involved meetings with the Duke of Norfolk, the Earl Marshal, the dean of St Paul's Cathedral, the

British Pathe

Pall-bearers carrying Churchill's coffin outside St Paul's Cathedral. From Pathe News.

police, the Ministry of Works, television, lighting engineers, Blenheim, where Churchill was to be buried – and sundry others. It took up a great deal of my time, for it was an ongoing project. As the months and the years passed, people changed, roads were altered, buildings appeared or disappeared, so every few months there were meetings to accommodate such changes. One major problem which occurred at every important event and in which only the police were involved was getting the negatives to the laboratories from the different positions as quickly as possible and at intervals so that everything did not arrive for processing at the same time. This meant several collection points and with roads closed over a wide area those points had to be very carefully planned. I made each of those places responsible for three camera positions. An assistant was to be with the first camera position, make his way on foot to the second and third positions and then if it was practical make for a motor bike nearby, which would take the negatives to the laboratories. If not he would go by tube to a point outside the closed area. The police were very helpful and when possible allowed us the movements we required.

When Churchill died in January 1965 all the arrangements made over five years were put into operation. Camera positions appeared magically, built by the Ministry of Works; lighting in the cathedral was placed in position without further discussion, and the necessary passes arrived on time. It was a massive undertaking, well thought-out in advance, and was on a scale in line with the funeral of a monarch. For deaths of royals there is a set programme of arrangements worked out over years, but Churchill was a one-off situation. In some degree it certainly followed the sort of arrangements made for the death of a king, including a state funeral. I had a cameraman at Westminster Hall to get the procession leaving after the coffin was taken from the lying-in-state and placed on the gun-carriage. That was a pre-arranged official position. I had cameramen in Trafalgar Square in high and low positions, in the Strand, in Fleet Street and at and in St Paul's. After the service the procession went by Cannon Street, Great Tower Street and Tower Hill to the Thames where the coffin was placed on a Port of London launch and taken upstream to the Festival Pier, thence by hearse to Waterloo Station and to Blenheim and Bladon cemetery for burial. All these places were covered. The burial was private but I had obtained permission for a camera on a stand some distance from the grave, which enabled us to get general shots of the proceedings at the graveside. A hundred and ten representatives of the world's nations attended the funeral. Detachments from all the Guards' regiments were in the funeral procession as were those from the navy and Battle of Britain aircrews. The pallbearers included Harold Macmillan, Sir Robert Menzies, Field Marshal Sir Gerald Templar, Lord Ismay, Earl Attlee, Earl Alexander, Earl Mountbatten and Viscounts Slim and Portal, indicating the regard in which Sir Winston Churchill was held. There was nothing I could do on the day of the funeral except to check that everyone was in position early on and to watch from one of our camera stands the procession, which was one of the most impressive I had seen in all my years of filming such occasions.

A lot of well-known people died during the years I was at Pathe. Pandit Nehru, Prime Minister of India, died in the same year as Churchill, and the Prime Minister of Iran was assassinated shortly before Churchill died. Somerset Maugham, Richard Dimbleby, Marilyn Monroe, Eisenhower and Hugh Gaitskill all passed on. Donald Campbell was killed attempting the world water-speed record and John F. Kennedy, Martin Luther King and Bobby Kennedy were all assassinated. All stories which kept me busy either securing footage or preparing obituaries.

Terry Ashwood decided to devote around a quarter of the reel to colour supplements which he called 'extras', devoted to a single subject that was in the news. These would appear periodically as suitable stories were found. With Beatlemania sweeping the country we made one based on youth. Carnaby Street, just off Oxford Street, was a shopping street – a must for the young. It gave us some useful shots. The Beatles at Buckingham Palace when they received MBEs and later at Downing Street gave us the news angle. A further story in 1965 was the opening of the 620-foot Post Office Tower, the tallest building in London at the time. Harold Wilson opened the elegant circular building, a landmark in the centre of London. It housed a telephone exchange, fourteen floors of transmitting apparatus and a viewing platform and restaurant at the top which was very popular but was subsequently closed on security grounds. The opening of the Forth Road Bridge, the longest suspension bridge in Europe, completed our main stories for the year.

Nineteen sixty-six proved to be exceptional. The first most important event of the year was on the Queen's birthday, 21 April. For the first time filming was allowed in the House of Commons at the state opening of Parliament. I spent weeks negotiating with television and the parliamentary authorities before we obtained permission to film the whole ceremony and most importantly in getting agreement to install enough lighting to film in colour. At first I had a lot of opposition from television which, operating in black and white, did not require as much light as we did and feared that my requests for the level we needed would jeopardise the whole of the arrangements. In gaining access to televise the historic scenes in the House of Commons, television, especially the BBC, was very much in the spotlight in the papers. I do not think we would have succeeded on our own, but eventually our use of colour coupled with complaints in the national press about the lighting by some members of Parliament turned the publicity in our favour. We survived the criticism and when the newsreel was issued we received many favourable comments about the coverage and quality of the colour.

In the House of Commons we had a position at the back of the seating and were able to show the Government benches, Black Rod entering the House to summon the MPs to the House of Lords and the members leaving the chamber to enter the other House. I also had a position in the passage between the Commons and the

Lords to show Black Rod approaching the Commons and knocking on the door and to get close-ups of the MPs as they filed through into the House of Lords. In the Upper House I had fully lighted the whole area for colour with the lamps installed high up whereas in the Commons they had to be at a lower level and were more obtrusive, causing the complaints. It meant the scenes were slightly underlit because of the limit in the numbers of lamps I was allowed to use. We filmed from a balcony in the House of Lords to show the Queen's procession to the throne and all the colourful uniforms, costumes and ceremony that attended a state opening of Parliament in London, somewhat different from those I had sometimes partly filmed on overseas tours. I obtained sound from a special BBC feed from its microphones to our camera for the reading of the speech by the Queen and other sounds such as fanfares.

The newsreel was shown to over 150 members of Parliament, including the Speaker, in the House of Commons. We had a private screening in our theatre for Edward Heath and Willie Whitelaw, the Opposition Chief Whip. Earl Mountbatten borrowed a print to show at his home Broadlands and a copy was requested by Buckingham Palace. The Lords had their own show. We had several more screenings in our private theatre to many more which included Captain Mackintosh, secretary to the Lord Chamberlain and with whom I had the most difficult of the negotiations; Barbara Castle, then Minister of Transport; the Prime Minister's press secretary; Sir Richard Colville; the Garter King of Arms and the Leader of the House of Commons. Altogether it was a very successful story.

To follow this in July there was another success – one that nearly was not – the football World Cup, and the final between Britain and West Germany at Wembley. The dramas began when the Cup trophy was stolen but that turned up in a garden shortly before the match. Pathe was the liaison company for the newsreels and it was my job to make the arrangements for camera and sound positions, car parking, collection points for the negatives, all the things necessary for covering the occasion. It meant frequent visits to Wembley to meet various officials and to see that the camera stands were properly built and sited. The Football Association was responsible for sending me the passes, car stickers, programmes etc., which arrived late in the afternoon two days before the match. I arranged with Movietone to pick up theirs at 10.00 am the next day – the day before the match. That meant that I had to sort them out before the morning. It was not a long job, but I did not want to delegate for I did not want any mistakes and only I knew exactly what to allocate to each position. I was particularly busy that afternoon so I decided I would take home everything the FA had sent me and quietly sort it all out ready for the next morning. At that time I was living on the south coast and travelled up daily by train to Victoria Station. The next day I carried my precious cargo in my brief case on to the train and placed it on the rack above my head and as I usually did leafed through newspapers on the lookout for stories. Each time the train stopped I glanced up to see that my case was still there. When I arrived at Victoria my case had an unfamiliar feel. It looked similar but it was not mine. Panic! I opened the case I had, praying there would be identification of the owner. Inside there were no papers, only a thermos flask and a packet of sandwiches. In exchange someone had got entry passes to the World Cup Final, car stickers, the lot! It was a ghastly thought. I would have to go to the office and tell my boss that I had lost all our passes and almost worse, Movietone's as well.

It would have been almost impossible to get replacements from the FA in such a short time and there would be the embarrassment of having to tell of the loss. I was frantic with worry when I arrived in Wardour Street and sat at my desk wondering what to do. I had to tell Ashwood and my secretary. As I write this now my mind goes back to those early pre-war Cup Finals at Wembley. Before the match they used to have community singing, which always ended with that lovely hymn, 'Abide with Me'. I always thought it strange and never understood why they chose that hymn to end the singing. Admittedly it was always sung loudly but its words are principally concerned with the ending of life. What would have been suitable and imaginative is if they had had singing and ended with the hymn at the last match at Wembley before the stadium was closed. A line from the hymn comes to mind which would have been appropriate as I sat at my desk in 1966: 'I need thy presence every passing hour'. Perhaps such a thought was subconsciously in my mind at that time for the phone rang. 'What brief-case?' queried my secretary who was not yet aware of my predicament. I grabbed the phone and asked the voice if he had taken the wrong case from the train at Victoria. He had and was very apologetic and was glad to find identification in mine. He was in Holborn and I sent someone to exchange the cases at once. I was very fortunate the chap was not a football fan and appeared to be uninterested in what he found. I expect he was glad to get his lunch back. I sat back and there and then vowed I would never take work home again and I never did. When I told Ashwood what had happened he laughed, but I do not think he would have if the passes had been lost. What would have happened if I had not got them back I really do not know. I suppose we would have got in somehow but it would have made a good newspaper story if it had leaked out.

The coverage of the match was superb and Terry Ashwood arranged with Sir Stanley Rous, president of FIFA and a good friend of his, that as we had won 4-2 the winning team should come to Film House the following morning to see the film of the match in colour. It was a Sunday and Sir Stanley arrived at the appointed hour of 11.00 a.m. I was waiting at the doors of Film House to conduct the team to our offices and was relieved to see a large coach coming up Wardour Street to stop outside our building.

One can never be absolutely certain when that kind of arrangement is made at the last minute whether those expected will turn up, particularly so in this case when a winning team would have many engagements. But, due at 10.00 a.m., the

British Pathe

Alf Ramsey, England's captain Bobby Moore, and on the right Terry Ashwood, when the England team came to see the World Cup film at Pathe's newsreel theatre in Wardour Street.

Technicolor print of the match had not arrived. Frantic calls were made to Technicolor, whose laboratories were way out of town near Heathrow airport. They told us they had done their best to get a good print and that it was about to be despatched. That was 11.15 a.m. We dared not tell the team we had nothing to show them for with their other engagements they would certainly have left. We had some champagne laid on for them after they had seen the film but, in the circumstances, we offered them a drink – to relax – before they saw the film. They were a good bunch and on top of the world after their win so we offered them another – and another – for the print had still not arrived. We began to run out of champagne and being a Sunday in 1966 the pubs did not open until noon. It was about that as I waited at the door of our local – The George – opposite Film House. The two elderly ladies who ran the pub responded magnificently and I returned laden with bottles and more champagne was served. By that time no one was thinking about the film except us and Sir Stanley Rous, who was getting anxious, as the team were due at Pinewood Studios at 1.00 pm. We told him of the problem and just as he was thinking of leaving with the team the print arrived. There was no opportunity of seeing the film before we showed it to our guests so we explained the delay as we quickly ushered them into the theatre before Sir Stanley could act. So finally they saw the match and themselves – at least I think they did – for they clapped enthusiastically at the end. After a final noggin, it was a very cheery crowd that climbed into their coach, and we waved them off to Pinewood just about the time they were due there. After calling the studio to say the team had been unavoidably delayed and were on their way, Terry Ashwood, our secretaries, the cutting editor and I left for a jolly lunch at the trattoria down the road. The World Cup had certainly produced some anxious moments but we received a lot of congratulations from the cinemas, the public and the directors of Associated-British Pathe.

In September 1966 I went up to Barrow-in-Furness, a small west-coast town on the edge of the Lake District, the home of the Vickers shipyard. The Queen Mother was to launch HMS *Resolution*, the 300th submarine to be built by that company. I had made arrangements previously for filming that important event and was at the yard at the launch to coordinate our coverage. This was the first of the Polaris submarines, vessels that combined nuclear power with the ballistic missile. It was an awe-inspiring warship, dark, menacing and slim as it lay stern-first on the slipway, designed to fire sixteen missiles from beneath the waters with a range of 2,500 miles in addition to its six torpedoes.

It is a naval custom for names of ships of distinction to be handed down through the ages. This submarine was the fourteenth to be named *Resolution*. The first was built in 1650, one of those beautiful ships carrying sail with eighty guns located in its sides. The last was the battleship which was lost in World War II and which I saw badly damaged by a French torpedo at Dakar. HMS *Valiant*, my favourite battleship in that same war carries her proud name forward as a nuclear submarine, launched in 1963. This launch was an impressive picture as 7,000 tons of steel slid gracefully into the water with hardly a splash, soon surrounded by tugs to take her to her fitting-out berth. With no more battleships or big ships being built it is a frightening thought that future wars at sea could probably be fought by ships one could not see, firing deadly missiles controlled by computers and many miles distant from the target.

Also in September the Queen launched the 58,000-ton *Queen Elizabeth II* at John Brown's shipyard on the Clyde. As these huge ships slip almost silently into the sea it is always spectacular and a proud if somewhat anxious moment for the builders. So we had two ships launched in the same month with very different roles. The submarine, the first of its class, built as a deterrent or an aggressor to operate beneath the waters; the passenger ship, said at the time to be probably the last of such big ships, destined to give pleasure to those who travelled or cruised above the waves.

In October of that eventful year of 1966 I had one of our cameramen, Ken Goddard, in Wales on a local story. I received an early call from him to tell me he had heard of a terrible disaster at Aberfan in which many children had been killed. It was not far from where he was so I told him to go there immediately and to let me know what had happened. Shortly after that call the door leading into Terry Ashwood's office opened and he came out. He had with him in his office one of Movietone's executives who had just received news of the disaster. Ashwood said we had better get someone there quickly by air and we would share the plane with

229

Movietone. I was able to say I already had someone on the way whom I expected to be there within the hour. It was a moment of glory for although the two reels worked together amicably it was always nice to get one up on the opposition. As well I knew it stressed how important it was for cameramen to keep in contact with the office and to keep an ear to the ground when on assignments. If Ken Goddard had not phoned and perhaps acted on his own initiative I would not have been able to get in touch with him and possibly have sent someone else to Wales. Aberfan was indeed a major disaster and we were able to get some dramatic early pictures. The story soon came up on the tape machine and has been well documented with 116 children and twenty-eight adults killed when a coal slag slid down, engulfing a school.

After the six-day war between Israel and Egypt in June the Middle East was very much in the news. Yasser Arafat became a key figure in Palestine. He had not yet become leader of the Palestine Liberation Army but was involved in training guerrillas in Jordan and was making hit-and-run raids on Israel from Syria and Jordan. Terry Ashwood thought if we could get some training pictures it would make a stunning 'extra'. I contacted the Jordanian authorities in London and, understandably, at first they were not cooperative. Eventually I managed to persuade them to help by pointing out that world pictures of the Palestinians training for fighting might influence the Israelis to give some ground. It was extremely complicated requiring great secrecy. I could not make arrangements by letter or telephone as to where we would find Arafat. Finally I obtained what amounted to a pass to film and a meeting place from where one of the Palestinians would conduct the cameraman to the training grounds. I gave the job to Pat Whitaker and we flew him to Jordan, taking on trust that the Palestinian would turn up at the appointed time and place. The man did arrive as planned but was reluctant to reveal where the training was taking place. However, Whitaker did very well in his persuasive powers and finally managed to get some very good pictures. It was quite a scoop, shot under very difficult conditions.

There was a trip to the South West in May to arrange positions for the return to Plymouth of Francis Chichester after his epic solo sailing round the world. We placed a cameraman on a boat which we shared with press photographers to get *Gypsy Moth* entering the harbour and scenes around the boat, one on the Hoe overlooking the harbour, one getting him coming ashore, one to take the drive into the town, and a truck with a sound camera and a hand-cameraman for civic greetings at the town hall. A big story which made a large section of the reel but took all our cameramen.

The International Newsreel Association (INA), established in 1957, held its meetings in a different country each time it met. The principals and editors-in-chief of newsreel companies from all over the world and who produced at least one newsreel a week gathered together periodically to discuss problems and to further cooperation and set up associations for the supply of material to each other. The meetings usually lasted around three days. After registering in the afternoon when one arrived and meeting old friends or making new ones, there was what amounted to a state banquet on the first evening with a speech of welcome from a highly placed government official. The next days were taken up with debates and speeches in the main hall with adequate translation facilities through interpreters. There were informal lunches and dinners for everyone to discuss individual problems with their associates, and there was an afternoon set aside for sightseeing and shopping. If possible on the last morning the secretary would arrange a meeting with the head of government. I had been to one meeting in Majorca with Terry Ashwood but in 1968 he was president of the association and Prague in Czechoslovakia was the chosen venue. We flew to that beautiful city on 15 August. The hotel was just off Wenceslas Square within walking distance of the hall hired for the meeting. The debates and speeches were interesting but nothing of any consequence was actually decided. I thought the main benefit of such an assembly, impressive in the number of members who attended, was the opportunity to meet in person the executives from the various newsreels with whom we were associated so that we could put a face to a voice on the phone. There were many promises of possible tie-ups with reels not already in our orbit but as generally happens at such gatherings they came to nothing after the meeting broke up. We met Alexander Dubcek, the president, on the last morning, a historic meeting for us as a week later he was deposed when Soviet tanks invaded the country and stormed through Wenceslas Square.

In November 1968 there was another world event at which Terry Ashwood was chairman. The 1968 World Newsfilms Awards were held at the National Film Theatre in London. This festival was the first international one of its kind and designed to pay tribute to the work and skills of cinema and television cameramen. Entries came from Great Britain, Europe, the USSR, the USA, Asia, Australia and New Zealand. The entries, divided into various categories, were pre-judged by a panel of ex-cameramen for films shot in the year ending 31 July 1968. The cinema Grand Prix was won by Pathe for our film of the European Cup Final and we won another first prize for the Derby and a second for the funeral of Robert Kennedy. The television Grand Prix was won by a Japanese broadcasting company. Terry Ashwood presented the prizes and I was on the stage receiving our awards from my boss for films taken by our cameramen.

We were coming under increasing pressure from television as we entered 1969. The BBC had been transmitting in colour from late 1967 and it was noticeably affecting our newsreels. Nineteen sixty-nine was a busy year, recording events destined for the history books. It was also to be the last full year for *Pathe News*, a reality of which we were unaware as the months passed to the next decade. In April

Concorde made its maiden flight. We were not certain it was going to fly but were at Filton, near Bristol, to get pictures of it taxiing fast down the runway with the possibility of taking off if test pilot Brian Trubshaw decided the conditions were right. They were. The nose lifted and the 100-ton body was airborne for the first time. It made a good story and one in which the COI was interested.

I was next involved in planning our extensive coverage for filming the investiture of the Prince of Wales at Caernarvon Castle at the beginning of July. It meant several journeys to Wales. I had a good contact there – Idris Evans of the COI – who became a friend when I was on the road. He was my Welsh liaison with the COI when covering stories for it in Wales but especially on royal stories in that part of the country as the COI coordinated press arrangements for Buckingham Palace. He was made director of information for the investiture and helped me secure the positions I wanted when meeting with the Earl Marshal, the Duke of Norfolk. Television was very much in evidence and had prime positions everywhere. Our sound camera had a good site on the battlements overlooking the dais. It enabled us to film the main part of the ceremony when Prince Charles was created Prince of Wales and Earl of Chester. The symbolic insignia were given to him by the Queen by placing a coronet on his head, a mantle round his shoulders, a gold ring on his finger, a sword on his waist and a gold rod in his hand. This was followed by a loyal address to the Prince and his reply in Welsh. The sound, fed to the camera by a special feed from the BBC, included the speeches, choirs singing, harps and brass bands playing, trumpets, fanfares and royal salutes. We had other positions when the Prince was presented to the people both outside and inside the castle and for the many processions in and to and from the scene. The weather was grey and looked very chancy but apart from occasional drizzle the rain held off. I was there on the day to coordinate our coverage and to see that the negatives left by air on time. It was a magnificient spectacle, made for colour. The heralds in their tunics, the lords in their ermine, the hats of the ladies, the mayors in their robes, the banners hanging from the battlements, the Yeoman of the Guard, the green uniform of Lord Snowdon, Constable of the Castle, the purple velvet mantle of the Prince, the vermilion chairs, the green grass and so much more were the ingredients making up that colourful pageant. It was sad for us to realise we were no longer the only news outlet in colour – television was transmitting live by our side in colour. We made a full reel, however, and it was very popular in the cinemas.

Three weeks later Neil Armstrong and Edwin Aldrin landed on the moon as the dramatic message came – 'The *Eagle* has landed.' I had to make many calls to America to secure footage of that historic event, which made another full reel for us and was very exciting and impressive on the big screen.

In November Independent Television began transmitting commercial adverts in colour, yet another nail in our coffin. And so it was. Nineteen seventy began, another decade, which was to bring still another change in my fortunes but this time unfortunately not with the newsreels. On 26 January 1970 Bernard Delfont, chairman of Associated-British Pathe, put out a statement to the press that the Pathe newsreel was to close, the last issue to be on 26 February 1970. Alongside this the company was also closing its television commercial division and the Pathe production group for documentaries – sponsored short films. Television, giving an immediate topical service against which the cinema newsreels could not compete, was given as the reason for the closures. So, as we had been aware through the late 1950s and throughout the 1960s that the increasing power of television and eventually its output in colour was a danger, it had now become a reality and finally defeated us. All the newspapers ran the story of our closure. 'Pathe rooster to retire,' said *The Times*; 'Pathe News reels into the past,' said *The Mail*; 'Pathe News killed by television,' said *The Telegraph*; 'It deserves a state funeral,' said *The Guardian*. In Parliament Gwyneth Dunwoody of the Board of Trade said *Pathe News* had become 'almost an institution ... the men who turned it out year in, year out have done a great job in the service they have offered to the community'. Commiserations indeed, which strangely had not been evident when the other reels closed. Only Movietone continued although not really as a newsreel, concentrating on short films and commercial subjects and using its comprehensive library until it too closed in 1979. Pathe's film library did survive and is still around today.

So for me, forty years in the film industry and thirty-four with newsreels came to an end. When I received the letter telling me my position would become redundant it was the first time in my working life that I was faced with unemployment. I was not at retirement age but old enough for it to be difficult to find another job, particularly at that time when anyone over forty was regarded as almost unemployable. Terry Ashwood was offered a job at Pinewood with Pathe library, but older than me, he turned it down and decided to take early retirement.

When I left Film House for the last time as an employee my thoughts went back to those first days all those years ago when I arrived on the fifth floor in publicity, when C.K. used to came to our office to see a girlfriend before I knew him as my boss with *Gaumont-British News*. It was a sad thought, for in this same year 1970 as my newsreel days ended, he died. I thought of the many stories I had filmed and how fortunate I had been in my assignments. I thought of the romantic places I had been to in privileged positions – India, South America, Canada, round the world in a royal ship. I thought of the war during which I had sailed in thirty ships – landing craft, torpedo boats, destroyers, cruisers and battleships; I had seen plenty of action but had come to no harm. How fortunate I had been by being with the navy rather than with the land forces. I always had a cover over my head for sleep, plenty of water, plenty of gin and plenty of food. And there was royal rota, one of only two cameramen to hold such a position. Then finally to have the job of running a newsreel from the other side of the desk. Television had finally shut us down but the cinema newsreels set the standard for much of the way television operates today in news coverage. Sometimes people had said there were frivolous items in the reels. Well, in essence we were part of an entertainment industry. In addition to many years of being the only visual outlet in providing live news of the day, perhaps sometimes a little lighter touch was permissible. I had indeed had a unique career which finally came to an end as I closed the door of Film House and, with my thoughts, walked down Wardour Street not knowing what I was going to do.

I came to a decision to set up my own company and stay in the film business. When the reel closed we had a number of documentaries lined up to make for an American air company – Pan-Am. They told me they would give me four fifteen-minute travel films they wanted on Lebanon, Hong Kong, Japan and Europe. The COI promised to give me commissions, and Terry Ashwood said he had a number of useful contacts and would use his influence to get sponsors. That seemed a reasonable start. It was a gamble, for making films was different from producing newsreels, but all the facilities one needed such as cutting rooms and editors, viewing theatres, sound effects libraries, music libraries and commentators were all available for hire in Soho. So John Turner Enterprises Ltd came into existence. It was gratifying to find how helpful people were when I told them I was starting a new business, especially in the basic facilities I needed like accounts with Kodak for film stock and laboratories like Technicolor and Denham. My bank manager was extremely helpful offering me substantial aid if I needed it while waiting for payment. He advised me to become a limited company as it would give me status when trying for sponsors. I made an arrangement with Terry Ashwood that he would join me when a film was to be made which he had helped to get. We worked together amicably for some years. Pat Whitaker and Ken Goddard both had acquired 35mm and 16mm cameras and had decided to go freelance so I employed them as my cameramen.

I managed to find a two-room office in Denmark Street, the street of the music companies and just across the road from Soho Square. It was a bit rough and on a top floor but it was in the West End, a good address and a good rent of £10 a week. Only Pathe was not generous to me. The furniture I needed for my office – desk, chairs, filing cabinet, typewriter, paper and the odds and ends I needed to equip an office mostly came from my Pathe office and was surplus to requirements after the closure and they made me pay for it with very little reduction on the price. My redundancy money after thirty-four years with the newsreels was almost negligible. They assessed it on the time I was actually on the Pathe staff, not taking into account the time I was partly employed by them on royal rota. Of course with hindsight I should have made sure I was protected against redundancy for the years I spent with Gaumont and royal rota. Apart from that, however, no one took advantage of a novice in business, for that was what I was at the beginning of my new career. What money I did get I used to start my company, helped by a first-class bank manager. I was my own secretary, did the VAT returns and only used an accountant when I had to by law as a limited company. My most difficult job was in costing films, for I had to make sufficient profit but not too much or too little to remain viable. I was successful for ten years with good clients for sponsored films such as banks and insurance companies, some shown on television through contacts Ashwood knew. I made four full length documentaries for actress Ann Todd, of which Jordan and Australia had cinema distribution. She got the money; I produced the films. It was a busy life.

The Pathe Sound Effects Library, owned by Pathe, was still being run by the librarian, Ken Nunn, but around 1978 the library was looking for a home. I made arrangements with Pathe and Nunn to continue to run it from my office; that is, it was sub-let to me, and all the transfer equipment and tapes were moved into my second room. After a while Ken Nunn, an elderly man, decided to retire and the library became almost a full-time job for me. It was a major problem at first learning where, among the hundreds of tapes, a particular effect was located, for the references were not always clear as to what exactly the sound was, and then transferring the effect in whatever way was required by the customer – and always working against the clock. However, it came at a useful time to aid my finances, as companies had begun to set up their own video departments, and the electronic age lessened the requirements for film as video tape took preference. Then in 1981 my office changed owners and I was asked a prohibitive rent. As by then I was past retirement age, I finished making films, the sound library went to KPM, and I wound up my company. It had been a very different life from that with the newsreels, without the excitement and interest of daily involvement with world events, but I had managed to stay in the film industry.

I was glad my office was so close to Soho Square, for I was working in the same area in which I had always been and that was a comfort. I was still able to see the large windows of the film companies in Wardour Street and Dean Street displaying their wares with posters and stills from their films. As I used the various facilities for making films and met my clients in pubs and restaurants in Soho I was at home, for as I said earlier, Soho was almost my lifeblood. It typified London for me, and still does, for I am a Londoner, born in London, as was my wife. We had our own private names for each other. She was SB and I was BB, so it is to SB, my lovely wife, that I dedicate this book. It is very sad and of great regret that she is not here to read it. She always wanted me to write of my experiences and I wish so much I had managed to do it earlier. I often wonder now whether all those days, weeks and months when I was away from her were worth it. Now my book is written, ever generous, she would probably have said, 'Yes, it was.'

John Turner today.

BUFVC/BUND

Further Information

This book has been published as part of the British Universities Film & Video Council's (BUFVC) on-going commitment to the British cinema newsreels and their importance to historical study and film research. Since 1974 the BUFVC has held a major collection of documents relating to news and historical film, the Slade Film History Register, which now forms the basis of its British Universities Newsreel Database (BUND). The BUFVC holds books and articles on British newsreels, an extensive collection of newsreel issue sheets, and a unique collection of newsreel production documents such as commentary scripts, shot lists and cameramen's dope sheets, which are available online. The BUFVC has published three volumes of *The Researcher's Guide to British Newsreels*, and has produced a wallchart detailing the history and ownership of British newsreels and cinemagazines. It has issued two CD-ROMs on newsreels, the *British Universities Newsreel Project Database* and *The Origins of the Cold War*. For further information on newsreels visit the BUND website at www.bufvc.ac.uk/newsreels or contact the BUND team on 020 7393 1508.

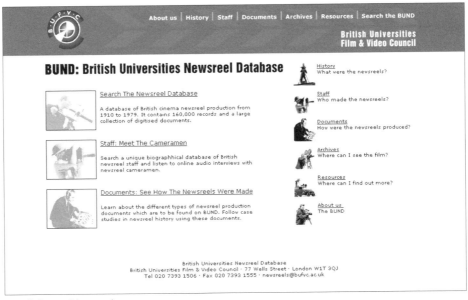

www.bufvc.ac.uk/newsreel.

General bibliography for the study of British newsreels and cinemagazines.

Aldgate, Anthony, *Cinema and History: British Newsreels and the Spanish Civil War* (London: Scolar Press, 1979)

Ballantyne, James (ed.), *Researcher's Guide to British Newsreels* (London: British Universities Film & Video Council, 1983)

Ballantyne, James (ed.), *Researcher's Guide to British Newsreels Volume II* (London: British Universities Film & Video Council, 1988)

Ballantyne, James (ed.), *Researcher's Guide to British Newsreels Vol III* (London: British Universities Film & Video Council, 1993)

British Newsreel Issue Sheets 1913-1970: the complete collection held by the Slade Film History Register reproduced on microfiche (London: Graphic Data Publishing/ British Universities Film & Video Council, 1984)

Fielding, Raymond, *The American Newsreel 1911-1967* (Norman: University of Oklahoma Press, 1972)

Fielding, Raymond, *The March of Time, 1935-1951* (New York: Oxford University Press, 1978)

Hammerton, Jenny, *For Ladies Only? Eve's Film Review: Pathe Cinemagazine 1921–1933* (Hastings: The Projection Box, 2001)

Jeavons, Clyde, Jane Mercer and Daniela Kirchner (eds.), *'The Story of the Century!': An International Newsfilm Conference* (London: British Universities Film & Video Council, 1998)

Low, Rachael, *Films of Comment and Persuasion of the 1930s* (London: George Allen & Unwin, 1979)

McKernan, Luke, *Topical Budget: The Great British News Film* (London: British Film Institute, 1992)

Mitchell, Leslie, *Leslie Mitchell Reporting...* (London: Hutchinson, 1981)

Noble, Ronnie, *Shoot First! Assignments of a Newsreel Cameraman* (London: George G. Harrap, 1955)

Pronay, Nicholas and D.W. Spring (eds.), *Propaganda, Politics and Film, 1918–1945* (London: Macmillan, 1982)

Reeves, Nicholas, *Official British Film Propaganda During the First World War* (London: Croom Helm, 1986)

Richards, Jeffrey and Dorothy Sheridan (eds). *Mass-Observation at the Movies* (London: Routledge & Kegan Paul, 1987)

Short, K.R.M. and Stephan Dolezel (eds.), *Hitler's Fall: The Newsreel Witness* (London: Croom Helm, 1988)

Smith, Paul (ed.), *The Historian and Film* (Cambridge: Cambridge University Press, 1976)

Smither, Roger and Wolfgang Klaue (eds.), *Newsreels in Film Archives: A Survey Based on the FIAF Newsreel Symposium* (Trowbridge: Flicks Books, 1996)

Wyand, Paul, *Useless if Delayed* (London: George G. Harrap, 1959)

The British Universities Film & Video Council does not hold any newsreel films itself. The existing British newsreels are held in the main by three commercial companies and two film archives. Contact details are given below, along with the newsreels and cinemagazines that each archive holds. **It is important to note that the commercial newsreel companies cannot normally handle academic research requests**, and such researchers should normally approach BFI Collections and the Imperial War Museum Film & Video Archive, both of which have extensive newsreel collections that often overlap the commercial collections, and which are designed for student research.

Associated British Pathe
New Pathe House
57 Jamestown Road
London NW1 7DB
Tel: 020 7323 0407
Fax: 020 7436 3232
E-mail: info@britishpathe.com
Website: www.britishpathe.com

Holds the newsreels *Pathe Gazette* and *Pathe News*, and the cinemagazines *Pathe Pictorial*, *Pathetone Weekly* and *Eve's Film Review*.

BFI Collections (National Film and Television Archive)
21 Stephen Street
London W1P 2LN
Tel: 020 7957 8971
Fax: 020 7580 7503
Website: www.bfi.org.uk/collections

Holds selected material for the newsreels *British Movietone News*, *British News*, *British Paramount News*, *Eclair Journal*, *Empire News Bulletin*, *Gaumont-British News*, *Gaumont Graphic*, *Gaumont Sound News*, *Pathe Gazette/News*, *Topical Budget*, *Universal News*, and others.

British Movietonews Library
North Orbital Road
Denham UB9 5HQ
Tel: 01895 833 071
Fax: 01895 834 893
E-mail: library@mtone.co.uk
Website: www.movietone.com

Holds the newsreel *British Movietone News*.

Imperial War Museum Film & Video Archive
Lambeth Road
London SE1 6HZ
Tel: 020 7416 5291/2
Fax: 020 7416 5379
E-mail: film@iwm.org.uk
Website: www.iwm.org.uk/lambeth/film.htm

Holds newsreels and cinemagazines for the First and Second World Wars: *Airfront Gen Operational Supplement*, *The Gen*, *Topical Budget*, *War Pictorial News*, *Warwork News*, *Worker and Warfront*, and war-time issues of *British Paramount News*, *Gaumont British News* and *Universal News*.

ITN Archive
200 Gray's Inn Road
London WC1X 8XZ
Tel: 020 7430 4480
Fax: 020 7430 4453
E-mail: archive.sales@itn.co.uk
Website: www.itnarchive.com

Holds the newsreels *Empire News Bulletin*, *Gaumont-British News*, *Gaumont Graphic*, *Gaumont Sound News*, *British Paramount News*, and *Universal News*.

Index